DISCARD

About Island Press

Since 1984, the nonprofit organization Island Press has been stimulating, shaping, and communicating ideas that are essential for solving environmental problems worldwide. With more than 1,000 titles in print and some 30 new releases each year, we are the nation's leading publisher on environmental issues. We identify innovative thinkers and emerging trends in the environmental field. We work with world-renowned experts and authors to develop cross-disciplinary solutions to environmental challenges.

Island Press designs and executes educational campaigns in conjunction with our authors to communicate their critical messages in print, in person, and online using the latest technologies, innovative programs, and the media. Our goal is to reach targeted audiences—scientists, policymakers, environmental advocates, urban planners, the media, and concerned citizens— with information that can be used to create the framework for long-term ecological health and human well-being.

Island Press gratefully acknowledges major support of our work by The Agua Fund, The Andrew W. Mellon Foundation, The Bobolink Foundation, The Curtis and Edith Munson Foundation, Forrest C. and Frances H. Lattner Foundation, The JPB Foundation, The Kresge Foundation, The Oram Foundation, Inc., The Overbrook Foundation, The S.D. Bechtel, Jr. Foundation, The Summit Charitable Foundation, Inc., and many other generous supporters.

The opinions expressed in this book are those of the author(s) and do not necessarily reflect the views of our supporters.

BIKE BOOM

BIKE BOOM

The Unexpected
Resurgence of Cycling

CARLTON REID

ISLANDPRESS Washington | Covelo | London

ISLAND PRESS is a trademark of the Center for Resource Economics.

Library of Congress Control Number: 2016959951

Text design by Maureen Gately
Typesetting by Carlton Reid

Websites: islandpress.org & bikeboom.info

⊛ Printed on recycled, acid-free paper

Manufactured in the United States of America
10 9 8 7 6 5 4 3 2 1

Keywords: Bicycle infrastructure; bike path; bikeway; Columbia, Maryland; cycleways; Davis, California; the Netherlands; New York City; shared streets; Stevenage, UK; vehicular cycling; Victory Bikes

About the Cover Image
"Power to the pedal!"

"CYCLING HELPS BUILD HEALTHY BODIES," asserted one placard. "Give Mom a bike lane," pleaded another. One held aloft by a young woman in stylish full-fingered red gloves with a matching satchel that simply said "PEDAL!" The placards were real, the San Francisco demonstration was real, but the pretty woman in the striking white dress and red accessories was a model, and the bike she was sat astride for this 1970s "Bike-in" was not hers, but one supplied by a local bicycle shop.

The image on the cover of this book comes from a 1972 fashion spread published in *Mademoiselle*, a Condé Nast magazine geared to "the smart young woman." The photos for the eight-page spread featured the fist-pumping brunette model wearing a "white-on-white cycle safari suit [with] button-down pleat skirt" as well as a blonde woman in a "black-and-white pin-dotted shirt jacketed over a matching stitch-pleat skirt." She also had Ruza Creations full-fingered gloves and a satchel from the same leather-design house—clearly, the magazine had just one set of red accessories between two models. In her hand the blonde model carried a placard affirming "BIKE POWER."

While the spread promoted high-end fashion brands, it also plugged cycling. "Cities are setting aside lanes for bicycling commuters," promised the magazine, and "towns and states are marking thousands of miles of secondary roads as Bikeway routes. . . ."

The year, 1972, was in the middle of the four-year-long American bike boom, and in the following year sales of bicycles would double. *Mademoiselle* was showing its readers it could spot a trend when it saw one, but didn't mention that its photo-spread had been shot at a real protest.

The archives of the *San Francisco Chronicle* show that the Bike-in took place on January 11, 1972. Black-and-white photos held back by the *Chronicle*—and taken by staff photographer Joseph J. Rosenthal, famous for his "Raising the Flag on Iwo Jima" image of 1945—reveal that the models mingled with real protestors and borrowed their placards. The "PEDAL!" placard seen on the cover photo actually stated "POWER to the PEDAL!" and during the demonstration was held aloft by a bearded middle-aged man in a suit. The placard was stiffened with a wooden rod, but was missing from the magazine photograph—the magazine's art department airbrushed the stick from the photo used in the magazine. Some of the other banners on the protest were politically charged, and not quite so suitable for publication in *Mademoiselle*: one said "Kill for bike paths."

Reporting on the demonstration, *Chronicle* reporter Jerry Burns wrote: "Bicycle riders and neighborhood groups demanded yesterday that plans for beautifying Upper Market street be changed to reduce the number of lanes for cars and to provide facilities for bikes."

The protesters wanted "Safe Bike Lanes on Market!" They didn't get them then, and there are still none today.

*For Robert "Bicycle Bob" Silverman,
and all of the other 1970s cycle advocates who tended cycling's
flame when planners and politicians were
trying to snuff it out.*

THANKS TO MY KICKSTARTER PATRONS

Rose Ades	James Moss
Jens Bemme	Hannes Neupert, ExtraEnergy
Chris Boardman	Simon Nurse
Denis Caraire	Michael Prescott
David Cox	Eric Robertson

See page 218 for all 461 Kickstarter backers.

Contents

Foreword

By Joe Breeze

WHEN I WAS GROWING UP IN THE United States in the 1950s and 1960s, cycling was at its nadir. Motorized personal transport was all the rage. The ill effects of automobile dependence—including air pollution, oil spills, traffic jams, and the health risks of a sedentary lifestyle—began to bring some recognition of bicycling as a solution. Most people, though, saw bicycles as kids' sidewalk toys.

I had a different upbringing. My parents were physically active. We hiked a lot and played sports. In the 1950s, my father owned the Sports Car Center in Sausalito and stayed in shape for auto racing by riding and commuting to work on his racing bike. By the age of thirteen, I had ridden one hundred and twenty miles in a day.

Our family's cycling habits were far from typical. Imagine this scene: 9:00 a.m. on a warm summer day in California's Central Valley, 1968. My brother and I, fifteen and fourteen years of age respectively, were sitting silently with our bicycles in tall grass alongside a highway sixty-five miles from home, peering at a highway patrolman. The radio of his patrol car crackled: "Parents say it's okay for Richie and Joey to proceed." The patrolman's jaw dropped a little. So we weren't runaways after all. Free to go, we continued our two-hundred-mile ride across the state. That's how it was in America before the bike boom: few people rode bicycles outside towns, and those who did raised eyebrows.

As Carlton Reid shows in this book, at least some of the 1970s bike boom can be traced to President Eisenhower's 1956 heart attack. The president's cardiologist, Dr. Paul Dudley White, recommended cycling. Eisenhower warned Americans that they were not getting enough exercise. This wake-up call led to the President's Council on Physical Fitness and Sports.

I was barely aware of these national events, but by third grade I certainly noticed when teachers had us out on the blacktop every day for invigorating exercise such as jumping jacks and running. In school we learned about London's deadly smog of the early 1950s and increasing pollution in other cities of the 1960s. For children my age, pollution of the air and the water brought environmental concerns front and center.

When the boom hit in the early 1970s, all vectors seemed to point to the bicycle as the solution. The bicycle hadn't been in the US spotlight since the 1890s, and now suddenly bicycles mattered. Everyone was talking about them. Many people who hadn't considered riding for decades suddenly found themselves plunking down bucks for bikes.

Unfortunately, the ubiquitous ten-speed racer of the day was not the best type of bike for most people. It was a skinny-tire, drop-handlebar machine that was uncomfortable for many. Most boom bikes soon gathered dust in garages across the nation.

Later, more-comfortable and inviting bicycles such as the mountain bike appeared on the scene. Later still, more-practical bikes came to the United States fully equipped for everyday transportation. Today, cycling is vastly expanded by such echoes of the bike boom.

I first met Carlton in 2012 at a French ski resort on the occasion of the twenty-fifth anniversary of the first World Mountain Bike Championships. Back at that 1987 event, Carlton had raced on the British team. Now he was interviewing me for a magazine article. I was immediately impressed with his depth of knowledge. We shared similar interests in all aspects of cycling: technical, social, and environmental.

Carlton's astute, interesting questions told me that he was a person who would delve into details, examine evidence thoughtfully, and come out with work of serious value. His five years of research was apparent in his book *Roads Were Not Built for Cars*. He uncovered crucial aspects of history that had long been forgotten. In *Bike Boom*, Carlton's research and insights provide key background to today's bicycle scene. No matter what the subject, history provides the best crystal ball for the future.

Joe Breeze is one of the founding fathers of mountain biking. As well as being the face of Breezer Bikes, he is curator of the Marin Museum of Bicycling in Fairfax, California.

Preface

"Learn from other's mistakes. You won't live long enough to make them all yourself."

—Groucho Marx

I HAVE BEEN WRITING ABOUT BICYCLES SINCE 1986, which means I have been professionally dependent on the health of cycling for more than thirty years. This pecuniary interest in getting "more people cycling, more often" is not my only motivation—I also want to see more people on bikes because I would like more people to love what I love. As a card-carrying *vélorutionary*, I've been immensely satisfied over those thirty years to report on cycling's steady elevation into the mainstream. That said, I have some bad news: despite what you might have assumed from book titles, there is no bike boom right now, nor has there been one in the United Kingdom or the United States since the early 1970s.

The mass media frequently mention that bicycling is booming, and when I'm interviewed by newspapers and radio stations I usually go along with throwaway comments about how well the industry and the activity must be doing. This book is a 79,000-word reaction to my timidity about not explaining why—despite appearances—bicycling may not actually be booming right now. One part of me (the PR half) wants to quit with the doom-mongering; the other part (the journalist half) wants to delve into the many reasons why all of the talk about booms is baloney. By acknowledging that there is no real boom we can better explore how to go out and create one.

BIKE BOOM is the follow-on from *Roads Were Not Built for Cars*, which covered the period 1870–1905. *Bike Boom* picks up where that book left off, and examines in some depth two seismic but underreported periods in cycling's history: the putative creation of English cycleways in the 1930s, and the hugely significant Great American Bike Boom of 1970–1974. Aftershocks from both periods are still being felt today. I also examine the story of how the Dutch got their bike paths, which also reaches back to both the 1930s and the 1970s.

Bike Boom, then, explores what was happening in cycle advocacy decade by decade. Here's a condensed timeline:

■ The Netherlands became the world's top cycling nation by 1906, and had already installed some cycleways; many more would be added over the next thirty years. The cycle paths were originally installed for the comfort and convenience of people on bicycles and not for protection from faster, heavier road users.

■ Germany also had a growing network of cycle paths by the 1930s. These, too, had originally been installed for the comfort of cyclists, but by the mid-1930s they were being used to shunt cyclists to the side, out of the way of a superior being: the Motorist.

■ Inspired by the Dutch example, in 1934 the motor-besotted powers-that-be in Britain started to install separate cycle tracks next to newly built arterial roads and bypasses; cycle tracks weren't always terribly comfortable or convenient, yet some politicians were readying to make them mandatory to use. Two million rich motorists were deemed to be worthier than twelve million proletarian cyclists. Organized cycling kicked back against the perceived enforced use of the often narrow and poorly surfaced paths, but it was the war against Hitler that stopped them spreading.

Stevenage's cycleway system has many underpasses.

■ Cycling made small comebacks in America in the 1920s and 1930s, and some bikeways were built by New York's "master builder," Robert Moses. But with cars getting cheaper, bicycles became "toys" for use, in the main, by children.

■ In the 1950s and 1960s, it was assumed—almost everywhere in the world— that cycling was on the same life-span curve as the dodo. On stony ground, the first buds of the American "bikeway" movement started to appear in Florida and California. Meanwhile in England, a separated cycleway network built in Stevenage from 1958 and through into the 1960s was the great hope for British cycle campaigners. (Organized cycling had warmed to "segregation" by the 1960s, especially as the cycleway network in Stevenage was so good and dense.)

■ The baby-boomer-fueled American "bike boom" of the early 1970s took almost everybody by surprise, most especially the bicycle industry, which couldn't keep up with demand—the market doubled overnight. The boom was over by 1974, leading planners and politicians to rein back plans for cycling, deflating the hopes of cycle advocates who had been pushing for the installation of high-quality bikeways. In fact, most of the cycle infrastructure that had been constructed prior to the bubble bursting wasn't very good anyway. Nineteen-thirties-style don't-force-us-to-ride-on-terrible-cycle-infrastructure campaigning became American cycling's loudest and most insistent voice.

◼ The poor infrastructure of the 1970s, as well as the equally dire stuff installed in the early 1980s, didn't get used by cyclists—and those who were calling, instead, for high-quality cycleways were shouting into the wind. Everywhere except the Netherlands, that is. Car use had taken off in the Netherlands in the 1960s, but a variety of campaigns in the 1970s—led by young anarchists at first, and later by parents worried about road safety for their little 'uns—encouraged an already cycling-aware nation to ramp up its funding for a denser and denser grid of high-quality cycleways.

◼ The cycleway-building dream of the 1970s soured in the 1980s. Cycleways in the United Kingdom and the United States had not encouraged cycling in the way their promoters had promised. Deflated, cycle advocates retreated. A number of advocacy groups folded; others went into hibernation. And as the Netherlands expanded its cycle infrastructure throughout the 1990s, the remaining British and American cycle advocates could only look on in wonder. These advocates worked tirelessly to keep the flame alive, but, outside of the Netherlands, the 1990s was largely a lost decade for everyday cycling. Campaigners started to stir again at the end of the decade, and the first signs of today's renaissance of cycling started to appear. But that story, dear reader, is for my next book, *People on Bikes*, which will be the third and final book in what has turned out to be a trilogy, and will be an examination of cycling and cycle advocacy from the 1980s through to today and beyond.

Many assume that the expansion of the Dutch cycleway network in the 1970s and 1980s must have led to a renaissance of everyday cycling in the Netherlands. In fact, it arrested a precipitous decline, with cycle use in the Netherlands in the 1970s being not a patch on what it had been in the 1930s. A graph (see color plates) shows this plainly: in 1925, cyclists in the Dutch cities of Amsterdam and Enschede accounted for more than 70 percent of traffic on the roads. Enschede's cycling "modal share" was closer to 90 percent (the graph doesn't include the pedestrian share of journeys). Between 1950 and 1970 cycle use fell off a cliff, but it stabilized after 1975 thanks, in part, to both a reallocation of roadspace away from motor cars and the expansion of cycle networks. Enschede now has a cycling modal share of nearly 40 percent, and Amsterdam a little over 30 percent. The easiest way for a city to achieve a cycling modal share of 25 percent is to start with one of 50 percent.

Falling in and out of favor is not something that can be controlled. Booms are controlled by prevailing fashions, and fashion, by definition, is fickle. Down through the years there have been many media references to bike booms. Such mentions usually need to be taken with a pinch of salt. What's notable about many of the postwar bike-boom media mentions is that—at least in the United States and the United Kingdom—everyday cycle usage did not tend to rise at the same rate as the puffery. For instance, as the journalist Joe Dunckley has shown with a UK-based graph plotting "cycling-is-booming" mentions against a decline in actual cycle mileage, there's often little to show for the boom claims.

For a start, there have always been massive differences among cities. For instance, the bike boom that many British newspapers say is happening right now is really only happening in London, where those national newspapers are based. The UK capital has most definitely seen a rise in cycle usage, and this is revealed in traffic studies. I can also attest that cycle usage has mushroomed in central London. I live 250 miles from London but visit frequently, and on my regular visits over the last thirty or so years I have indeed seen a rising number of cyclists. While, in the 1980s, I might have pulled up at traffic lights with just one other cyclist for company (probably a messenger, who likely didn't stop at the lights at all), by the 1990s I would have been joined by ten others. Now, the line of cyclists at traffic lights can be so long that not all of us can progress before green turns to red again.

Yet even London's latest bike boom may not be as impressive as it appears from the photos shared on social media, or from anecdotes such as mine. True, there are amazingly high counts of cyclists at key points during the "rush hour," but cyclists are not this thick on the ground throughout all of London, and they're almost literally an endangered species in Outer London.

Cycling's modal share in London still remains at 3 or so percent, and cycle advocate Mark Treasure has estimated that, at the current rate of progress, it will take London about 340 years to reach a 25 percent cycling modal share, which is the current level in Rotterdam, one of the Netherlands' worst-performing cities for cycling.

"This should cause those who proclaim that we have reached the promised land to pause for thought," remarked Treasure. "While it might be impressive to see 45 cyclists at one traffic light during the morning rush hour, this is by no means a revolution. The reason it might appear to be so is because we've gone from seeing practically no cyclists at all to quite concentrated pockets of fit, male 25- to 44-year-olds commuting into work on certain routes in central London."

Since Treasure wrote that in his blog, *As Easy as Riding a Bike*, London has installed Mark II versions of its Cycle Superhighways. Mark I's were protected with paint, not curbs. Undoubtedly, cycling's modal share will now rise faster as a result, but—despite newspaper headlines such as "Move Over Amsterdam, the London Cycling Revolution Is in Top Gear"—London still has a long way to go before it reaches Dutch levels of cycle usage.

Agreeing that "cycling is gaining popularity," sociologist Dave Horton, writing in 2012, warned about taking the United Kingdom's supposed current bike boom too seriously:

> There are two clear and present problems which bedevil UK cycling advocacy: one is the requirement to trumpet any and all gains, however minor or potentially imaginary, in order for us to legitimate and reproduce ourselves as advocates; the other is a rush to interpret any sign of growth in cycling as both "good" and a clear sign that investments in cycling are paying dividends, when a wider and more critical analysis might concur with neither.

A genuine critical analysis of how we actually travel shows that in the United States and the United Kingdom the active-travel modes are far from booming. Sidewalks are ubiquitous and of generally high quality in Britain, yet even with such separate and curb-protected infrastructure the modal-share for walking has been in steep decline for many years. In fact, walking trips are falling at a steeper and faster rate than are cycling trips.

Bike Boom is not a rose-tinted promotion of the joyful practicality of cycling; it is a work of history, unafraid to reveal some inconvenient truths. Some may say that by discussing these inconvenient truths I am, in effect, promoting them, perhaps even endorsing them. This would be both wrong and unfair. History has much to teach us. As always, to be forewarned is to be forearmed. It is instructive to study the market and mileage expansions of the past, and to work out why, despite appearances, there haven't been any actual booms for quite some time. What can we learn from the period of the 1970s, when the United States and the United Kingdom had the chance to follow the Dutch and Danish examples, but didn't? Can we really tame the monster that is the motor car, and replace it with the sustainable and swift bicycle? Why is it that, even with cycleways in place, cycling is not as popular with women, ethnic minorities, and the urban poor? How can cycle and pedestrian advocates convince uninterested governments to switch from designing only for motorists? Will America, Britain, Australia, New Zealand, and the rest ever make decisions based on Dutch-style long-term nation stewardship? And while cycling may only bloom once cities provide cycleway grids, how will such grids be provided in those cities where cycle usage is currently low? The historical background to such questions is what I set out to examine in *Bike Boom*.

Carlton Reid
Newcastle upon Tyne
May 2017

Introduction

*"No one has ever recruited activists to a cause by announcing
that things are getting better . . ."*

—Steven Pinker

HOW DO WE MEASURE WHETHER A BIKE BOOM IS, or is not, happening? By
mileage cycled, or bicycles sold? There are good stats for the latter, fewer and
often less reliable ones for the former. Or how about modal-share, the percentage
split between different modes of transport? Some cities have certainly seen
expanded cycle usage—for instance, between 2000 and 2015 New York City
witnessed a 381 percent growth in its bikeway network and a 207 percent rise
in bicycle trips—but dig down and the impressive jumps often turn out to be
starting from pitifully low bases. Going from, say, 1 percent of all journeys to
2 percent is, indeed, a doubling in cycling use, but in big-picture terms it's more
of a blip than a boom. And not all of the increases in cycling trips can be put
down to the provision of bikeways. Seattle has seen a 235 percent growth in its
bikeway network over the last fifteen years and a 123 percent uptick in bicycle
trips, whereas Portland, Oregon, saw a 391 percent growth in bicycle trips in the
same period, even though its bikeway network grew by "just" 53 percent.

By *cycling* I mean *everyday cycling*—using bikes for transportation, nipping
to the shops as well as riding to work and school. The late-1970s BMX boom,
the 1980s mountain-bike boom, and the more recent Lance Armstrong–inspired
road-bike boom were all recreational, and the focus in this book will be on towns

Even before the installation of London's curb-protected
Cycle Superhighways, the number of cyclists had increased. (Toby Jacobs)

and cities, and the *reasons* for the building—or non-building—of cycleways and similar. (Mountain bikes and road bikes are also used for transportation, of course; BMX bikes less so.) Suburban and rural cycling is generally neglected—cycle infrastructure is deemed to be for central business districts, and those who wish to ride in the suburbs, or between villages, are frequently ignored. Naturally, this isn't the case in the Netherlands. In fact, the first Dutch cycleways were built in the early 1900s for countryside recreation; urban cycleways came later, with significant network expansions in the 1970s through to the 1990s.

Cycling as a form of everyday transport for all has boomed on and off since the 1890s, with national differences even between topographically identical countries, as a look at a European cycleways map demonstrates (see color plates): the Netherlands has a dense network of cycleways, but neighboring countries do not. Booms, it seems, respect borders, suggesting that cultural differences play a key role in whether one country provides cycleways and another does not.

In the Netherlands, cycling is so normal as to be almost unworthy of study. "Cycling is just something you do," a Dutch traffic engineer told a US audience. "You get on your bike and you ride. It's like a toothbrush. You get up, you brush your teeth. What's the big deal? Do you subscribe to *Toothbrush Times*? Join a toothbrush club?"

Cycling academics John Pucher and Ralph Buehler claim in their influential book *City Cycling* that there's "booming interest in cycling around the world" and that North America is experiencing a "bicycling renaissance." Tapping into this renaissance and hoping to take it even further, Peter Walker, a political journalist for the UK's *Guardian* newspaper, has written a book called *Bike Nation: How Cycling Can Save the World* (2017). Cycling most certainly *is* transformative, and bigging up any rise in everyday cycling as a "boom" or a "renaissance" is *not* counterproductive. As Oscar Wilde said, it's better to be talked about than not talked about. What's amazing about cycling is its very survival, which is perhaps one of the reasons for the multitude of boom tales in the first place. Cycling has been written off many times, yet it's still with us, "always ready to thrive," wrote Jeff Mapes in his 2009 book, *Pedaling Revolution*, like a "plant that will flourish if given half an ecological niche."

THE LAST full-on bike boom was between 1970 and 1974. Cycling had been building in popularity throughout the 1960s thanks to health concerns, and when baby-boomer ecological concerns merged with a fitness kick the American market for bicycles doubled within a couple of years. Everybody, it seemed in the early seventies, rushed out to buy ten-speed drop-handlebar bicycles, and the number of urban cyclists became so great that the United States, and to a much lesser extent the United Kingdom, *almost* started to do what the Netherlands was doing at the same time, and that's build networks of cycleways. (The seemingly impractical ten-speed bike was also popular in the Netherlands in the 1970s; the practical black *omafiets* Dutch bike wasn't as ubiquitous back then as it is today.)

"The continuing bicycle boom [is] beginning to be heard by city, state, and federal bureaucrats," highlighted an American newspaper in 1972: "The phenomenal rise in bicycle sales has generated a bicycle lobby that is demanding better breaks for cyclists—their own traffic lanes . . . and a general admission that the auto is not automatically king of the road. . . ." This lobbying had its successes. A "bicycle bill" was passed by the Oregon legislature in 1971, directing the state to spend 1 percent of its highway money on cycleways. Davis, California, installed a network of Dutch-inspired barrier-protected cycleways that, from 1967 onwards, was promoted as the model for other American cities to follow. The US secretary of transportation rode to work on a folding bike, and he advocated for bikeways. British and American planners, engineers, and politicians went on early-1970s study tours to the Netherlands to learn how to "go Dutch." Ambitious plans were drawn up for urban cycling networks, especially in North American cities. And then the bubble burst: sales collapsed, and most of the bikeway plans were shelved. No modern "bike boom" has come close to the 15 million bicycles sold in 1973, the high-water mark for cycle sales in the United States, triple the size of the market just eight years previously. At this peak there were 95 new bikes per 1,000 American adults; it is now half that.

Compared to the 1970s boom, today's is illusory. Over the past ten to fifteen years, sales of bicycles in English-speaking countries have been declining, and, even though there has been a steady expansion in the number of cycleways, bicycling is growing in very few places in the world. We are a long way from Utopia (which is not a town in the Netherlands).

The building of cycle infrastructure—and that can mean physically separated cycleways as well as cycle-priority streets, cycle parking facilities, and separation-by-time traffic signaling—is absolutely necessary for everyday cycling to grow, but I wouldn't go as far as two academics in the 1970s who warned "no bike paths, no bicycles." For a start, curb-separated cycleways are not necessary on every single street. For a large city, Amsterdam has wonderfully high cycle usage, but the riding is not all done on separated cycleways—there's also a lot of cycling on streets where the only protection is paint, and there's plenty of riding next to (or just as commonly, in front of) motor vehicles. And even on the best of Amsterdam's separated cycleways, cyclists are beeped and buzzed by motor scooters and micro-cars. Amsterdam's 110-year history of being a cycling city is inescapably the most important reason for why it remains a cycling city.

Nevertheless, the provision of cycleway networks is a measure of how welcoming a city wants to be to space-efficient non-polluters such as people on bikes. In the last ten years, there has been a growing consensus among those leading and taking part in the various bicycle movements around the world that high-quality cycleways are a Good Thing. There has been a substantial shift away from advocating for the 1970s-era swimming-with-the-sharks riding known as "vehicular cycling." This notion holds that "cyclists fare best when they act and are treated as drivers of vehicles" and that cyclists should mix with cars and trucks on roads, "which go everywhere." Instead, in cities around the world there is a deepening desire for a dense, Dutch-style grid of cycleways where people on bikes are protected from motorists and their often erratically and dangerously driven motor vehicles.

However, the provision of cycle infrastructure—known to most bicycling advocates as just "infra"—is not a silver bullet. Infra alone does not bring the masses to cycling. In general, the masses (unless they're Dutch, or from Copenhagen) appear not to want to cycle, especially when motoring is lavishly catered for, intensely marketed and, above all else, cheap. Naturally, there's a measure of suppressed demand for cycling, and the provision of high-quality cycleways has been shown to lead to an uptick in pedaling, but it cannot be denied that cycling has some physical drawbacks. The many benefits of cycling are well known, but it's also important to acknowledge the negatives, perceived or otherwise. Cycling involves effort: you sweat, and not just in hilly, hot, or humid cities (the e-bike could be one solution). It might require wearing helmets in some cities, which suppresses everyday cycling. Cycle in the rain and, even when you're dressed for it, you may get wet. You sit on a lump of leather: "my bum hurts" is a greater disincentive to cycling than many cycle campaigners ever stop to consider. There's no roof on a bike, no air-conditioning, no airbags. Carrying passengers is out of the question, and there are no doors to keep out ne'er-do-wells. And nor can you, comfortably, have sex on a bicycle.

These drawbacks are often described as "myths" by bicycle activists, and they—rightly—point to the fact that many global cities once had thriving cycle ecosystems. For instance, prior to the Second World War Christchurch in New Zealand was celebrated as the "Copenhagen of the Pacific" because—even without cycling infrastructure—so many of its residents dotted around on cycles. Today, the city has a (reasonably decent) cycling modal-share of 6 percent, but it's a (sad-for-cyclists) example of how, once a "cycling culture" is allowed to lapse, it's very difficult to bring it back, especially if motoring is cosseted, subsidized, and, frankly, preferred.

There are hard-to-shift socio-psychological reasons why many people won't ever take to urban cycling, including the very un-Dutch belief that riding a bike instead of driving is an affront to self-identity. In 2016, this palpable drop in status thanks to pushing pedals allowed the *Daily Mail* to lead with a front-page story claiming that protected cycleways, which have been installed on just 0.2 percent of London's roads, are the "new blight paralysing Britain." Motoring is deemed to be "normal," cycling is not. Cycling might be fine for kids (in parks and on trails) goes the thinking, but it isn't something for adults. In addition, cycling's association with sport and exercise can lead to it being framed as an illegitimate use of roads compared with use by motorists who "just need to get somewhere"—as if cyclists don't.

Cycle advocates sometimes state that a significant number of others share their enthusiasm, believing that the key thing that's stopping loads of people getting on bikes is the hostile road environment. It's far more complex than that. London's recent spike in bike use (confined to central London, and along a few corridors where cycling's modal-share, at peak times, can be as high as 70 percent) came about *before* the provision of short stretches of world-class infrastructure—in other words, when the road environment was still hostile.

"Build it and they will come" is a dead cert for motoring, but is not yet a given for cycling. It's possible that a great deal of the stellar usage witnessed on high-profile non-Dutch cycleways—such as Dearborn Street in Chicago, London's Embankment, and Multnomah Boulevard in Portland, Oregon—is the channeling of existing cyclists. Where before riders used a bunch of diffuse routes, they now go out of their way to ride on protected infra.

According to the US advocacy organization People for Bikes, the provision of protected bike lanes has been doubling every two years since 2009, but American cities still only have a few hundred miles of such cycleways. Sadly, there are also examples of cycleways being dug up, and if this fate is not to befall more of them—as happened in New York in 1980 (see epilogue)—usage has to be seen to be healthy. Motorists do not remark when a road is empty (except maybe to do a happy jig), but they very much remark when a cycleway is empty. London's curb-protected Cycling Superhighways are full to bursting in rush hour, but can appear empty at other times, which is distressing to cycle advocates, and ammunition for anti-cycling shock jocks.

Some things sell themselves. Motoring is one of those things. Cycling is not one of those things. Those who don't have access to cars are often regarded—and frequently regard themselves—as disadvantaged; only enthusiasts think the same about having access to bicycles.

Millennials may be turning away from cars because they'd rather be plugged into social media, but that's a fillip for sit-and-play public transit, not cycling. And the theory of "peak car"—that motor-vehicle use has peaked, and is now falling—is not as statistically solid as it looked during the last recession,

The joyful practicality of cycling.

when driving most definitely dipped. Terrible for the planet, and bad for both congestion and health, but car purchasing and car use are on the rise again.

This is due, in great part, to the built environment. Over the last sixty years, planners designed for "King Car" to the exclusion of all else, and we now have toxic, congested cities where one of the obvious solutions (obvious to cycle advocates, that is) is to plan for the bicycle. Dutch cities do such planning, so why can't others? It might come as a surprise to find out that cycle use in the Netherlands did not "boom" when the good existing network of cycleways was upgraded in the mid-1970s to became a dense grid. Cycle usage stabilized, it did not explode, as pointed out by the lead author of the *Dutch Bicycle Masterplan* of 1999: "Since 1990, the total length of cycle paths . . . increased to almost 19,000 km . . . double the length in 1980. Results: In 1994, the total distance cycled was 12.9 billion km, compared with 12.8 billion in 1990. . . . Expansion and improvement of the infrastructure does not necessarily increase the use of bicycles."

An expert from the Dutch Ministry of Infrastructure—which, critically, has been in the business of nation-building since 1798—made a similar point: "One of the beliefs in the bicycle world is that complete city networks for bicyclists stimulate people to make more use of the bike. . . . [In fact, after a] re-evaluation . . . only marginal positive effects upon bicycle use could be determined." Cycle usage in the Netherlands has steadily increased since the 1990s, but not as dramatically as is sometimes claimed, which is an uncomfortable fact for cycle advocates—such as myself—who assure planners and politicians that spending on cycle infra is a rock-solid investment that will bring in its wake social, economic, and health benefits. True, it *can* be a good investment, but we have to be careful not to oversell the likely growth in cycle usage. We may claim that the provision of high-quality cycle infra will lead to an upsurge in users, but this will not be the case in every locality (cycleways still work best in middle-class areas, but they often bomb in working-class ones), and it's going to take much more than providing infra to get people out of cars—and buses—and onto bikes.

If we tell politicians that "cycling is booming, so start building infra for it," politicians can say, "Great, it's booming, we don't need to do anything, it's clearly doing fine without any money or thought from us." If we say that "cycling is stagnating, so start building infra for it," politicians can say, "Oh, it's flatlining, is it? Well, no point throwing good money after bad, let it continue to flatline." This is a dilemma that has troubled cycling for nearly ninety years.

NOT MANY people think it is sensible to put their heads in the way of flailing lump-hammers, so it's no real surprise that survey after survey in America, Australia, and Britain finds that the fear of fast motor traffic is the number-one factor keeping people off bikes. No matter how often it's repeated that cycling is *statistically* safe—which it is—and that it's healthier to cycle than not cycle—which it is—people tend to consider *subjective* safety alone, and conclude that a near-miss is one near-miss too many. The building of short stretches of even superlative cycleways may not get these folks cycling because, they point out, not unreasonably, potential riders need a joined-up network before they'll take to pedaling. To make the point that road networks are only as strong as their weakest links, the British transport academic John Parkin asks his students to consider how the volume of traffic on the M6 motorway in northern England might be affected if there were a permanent closure between junctions 16 and 17. After allowing this to sink in, he adds: "Growth in cycling numbers will only become significant when networks for a wide range of cycle users reach completeness and maturity," but he complains that "the most difficult (and yet crucial) elements of cycle networks are left until last because of financial or political pressures. . . ."

And even when networks are complete, that doesn't necessarily mean people will use them, if, that is, the alternatives are more attractive. Stevenage in England has a dense grid of cycleways, fully separate from motor traffic and pedestrians, but those who live, work, and study in this postwar New Town don't cycle very much, and, comparatively speaking, they didn't even in the 1960s when the network was shiny and better looking than it is today. It's now an ossified network, unknown and largely unloved by residents, most of whom prefer to drive because driving in Stevenage is quick and convenient. People who say they'll start to cycle once a cycleway network is on the ground may, in fact, end up not cycling that much at all should driving—or getting the bus—be even easier. They may also say that there are long distances to cover (even when there are not) and multiple "trip-chaining" tasks to be carried out that, it's claimed, are only possible by using a car.

Citing "dangerous traffic" as a reason for not cycling is most certainly valid, but it also probably masks many other reasons why people don't cycle, reasons that surveys are not always very good at teasing out. People lie, hiding their real motivations from researchers, and perhaps even from themselves.

There's a great one-liner to counter the argument that there's no significant existing demand for cycleways: "You don't justify building a bridge by counting the number of people swimming across a river." This is true, but it's not how planners tend to think. Many of them—and the politicians who commission them—see their role as providing for the ways they see people traveling *now*, not for a way those people *might* travel if provided with other choices. Unsurprisingly, the majority of advocates for cycling are cyclists, and by definition, they believe cycling is better than not cycling. However, being a "cyclist" is often seen as a sin by some cycle advocates. Back in the 1970s many of the leading advocates for cycling were not cyclists—they were environmentalists. The Friends of the

Earth was at the forefront for calling for cycleways in Britain in the early 1970s, and in America during the same period there were groups such as the Friends of Bikeology. Most of these eco-warrior groups lost interest in cycling within a few short years, and it was the "hardcore" cyclists who remained as evangelists, but according to some modern cycle campaigners these "old guard" advocates are somehow the bad guys.

THE REASON the Netherlands now has a cycling modal-share of 26 percent is that it had one more than double that in the 1920s. Similarly, Copenhagen's status as the world's leading "cycling city" is due to the fact it was already thus in the 1930s. "Cyclists overrun the city . . . and rule the streets," explained an American filmmaker in a 1937 tourism newsreel. Copenhagen's current high cycling modal-share is the result of more than 100 years of continuous improvements. The growth of cycle usage in Copenhagen since 2010 has been impressive, but it was from an elevated base. Even at its worst in the 1970s, when cars started to overrun the city, Copenhagen had a cycling modal-share of 23 percent.

Meanwhile, in the United Kingdom and the United States, Australia, and New Zealand, it's surprising that transportation cycling has survived at all. The assumption in the 1960s was that cycling—dismissed by planners as an archaic, anti-progressive form of human-powered transport in a motor age—would have all but disappeared by the 1990s. Cycling was ignored, forgotten, left to rot.

In some locations, though, cycling appears to be healthy today. These places tend to have dense networks of cycleways, municipal car-restraint policies that have been in place for some time, and cultural acceptance of travel by cycle. Where cycling is prioritized—in paternalistic, socially minded towns and cities such as Münster and Freiburg in Germany, Groningen and Zwolle in the Netherlands, Västerås and Lund in Sweden—the quality of life tends to be higher than the national norm. The air is certainly cleaner, there's less noise, and there are far fewer road deaths.

We should take heart from what has happened in the last ten years in cities such as Seville in Spain, and Canada's Vancouver. Seville grew its cycling modal-share from a low base, thanks to a three-year "overnight" installation of a cycle

Motorists don't complain when a road is empty. . . .
Dual carriageway, Gateshead, northeast England.

network. Similarly, Vancouver has made deep investments in protected cycle infra in a relatively short space of time, and has seen a doubling of modal-share to 7 percent. There are also encouraging signs that new cyclists are attracted to the city's growing network of cycleways, and there are ambitious plans to grow the infrastructure even further. But spells of wet weather in Vancouver can result in reduced riding, allowing critics to argue that cycle infra takes valuable space away from all-weather motorists.

In low-cycling cities the *desire* to ride does exist—academics call it the "propensity to cycle"—but for cycling to flourish it will need cultural shifts, not just engineering ones. If infrastructure never attracted newbies, and if it *only* protected existing cyclists, that would still be of inestimable worth, but infra by itself does not always bring the huge jumps in modal shift often demanded by politicians keen to justify capital expenditure to cynical voters. "Soft" measures, such as cycle training, marketing, tougher enforcement of road laws, and suchlike, also do not work in isolation. The trick is putting a mix of measures into action.

Bike Boom chronicles how cyclists have been in the vanguard of trying to change cities for the better, but, as you will read, bike battles have raged for

SIDEWALK/PAVEMENT

In Britain, the word *pavement* is not anywhere near as descriptive as *sidewalk*, the American term for the same sliver of pedestrian infrastructure. When Americans—and all nationalities of road engineers, including British—talk about *pavement*, they mean the road, not the sidewalk. For clarity, in this book I use *sidewalk*. I also use American spellings throughout.

an awfully long time, and victories, sweet as they are, have been few and far between. Keep aiming for the stars, but be aware that interstellar travel is a long haul. Bike advocacy professional Dave Cieslewicz, a former mayor of Madison, Wisconsin, said in 2016 that "part of being a movement is creating a vision and that means asking for things that you know you won't get this time. It means pushing the envelope, aiming high so that if you fall short what counts for 'short' is . . . a pretty long way from where you started."

Cycling has made remarkable progress over the last fifteen years. In the late 1990s, there were very few MAMILs ("middle-aged men in Lycra") cycling to work on expensive carbon road bikes; "cycle chic" had to yet be commodified; and public bicycle-hire schemes were only just starting to appear in the "global city" form now so beloved by civic leaders. But in English-speaking countries, cycling is still far from being a normal, everyday form of transport that starry-eyed advocates, myself included, plug that it has the potential to be. Anti-cycling stigma runs deep. When even the *New York Times* felt it was fine to headline a story with "Is It OK to Kill Cyclists?" it's not at all clear that the word *cyclist* can be sanitized, as many advocates try, by replacing it with "person on a bike." A new protected cycleway in Scotland might have been promoted in photographs with small children cycling along it, but that didn't stop the *Daily Record* from running a story on how it parked a van on the "unwanted" cycleway in order to bring it to a "grinding, crushing halt." And a London magistrate told a 53-year-old investment banker that his crime of "furiously riding" on a sidewalk "diminishes the really rather low esteem cyclists already have. People do not like cyclists."

Stereotypes of people on bikes are often maddeningly contradictory: urban cycling is done by the cash-strapped carless *as well as* the rich elites who can afford expensive cars and fleets of bikes. In this poisonous worldview, protected cycleways are not safe corridors of rosy-cheeked health built to enable use by eight- to eighty-year-olds; rather, they are pork-barrel handouts for middle-class treehuggers *and* supposed wastrels. To many people all cyclists are the same, they are the "other," whether that's the Washington, DC, executive who commutes on the C&O Towpath to Georgetown on her $4,000 gravel bike or the low-paid Hispanic rider on his $130 Walmart bike carting clicker-cards along the sidewalks of Las Vegas.

Some advocates argue that the stigmatization of cyclists is the *result* of the famous "crap cycle lanes," but how then, in chicken-and-egg fashion, will such an out-group ever be provided with normalizing infrastructure?

DESPITE THE painful reality checks noted above, cycling *does* have massive potential, partly because of its current cachet, but most especially because the cities of the future look certain to grind to a halt if they continue with their present planning priorities. The unstoppable growth of urbanization is probably cycling's greatest chance to become a throbbingly vital transport mode. Over half of the car journeys people make in the UK, and most other places, are less than five miles long—easy cycling distance. Cities are set to become more crowded, and you don't have to be Nostradamus to predict that urban driving is going to be restricted in the years ahead, either by glut or design. Intelligent cities will do it by design, restricting the entry into central business districts of space-inefficient motor vehicles. (And that includes not just private cars, the use of which is falling in cities such as London anyway, but also vans, trucks, and taxis.) Global car production has almost doubled in ten years and is expected to double again by 2035. Carmageddon awaits for those cities that aren't planning for a vehicle-free future.

Driverless cars will work well on grade-separated, go-faster motor roads, but they have a far less certain future in city centers where cyclists and pedestrians could easily block their progress, thanks to the knowledge that autonomous vehicles are programmed not to bully humans out of the way, resulting in what

risk specialist John Adams calls "deferential paralysis." Even if pedestrians didn't play "chicken" in front of them, driverless cars would still be wrong for cities: if even a quarter of the 1.3 million daily commuters into central London switched to driverless cars, the roads would seize solid. For many cities, providing for cycling will become as necessary as providing for public transit and walking. And compared with the costs of pandering to cars, or building intra-urban bullet-train networks, providing infra for cyclists has off-the-scale benefit-to-cost ratios.

Providing such infra at a national scale—not just protected cycleways, but cycle parking and all the other necessities—is something that some bright non-Dutch politicians are going to do at some tipping point in the future. It won't happen quickly: it will take time to nibble away at the hegemony of the car, but there's a growing consensus—including from businesses—that we can't carry on providing only for cars.

Just don't think these are new concerns, or that lobbying for protected cycleways is a blogosphere-era revolution, or that the famously fantastic Dutch infrastructure fell from the sky forty years ago. It's too often forgotten, but today's cycle advocates stand on the shoulders of giants, and even the now-discredited "vehicular cyclists" tended cycling's flame when all around them planners and politicians were trying to snuff it out.

NOTES

The notes and references for this book are online at bikeboom.info/notes

---

(Left) The National Museum of the Netherlands—
the Rijksmuseum in Amsterdam—has a cycleway
running through it.

CYCLEWAY vs. BIKEWAY: Some definitions

There is no universally accepted name for cycle-specific infrastructure. Take your pick from *bike lane, bike route, bikeway, bike path, bicycle boulevard, green lane, blue lane, protected bike lane, "crap" cycle lane, buffered bike lane, cycle facility, shared-use, wheel way,* and *cycleway*. The National Association of City Transportation Officials (NACTO), in their *Urban Bikeway Design Guide*—America's official design guide for cycling infrastructure—calls protected bikeways *cycle tracks*. "Cycle tracks, as the Ministry of Transport persists in calling them . . . [risk] confusion with racing tracks," complained Britain's Cyclists' Touring Club in 1963. Nowadays we have the *cycle superhighway,* although the "super" was once very much open to question (though many of London's Cycle Superhighways were once paint-only, they now benefit from protection).

There are also *rail trails,* most of which were converted from the 1960s onwards, and, from the 1890s, *sidepaths,* built and paid for by American cyclists via sidepath commissions.

At the end of the nineteenth century, America had the world's best cycle infrastructure—the California Cycle-way and the Coney Island Cycle Path. I reckon *way* is a far more powerful word than *path*. In America and Britain, *path* became low-status: a path is deemed to be narrow and for walkers. (The words *path* and *pad* indicate earth beaten down by feet—either human or animal.)

The use of the right terminology can be important, especially in cultures that later downgraded the bicycle. In the Netherlands, a *fietspad*—or "bicycle path"—is not low-status.

Way denotes moving or traveling and comes from the same Sanskrit root (*vah*) as the words *wagon* and *vehicle*. Perhaps Eric Claxton, designer of the New Town of Stevenage in the 1950s and 1960s, had the right idea when he insisted that the separated cycle infrastructure he created had to be called *cycleways*. Claxton's granddaughter Joanna Brown told me he was very proud of his cycleways, and insisted on calling them that: "I remember as a child being pulled up for using the wrong term and being told 'paths are for pedestrians, tracks are for horses, I built cycleways.'"

Way is used a lot for roads: think of *freeway* and *motorway*. When I use the word *cycleway*, I mean a way for bikes away from roads as well as one that runs beside roads. Generally, a cycleway will offer some form of protection, either by running wholly away from a road or being bordered with curbs or other such barriers.

The commonest term in the 1970s in the United States—and which was used by legislators, although only ever loosely defined—was *bikeway*. From reading period texts and then looking at photographs of the infra in question, it's clear that *bikeway* could mean on-street painted bike lanes, on-street signed bike routes, off-street bicycle paths, and more.

Most US legislators still use the term *bikeway*. California's Department of Transportation once defined a fully protected cycleway as a "Class IV Bikeway." Because *bikeway* was rarely defined it was flexible: it could mean many things, allowing advocates to call for the provision of bikeways without specifying what they actually wanted.

Godfrey and Lillian Frankel used the term *bike-ways* in their 1950 guide *Bike-ways: 101 Things to Do with a Bike*, but they clearly meant ways of riding bicycles such as hosteling, bicycle games, and "bicycle safety meets." In the late 1960s, the US Department of the Interior used the term for rail-trails, cycle routes in parks, and tracks alongside urban roads. Bikeways were also described as Dutch-style "special bike roads" in 1973—even though they didn't actually exist in America.

And just as *cycleway*, *cycle track*, and *bikeway* can be used in different ways by different users, so too can modern advocacy phrases such as "space for cycling" (shared on social media as #space4cycling). Infrastructure-first advocates state that space for cycling means *curb-protected* space for cycling; others say it means "share the road"–style space carved out by lane-claiming "vehicular cyclists" on unreconstructed roads shared with motor traffic. You pays your money, you takes your choice.

1 | How Cyclists Became Invisible *(1905–1939)*

"Take care to get what you like or you will be forced to like what you get."

—George Bernard Shaw

THE BICYCLE IN THE BOOM OF 1896–97 was the plaything of the American and European elites, a signifier of status, health, and wealth. In post-boom America, the bicycle regressed, becoming a vehicle solely for juveniles. In 1920s Europe, the mass-produced bicycle evolved into a transport tool for working stiffs. On both sides of the Atlantic, cyclists faded from view. They became invisible in the Netherlands because bicycles were classless and ubiquitous; and they became invisible in Britain and America because bicycles were deemed to be proletarian or for play.

In 1912, a Dutchman resident in America asked a local how wise would it be for him to cycle in Washington, DC. "Such an attempt . . . would be tantamount to a revolution," came the tart reply. "In the past few years, so few respectable people have been sighted on a bicycle, that one runs the risk of earning sudden newspaper headlines that few would wish for."

Bicycling might have been beyond the pale in America, but elsewhere it was still a transport mode with muscle. By the end of the 1920s, the many advantages of cycling, including speed and thrift, brought millions of new cyclists onto the roads of Britain. Some cycle manufacturers promoted bicycles to blue-collar workers as tools of escape. "Is your life spent among whirring machinery, in adding up columns of figures, in attending to the wants of often fractious customers?" asked a 1923 Raleigh catalog:

> Don't you sometimes long to get away from it all? Away from the streets of serried houses . . . only a few miles away is a different land, where the white road runs between the bluebell-covered banks crowned by hedges from which the pink and white wild rose peeps a shy welcome. Sheltering amongst the trees you see the spire of the village church—beyond it that quaint old thatched cottage where the good wife serves fresh eggs and ham fried "to a turn" on a table of rural spotlessness, for everything is so clean in the country. . . . Rosy health and a clear brain is what Raleigh gives you. . . .

Hercules, by contrast, pitched its wares at working-class cycle commuters. In 1922, just before the start of a working-class bicycle boom, Hercules was making 700 machines a week. By the mid-1920s, a bicycle could be bought new for what the average laborer earned in two weeks—it was becoming an affordable luxury. By cutting prices even further, and advertising the fact, Hercules sold 300,000 bicycles in 1928. Five years later this had risen to 3 million sales per year. At the end of the 1920s, while manufacturers such as Raleigh continued to make and market bicycles for touring and leisure use, Hercules mostly made utilitarian bicycles. A Hercules bicycle was a workhorse, cheaper than its rivals, but still reliable. In 1939, Hercules made 6 million bicycles, making it one of the largest cycle manufacturers in the world.

With falling prices and rising wages, more and more people became able to afford bicycles. Yet the market growth in Britain, as we'll see later in the chapter, came at the same time as the government was actively marginalizing cycling.

American cyclists were even more marginalized, even though in a few US cities in the early twentieth century cyclists remained relatively numerous. A traffic count by the Minneapolis city engineer discovered that 1,258 cyclists passed a busy downtown intersection on one day in July 1911, and he counted an average of 669 cyclists per day during a full year of observing the city's traffic. Horse-drawn wagons dominated, with nearly 3,000 teamster wagons counted, and the number of people on bicycles was only 200 less than the average number of automobiles.

Columbia, one of the oldest and still at this time the leading American manufacturer of bicycles, switched from making high-end recreational cycles to workaday ones. The company's 1911 catalog suggested: "As a vehicle of daily use, and as a saver of time and . . . fares for those who would otherwise ride in the street car, there is nothing that gives so much return for a moderate investment as the bicycle." And these frugal machines were targeted at blue-collar workers:

> A great army of men and women daily ride to and from the store, factory, and office; by its means policemen cover long beats and are employed in a variety of service; the letter carrier finds his long route a comparatively easy matter to cover; telephone and telegraph linemen quickly and more easily reach the scene of their work; and thousands of boys on bicycles give to merchants the most economical of any quick delivery service.

A 1905 US census report on the cycle industry stated that the automobile's "remarkable growth is not, like that of the bicycle, based on a fad, and so liable to as sudden a decline," but it remains a stretch to claim, as some historians have done, that it was the automobile that killed the bicycle. The great nineteenth-century bicycle boom fizzled out some eight years before any significant rise in the sale of automobiles. The leisured elites who had flocked to the bicycle at the height of its popularity had rejected it before they sashayed over to motoring. This was exemplified by the fate of the California Cycleway, an ambitious elevated cycling highway built in 1899, but largely abandoned by the following year.

Promoted as an "ingenious scheme" that was to be an uninterrupted "paradise for wheelmen," the plans for the first elevated highway between the cities of Pasadena and Los Angeles were grandiose, but the grade-separated toll highway that towered over train tracks, road junctions, and slow-poke users of the rutted roads beneath wasn't completed to length. Only the first mile-and-a-bit was erected, which wasn't long enough to attract sufficient paying customers. Within just months of opening, the cycleway had become a loss-making stub of a route rather than a profitable cycling road for Pasadena's many wealthy cyclists. Had it been built to length in 1897, the year after it was first proposed, the cycleway might have turned a profit, and could have become the "splendid nine-mile track" that, in 1901, *Pearson's Magazine* (falsely) claimed it was.

Built with pine imported from Oregon, and painted green, the would-be superhighway had a lot going for it. For a start, it had high-society support: it was constructed for a company controlled by Horace Murrell Dobbins, Pasadena's millionaire mayor, and the investors included a recent former governor of California, as well as Pasadena's leading bicycle-shop owner. The cycleway was meant to run for nine miles from the upmarket Hotel Green in Pasadena down to the center of Los Angeles. The first short stretch opened to great fanfare on New Year's Day, 1900, as part of the route of that year's Tournament of Roses Parade. Three hundred and fifty bicycles, decorated with floral displays, took part in the main parade, and no doubt many of them were ridden down the wooden track by some of the 600 cyclists who took part in the cycleway's inaugural ride.

Because the truncated cycleway wasn't terribly long, didn't go where people wanted to go, and didn't have enough entry and exit points, it was of little practical value, and hence not used. In October 1900, Dobbins told the *Los Angeles Times*: "I have concluded that we are a little ahead of time on this cycleway. Wheelmen have not evidenced enough interest in it. . . ."

Despite the fact the California Cycleway was a dud before motoring became popular, newspapers and blogs claim that the cycleway was killed off by the automobile. "The horseless carriage . . . caused the demise of the bikeway," wrote the public information officer for the city of Pasadena on her blog in 2009. In 2005, a feature for the *Pasadena Star News* claimed that "Automobiles spelled doom for the cycleway." Numerous online mentions of the cycleway have trotted out the same angle. In January 2014, the architecture correspondent for Britain's *Guardian* newspaper even claimed that the structure, abandoned in 1900, was "destroyed by the rise of the Model T Ford," a car not introduced until 1908.

There's no proof that the advent of the automobile had anything whatsoever to do with the financial collapse of the cycleway. In 1900, motorcars were still fresh on the scene and very few people thought they had a certain future—even fewer thought they had an all-dominant future. By 1905 the scene had shifted, and a writer in that year could truthfully claim that in America at least, "[the] Bicycle [had] had its day." The pro-motoring author continued: "An Interregnum followed. The ale houses again sank into desuetude and scores of them were not

California Cycleway, Pasadena, 1900.
(Pasadena Museum of History)

aroused until a year or two ago when the prolonged toot, toot for the automobile horn told them that good times were coming round once more." In fact, the "interregnum"—a transitional period between two reigns—lasted longer than this automobilist claimed. Elites did not immediately transfer their affections from expensive, status-enhancing bicycles to even more expensive and status-enhancing automobiles: the transitional period lasted from 1898 through to about 1905. This wasn't because the elites bided their time; rather, it was more of a reflection of availability—there were very few motorcars made in this period, and most of them were made in France.

Bicycling went through a tough period of slackening demand, and it took some years before bicycling became a transport choice for working people. There was a thriving market for secondhand motor cars in America before there was even a sniff of an automobile boom in most European countries, and it was not until 1913 that motorcar sales in America overtook bicycle sales.

Then came darkness. "The lamps are going out all over Europe, we shall not see them lit again in our life-time," British Foreign Secretary Sir Edward Grey remarked to his friend on the eve of Britain's entry into the First World War.

The privations of this war led to a reawakening of interest in cycling in Britain (the same happened during the next war, too). "With the present decay of motoring," wrote a correspondent for the *Guardian* newspaper, "the push-bicycle has temporarily returned to its own."

> It is now possible for the weary cyclist to push uphill, taking the whole width of the road in his meanderings, without being irritated from the rear by the snappy snort of a car while he is smothered at the front by a plunging motor-bicycle. Three years ago the "push bicycle" had become a mere hack. . . . With the restoration of our highways and byways to civilisation, the old "tandem" for man and wife has awakened from its sleep; while children, "flappers," and timid-looking ladies are once more to be seen on their "wheels" as they were about a decade ago, there being little to scare them.

"But," warned the reporter, "all this is only for the duration of the war, unless road reform includes . . . special tracks for bicycles like those that run along many roads in Germany and some other Continental countries."

Special tracks for bicycles had been a feature of roads in the Netherlands since the late 1890s, and as I'll show in chapter 8, the provision of such cycle-specific infrastructure would continue, in fits and starts, for much of the twentieth century.

IN 1916, in an attempt to revive interest in American cycling, the cycle industry created a promotional platform: Bicycle Week. "The men and women who have persisted in their affection for the two-wheeled friend of mankind will work wholeheartedly for a rejuvenation of its popularity," wrote the *Washington Times*. "The bicyclists declare that the wheeling population hasn't decreased very

Bicycles were for boys. Howard Williams, thirteen-year-old delivery boy for Shreveport Drug Company. "Goes to the Red Light every day and night," Shreveport, Louisiana. (Library of Congress)

much. . . . Bicycle Week is to be observed in all sections of the people who deal in bicycle specialties."

The promotion wasn't terribly successful. As one observer put it three years later: "Today bicycling has its place. The young, the strong, those too poor to own motor cars, ride bicycles."

And for "young" and "strong" read: teenage boys. The US Tariff Commission remarked in 1921 that there "has remained a steady demand for the bicycle as a utility, widely used as a means of cheap transportation by laboring people and by boys." The Cycle Trades of America advertised to this demographic through the pages of *Boys' Life*, suggesting in 1925 that: "The BICYCLE is your best PAL! . . . The bike is your birthright." Such ads mostly targeted middle-class boys, but the bicycle was an essential tool for many working-class boys, with the telegram-delivery boy on his often-oversize bicycle being a common sight in American cities from the early 1900s through to the late 1930s. "Western Union Messenger Service is the BOYS' BUSINESS with a future," declared an ad in 1926. As historian James Longhurst has suggested, "the telegraph companies might have benefited from emphasizing this idea in order to keep wages down: work done by children certainly didn't merit a man's wage."

The association of bicycling with children—and especially with boys—reinforced the perception in America that bicycles were not for adults. And as the bicycle was now portrayed as a vehicle for mostly children, its presence on roads getting busier and busier with automobiles was increasingly questioned.

Road markings—or the lack thereof—were an effective way to marginalize the bicycle, yet, ironically, they had been introduced by a former cycling club official. Edward N. Hines of Michigan devised the painted highway center line, still one of the world's most important road-safety features. The first was installed on a rural highway in 1911, on the aptly named "Dead Man's Curve" along the Marquette–Negaunee road in Michigan. Hines conceived the separation idea when he was a motorist, but his interest in roads had started when he was a cyclist. Back in the 1890s, Hines had been chief counsel of the League of American Wheelmen's Michigan division, a vice president of the national organization and also president of the Detroit Wheelmen cycling club.

Such lines later marked out lanes for automobiles and parking areas, but few American cities before the 1950s striped their roads to show that cyclists belonged. Washington, DC, was an exception to this. "Another measure on the cyclist's behalf is marking of special lanes by white lines," reported *Collier's Weekly* in 1939. "You can sight-see in Washington on your bike by sticking to the streets marked off in this fashion."

However, such cycle-specific striping was rare, and in 1936, the League of American Wheelmen—an organization much reduced from the influential one of the 1880s and 1890s—reckoned that the development of on-street parking for automobiles was detrimental to cycling, complaining that cyclists "were finally deprived of the use of the roads they helped to build by the speeding motor car, plus the fact that our streets have . . . become public parking places."

By this time the League was a club for old-timers. The members may have bemoaned the encroachment of automobiles on the roads they had earlier helped to rejuvenate, but nevertheless most of them traveled to the decreasing number of meets in their motorcars. And such motorcars were rapidly taking control of the streets, both in town and in the countryside.

As Peter Norton has shown in *Fighting Traffic*, automobile interests invented the term "jaywalking" to shame pedestrians into keeping off the street. These interests joined forces after 1923, when the city of Cincinnati, Ohio, threatened to pass a law requiring speed governors on all motor vehicles, limiting them to 25 miles per hour. "Motordom" defeated the Cincinnati referendum and went on to develop a masterful, coordinated campaign to redefine what—and who—streets were for. Cyclists were labeled as "jay-cyclers"—a name that didn't catch on—but they too came to be seen as illegitimate users of the roads supposedly built for motorists.

Such reframing was most explicit during the development, in 1920, of the Uniform Vehicle Code: this was a set of national driving standards that were expected to be adopted by states and adapted to their statewide or city requirements. Bicycling was steadily downgraded by a number of versions of this code. Slow-moving cyclists came to be seen as "impeding" the progress of the more rightful user of the roads, the motorist. The 1930 UVC stated that "it shall be unlawful for any person unnecessarily to drive at such a slow speed as to impede or block the normal and reasonable movement of traffic." The 1938 revision judged that cyclists should "ride within a single lane." A further revision in 1944 redefined bicycles as "devices" and stated that "Every person operating a bicycle upon a roadway shall ride as near to the right side of the roadway as practicable. . . ." No exceptions were originally given, meaning cyclists had to ride in the gutter. The 1944 UVC also stipulated that "Wherever a usable path for bicycles has been provided adjacent to a roadway, bicycle riders shall use such path and shall not use the roadway."

"Usable"—then and now—was and still is open to interpretation. "Cyclists had no part in these decisions; they were made by motorists," claimed cycling engineer John Forester in 1994. "These rules meant that cyclists had to stay out of the way of motorists just as much as was physically possible, just in case a motorist might happen to come along and be delayed."

Known by its detractors as the Far to the Right law, or FTR, the 1944 revision remains controversial with so-called vehicular cyclists. They claim it led to cyclists being squeezed off the roads and onto substandard "sidepaths" (see chapter 6).

"THE BICYCLE of today has staged an amazing come-back in the past two years," wrote John E. Lodge in an article in *Popular Mechanics* in 1935. "Four million Americans now pedal along streets and highways," he wrote, perhaps a little optimistically. "Instead of subsiding, the tide of cycling popularity continues to rise," he continued, and remarked that "publicity agents" were behind the craze:

> About 1932, it is pointed out, publicity agents for Hollywood movie stars began to run out of ideas for "different" pictures that would be printed in newspapers and magazines. The actors and actresses had been shown engaging in every form of athletics, wearing almost every known costume, and riding in almost every kind of motor vehicle. The publicity men hit on the idea of having their stars photographed riding bicycles. Almost overnight, Hollywood became "bicycle conscious." What started as a mere publicity stunt, turned into an authentic cycling craze.

The *Popular Mechanics* piece may have been cobbled together from press reports, but it's interesting that it also stated that cyclists were now lobbying for their own space:

> Another outstanding development of the bicycle boom is the establishment of cycle paths in city parks. In the nineties, it was the bicycle rider who led the agitation for better roads. Now, the present-day enthusiast argues, the automobile age can repay its long-standing debt by providing such paths for bicyclists away from the dangers and fumes of the motor traffic which monopolizes our highways. At Chicago, in response to a monster petition signed by 165,000 bicycle fans, 100 miles of cycle trails are now being established. . . . To safeguard bicycle tourists riding on main highways, cycling organizations are now strenuously advocating that states authorize the construction of special paths along the shoulders of roads.

Of course, cycling organizations could advocate all they liked, but it didn't mean "special paths" would be provided, at least not on high-speed highways.

Rental bicycles in New York's
Central Park, 1942. (Library of Congress)

However, some cities did provide facilities for cyclists, some modeled on the burgeoning cycleways appearing in Europe at the same time.

Prompted by the 1933 opening of the St. Anna bicycle tunnel under the River Scheldt in Antwerp, Belgium, the famous *New Yorker* columnist E. B. White—author of *Charlotte's Web* and *Stuart Little*—wrote that he'd like to see the creation of a system of cycleways in New York City:

> We would like to see a network of permanent bicycle paths built throughout the East, to serve bicyclists in the special way that bridle paths serve equestrians. A great many people have now reached forty years of age in this country, despite all the handicaps, and they are the ones who specially enjoy bicycling, the men being somewhat elated on discovering that they can still ride no hands.

Just five years later the trick-riding White got his wish, thanks to Robert Moses. Possibly New York's master builder built for bicyclists because, as *Collier's Weekly* reported in 1939, he was a "bicycle bug" himself.

Moses is best known today as the planner whose plans for expressways through Manhattan were thwarted in the 1960s by urbanist Jane Jacobs. A journalist for the *Architectural Forum*, Jacobs rode around Greenwich Village on a bicycle, her handbag stashed in a wicker basket on the front. With her grey thatch and owlish glasses, and her undeniably brilliant writing, she is now usually portrayed as a David-vs.-Goliath heroine, with Moses as Goliath. In fact, the two only sparred in person once, and Moses appears only fleetingly in Jacobs's great 1961 work, *The Death and Life of Great American Cities*.

Moses is usually painted as a monster intent on putting cars where we now know cars shouldn't go, but this ignores his massive earlier influence on New York. For 44 years, from 1924 until 1968, Moses built parks, highways, bridges, playgrounds, housing, tunnels, zoos, and exhibition halls. The job of parks commissioner was just one of many he held simultaneously.

In *The Power Broker*, his 1974 biography of Moses, Robert Caro called Moses a genius and "perhaps the single most influential seminal thinker" in twentieth-century urban renewal, but Caro was also highly critical of the commissioner's autocratic style and bombast. After he forced the New York Aquarium to up-sticks to Coney Island a wag wrote:

> No one opposes Commissioner Moses,
> Even the fishes accede to his wishes.

Caro's Pulitzer Prize–winning book was dismissive of Moses' 1930s-style belief in the hegemony of the car. Moses' Triborough Bridge complex—the "biggest traffic machine ever built," according to Caro—was built without sidewalks or bike paths, and his New York was one of automobiles and skyscrapers, a vision of concrete that came to be discredited by later planners.

In a rebuttal to the Caro book, Moses countered that "we live in a motorized civilization." He may have been the car-loving destroyer of much of New York, but he couldn't himself drive—he had a fleet of cars and a number of chauffeurs at his beck and call. He was also instrumental in providing New York with a great many bikeways. In August 1938, Moses submitted plans for building 58 miles of bicycle paths within New York City's parks, with some as long as nine miles, that would join parks together. In a letter to Mayor La Guardia, Moses explained that he wanted to "turn back the calendar forty years" and cater again for cyclists, the numbers of which had increased dramatically in the early 1930s.

Moses wrote that "we have taken into consideration that nothing could be more exhilarating than riding up and down a short straight stretch of road" but that he also planned to create "winding layouts which will lead . . . from somewhere to some other place, and of such length and design that there will be no feeling of monotony to a person who rides his or her bicycle. . . ."

The Central Park roads would be narrowed to make way for "paths . . . wide enough for two lanes in each direction" and with "grade crossings at park drives . . . protected with traffic lights and definite barriers. . . ." Moses said that the park's roads were "unnecessarily wide, and reducing their width by one lane will have no material benefit on the movement of [motor] traffic through the park."

New York's separated bikeways were built next to the "parkway" roads commissioned by Moses, and some were used for utilitarian purposes. In one period photograph, the Belt Parkway bikeway was shown being used by seventeen or more cyclists, while the Belt Parkway itself was being used by just a few cars. Many of the cyclists using the wide bikeway—which was separated from the road by a barrier and from pedestrians by a raised curb—look as though they are riding to work.

However, most cycling in this period was recreational. There was an increase in adult bicycle purchases in the 1930s. The *New York Times* reported that just 180,000 bicycles had been sold in 1932; 643,000 were sold in 1935, rising to 1.3 million in 1937. A doubling of market size might seem impressive but the increase was short-lived, and even at the peak of this micro-boom the numbers of people cycling in America were tiny compared with the numbers of people cycling in Europe, where "pappa, mamma, and the children never forsook the bike," reported the magazine of the US Rotary Club in 1938. The *Rotarian* stated: "In Europe, where bicycles are economically important as means of transportation, special cycle lanes have long been in use."

UNLIKE IN America in the 1920s and 1930s, cycling in many European cities remained both popular and normal. Bicycles were not just for children, they were for almost everybody—ministers and midwives, doctors and dentists, bakers and butchers, schoolchildren and soldiers, postmen and pilots. In the mid-1930s, there were 15 million cycles in daily use in Germany, and 7 million in France. In the Netherlands every second citizen owned one—a Dutch Ministry of Transport report of 1934 revealed that bicycles represented a staggering 95 percent of the vehicles in regular use. In Britain, there were 12 million cyclists, and fewer than 2 million motorists. Cyclists dominated on many British roads, including the new "arterial" ones. On approaches to large factories and dockyards, cyclists at clocking-off time would clog the roads solid. According to a 1935 Ministry of Transport census, cycles accounted for 80 percent of the vehicular traffic in some English towns. The minister of transport admitted: "It is indisputable that the number of cycles on the road is far in excess of the total of all other classes of road vehicle, public and private, passenger and goods."

Despite this dominance, British motorists demanded that the majority users of the roads should step aside for their betters. Cycling organizations felt that if anybody should be corralled it ought to be motorists. Policy makers and urban planners—most of whom were rich motorists—begged to differ, and they wished for cyclists to be provided with their own infrastructure. While cycleways beside major roads were by now rather normal in the Netherlands (and mandatory), they were deeply controversial in England (partly because of this compulsion).

Framed as a measure to reduce what was a dreadful death toll among cyclists, cycling organizations believed the true motive of the "experimental" cycle-track building was to force cyclists to use narrow, inferior paths in order to increase the utility of motoring. A pamphlet produced by the Cyclists' Touring Club voiced this concern:

> Most people and organisations who advocate cycle paths are not actuated by motives of benevolence. . . . If they did recommend them merely because so many cyclists were being killed they would recommend separate paths for motor cyclists as well, for the death rate among motor cyclists is the highest of all road users and fifteen times as great as that among cyclists. A great deal of the cycle-path propaganda is based on a desire to remove cyclists from the roads. That is why the request for cycle paths is so often accompanied by a suggestion that their use should be enforced by law. Therein lies a serious threat to cycling.

London's Western Avenue cycling tracks, c. 1936, before the surrounding fields were turned over to factories and houses.

The CTC also believed in the out-of-sight, out-of-mind theory that once cyclists were removed from some roads, motorists would not want to see them on *any* roads:

> The provision of some roads with cycle paths would naturally confirm inconsiderate motorists in a false belief that they need have less regard for other classes of road users. Driving would become faster and more reckless on all roads, including the majority of roads that could not be provided with cycle paths.

Transport minister Leslie Hore-Belisha admitted that cycle tracks would not be built on every road, but denied there was any plan to banish cyclists from the highway. His private secretary told one letter writer: "It should be obvious that it will never be possible to provided separate tracks for cyclists on more than a small percentage of public highways of Great Britain and there is therefore no question of the permanent exclusion of cyclists from the roads as a whole. In view of these facts it is Mr Hore-Belisha's earnest hope that the cycling organizations will not persist in opposition to these cycle tracks."

Nevertheless, a road network freed of cyclists was the ardent desire of motoring organizations, leading police officers, county council officials, road engineers, and newspaper editorialists. Cyclists ought to be compelled to use cycle paths when provided, argued motorists and organizations other than cycling ones. In 1935, Sir Charles Granville Gibson, the Tory MP for Otley, wrote to Hore-Belisha suggesting that cyclists would welcome the provision of tracks, and those that didn't should be chastised:

> I have received letters from the chairmen of the Hercules Cycle & Motor Company, and they both oppose the provision of walks allocated for pedal cyclists only. Now these two people must be prejudiced people and interested in selling cycles, or else they would not write the nonsense they do. If they have travelled in Denmark and Holland . . . they will have realised that a cyclist gets all the liberty he wants . . . As cyclists [here] become accustomed to [the tracks] they will not raise the slightest objection. I believe in Holland, cyclists are prosecuted if they travel on the main highways.

IN FEBRUARY 1934, Colonel Bressey, the Ministry of Transport's chief engineer, contacted the director of the Dutch infrastructure ministry to ask him about the wide cycle tracks the Rijkswaterstaat had built beside a number of new arterial roads in the Netherlands. W. G. C. Gelinck responded with a number of plans, maps and other advice, all in English. "In Holland, with the great number of cycles . . . all modern roads are provided with special cycle-tracks apart," Gelinck told his counterpart. "No traffic betterment for motor traffic can work unless the cyclists have left the main roads. [They are] a perpetual danger for themselves and for the traffic."

Impressed, Bressey commissioned the building of Britain's first off-carriageway cycle track, a two-and-a-quarter-mile stretch of uneven concrete from Hangar Lane to Greenford Road in Ealing, London, kept separate from but adjoining Western Avenue, a relatively new arterial speedway (today's A40). The nearly 9-foot-wide cycle track was operational by May 1934. A brochure

Days after this photograph of the Amsterdam–Haarlem road appeared in the *Times* of London in February 1934 the Ministry of Transport sought cycle track advice from the Dutch infrastructure ministry.

produced for the official opening in December of that year puffed: "For workers traveling between their homes and the factory, for children proceeding to and from school, for holiday-makers intent on a country jaunt, these tracks should prove a boon and a safeguard."

A voiceover on British Pathé cinema news said the Western Avenue cycle track was "a new safety innovation" and that "motorist users of the road will be equally appreciative of this new boon." A small crowd witnessed Hore-Belisha cutting the ribbon officially opening the experimental "cycling track." He said the track was for the "comfort and safety" of cyclists.

Hore-Belisha was no fan of cycling—he believed cyclists were the "most dangerous people on the roads today" and, in Parliament in July 1934, when Viscountess Astor asked whether a "system could be devised to prohibit pedal cycling in very crowded areas," he answered: "I quite appreciate her humanity of view." Opposition to the Western Avenue path came from the Cyclists' Touring Club, the National Clarion Cycling Club, the National Cyclists' Union, bicycle manufacturers such as Hercules, and the bicycle industry's representative body.

Hore-Belisha described representatives of such cycling groups as "hysterical prima donnas."

The Perils of the Cycle Path, a CTC leaflet produced in 1935, made it plain that club cyclists did not want to be fobbed off with substandard cycle tracks, and they feared being compelled to use them, as had happened in Germany, Belgium, and the Netherlands. The leaflet, subtitled "How Confusion Would Occur at Road Junctions," complained that the proposed paths provided protection on the straights, but none at junctions or side roads. One early cycle track design, which was implemented at least once, had a central cycle track sandwiched in the middle of two carriageways—with cyclists left to their own devices at crossroads. "The Club upholds the view that special paths would not prove a remedy for the existing problems of the roads—would, indeed, increase and complicate them."

While club cyclists were opposed to cycle tracks, it's probable that "casual" cyclists preferred them. In 1935, Hore-Belisha told parliament that "over 84 percent of all cyclists proceeding along the section of Western Avenue, where cycle tracks have been provided, used the tracks. Signs have been erected at intervals stating that the tracks are for cyclists only." A 1937 traffic census on the Great West Road cycle track found that, at one measuring point, on an August Monday, 1,187 cyclists used the track, with 816 preferring to duke it out with motors on the road. However, at another point, 1,049 cyclists used the track and 1,303 used the road, suggesting that some sections of the track were deemed to be more practical to ride on than others.

Media commentators saw things differently, claiming to witness greater use of the road. "On the Great West-road only one cyclist in ten was using the traffic lanes provided for them," griped 'Peterborough' in the *Daily Telegraph*. "Doubtless the screeching of car brakes is stimulating to them."

Another newspaper was incredulous that cyclists would be opposed to "special tracks" and that compulsion to use them would, therefore, be required:

> It is evident already that this innovation is strongly resented by a section of cyclists who see in it a formidable conspiracy to deprive them of their right of access to the roads. [The] National Cyclists' Union passed a resolution calling for a united front against "any attempt to curtail their rights on the King's Highway" and suggesting, besides monster meetings and a national petition, mass rides along highways where cycle paths are being built.

The *Western Morning News* then editorialized: "One trusts that when it comes to the point, more prudent tactics . . . will prevail." Admitting that cyclists were a "numerous contingent"—but not stating they were, as most people would have understood, the majority users of the road—the newspaper claimed cyclists "have nothing to gain by closing their eyes to the tremendous changes that have taken place on the roads during recent years and which make further rationalisation unavoidable."

The newspaper's editorialist was in all probability a motorist, and he (most newspaper journalists at this time were men) was keen for cyclists, many of whom were women, to get out of the way. "Mere windy assertions about the inviolable rights of true-born Britons to go as they please lead nowhere," he fumed. The paths were coming, he believed, and they would soon be compulsory so "it might be better if cyclists were to concentrate on ensuring that the tracks to be constructed fulfil the conditions which are necessary for safe, speedy, and enjoyable cycling."

The impetus for building such tracks came from motorists, who wanted to drive fast on the new arterial roads that had been built in the 1920s. The first, and greatest number, of these roads radiated out from London, where there were the greatest number of motorists but also where political power resided. London's new arterial roads were often used by members of the upper classes to speed them twenty miles or so from Mayfair to novel and decadent "roadhouses" with their swimming pools, clubrooms, and all-night drinking, where "high-rolling, metropolitan members of London society" would "race down" for a night of debauchery. "Their number included . . . the Prince of Wales, which gave the royal seal of approval for attending roadhouses rather than his more usual choice, the Embassy club in Piccadilly." The Ace of Spades roadhouse at Heston on the Great West Road, close to Western Avenue, did a "roaring trade" with these high-rollers, and had been built at a time when many parts of Britain were enduring desperate poverty. "One of London's richest men, Lord Londonderry, who kept four chauffeurs for his Park Lane home, was happy to drive himself along arterial roads at great speed," recounts the motoring historian Michael John Law.

The high-speed socialites were often the same politicians who demanded that cyclists should be removed from roads "for their own comfort and safety." They blamed cyclists for the fact that fast travel on the arterial roads was becoming more and more difficult. The numbers of cyclists on these roads did, indeed, increase in the 1930s—the average number of cyclists on Western Avenue at one point increased from 1,772 in 1931 to 6,515 in 1935—but there were other, probably greater, reasons for the slowing in driving speeds, including the increasing number of cars on the roads. In London's Home Counties there was a 400 percent increase in car ownership between 1926 and 1938. As suburban car ownership increased, progress on the arterials was interrupted by motor vehicles entering from the side roads that housed new homes and factories. Cyclists, in effect, became scapegoats for the congestion that they didn't cause, a blame game that's still played today.

"THERE IS a universal demand made upon me . . . for cycling tracks," Hore-Belisha told the British Electrical Development Association in 1938. "I find the pressure irresistible." Ernest Snowden of the Anfield Bicycle Club suggested this was so motorists could drive faster: "It needs no prophetic ear to detect the knocking of the enemy at our gates . . . clamouring that we should forfeit our freedom of the roads, that he may . . . hurl his death-dealing machines across this fair land of ours, utterly regardless of the lives and rights of the great non-motoring majority. . . ."

Snowden urged that individual cyclists and cycling groups should stand together to fight against the tracks. "We are a disintegrated whole, possessing neither abundant strength, nor far-reaching power, yet by unity both may be attained. Already the two great bodies which represent cycling interests are joining forces against the common menace. . . ."

A mass meeting of cyclists was held in the center of Liverpool in January 1935. Another was held in London—500 club cyclists met in Hyde Park before riding to the cycle tracks on Western Avenue, which they pointedly refused to ride along, choosing to cycle in formation on the main carriageway, three and four abreast. "It is no use grousing that the cycling organisations should do this and that: ask yourself what *you* are doing!" thundered Snowden. "If you are driven off the roads onto cycle paths, you will only have yourself to blame. . . ."

The Cyclists' Touring Club organized protest rides against cycle tracks, including a 1937 action that blockaded the York-to-Malton bypass. "The proposal is to make a demonstration of a refusal to use the [cycle tracks]," John Bevan told the *Yorkshire Evening Post*. Bevan, who was secretary of the county

A caption in *Cycling* magazine beneath this photograph of a wide, curb-protected track in Manchester recommended that "In their own interests cyclists are advised not to use them."

branch of the Cyclists' Touring Club, said the mass ride would "take place on a very busy day" and suggested that club cyclists might station themselves at the entrances to the cycle tracks on weekends, handing out literature urging "private cyclists" not to use them. "Following our usual practice when the rights and privileges of cyclists are threatened, we raised objections when the scheme to make these tracks was first mooted," Bevan pointed out. He disputed that the cycle tracks would offer much safety and added that "we believe that if these come about generally, the next move will be a tax on cyclists to pay for something we do not require."

County surveyor R. Sawtell told the newspaper: "The County Council has been generous to cyclists in the provision of tracks on this section of road. The Ministry of Transport laid it down that we should provide tracks six feet wide. We have made the tracks nine feet wide." He stressed that "the provision of cycle tracks is the declared policy of the Minister of Transport." He also revealed that the Transport Ministry had ways to make local councils play ball—central government grants for bypasses and arterial roads would only be provided to those schemes that included cycle tracks.

When asked whether cyclists used the tracks on the York–Malton road (today's A64) Sawtell replied: "What you may term the 'private cyclist' is using them. The club cyclists are not using them. It is a pity . . . we have done everything possible to make the tracks beyond the criticism of cyclists. I have heard that on Whit Monday club cyclists were trying to induce the 'private cyclist' not to use the tracks."

There were many other efforts at dissuasion—a caption in *Cycling* beneath a photograph of a young woman cycling on a wide, curb-protected track on a residential Manchester road recommended that "In their own interests cyclists are advised not to use them."

Most of the pre–World War II cycle tracks were short (two to four miles usually, although the one built along the Southend Arterial Road was—in fits and starts—23 miles long), and didn't usually link in to wider networks of such tracks. Club cyclists thought them to be a poor substitute for the roads they were used to riding on. Even one of the designers wasn't impressed. Eric Claxton, then a junior engineer in the Ministry of Transport (whom we shall meet again in chapter 7, but in a different era), was an everyday, practical cyclist. The cycle tracks he worked on in London were substandard. "As a cyclist, they gave me no satisfaction," he complained:

> They were too narrow. They were made of concrete and suffered from either cracking or construction joints. They provided protection where the carriageway was safe but discharged the cyclists into the maelstrom of main traffic where the system was most dangerous. For me worst of all the tracks were uni-directional either side of the dual carriageways; thus if for any reason one needed to retrace one's way, one was compelled to run the gauntlet of crossing the streams of traffic on both carriageways to return on the far side—woe betide the person who left money, keys, books, tools or even lunch behind.

But it wasn't just cyclists who thought the eight-and-a-half-foot-wide path on Western Avenue disjointed and bumpy. The Automobile Association, the Royal Automobile Club, the police, and many others, also said Britain's first modern cycle track was poorly executed. Better ones should be provided, were

This 1-mile cycle track was built in 1937 beside the A1 trunk road south of
Neville's Cross in northeast England. (Durham County Archives)

"segregation" to be compelled by law, a parliamentary committee chaired by
Lord Alness was told in 1938. When the committee's report was published, one
of the chief recommendations was that cyclists should be provided with wide,
well-surfaced cycle tracks, separated from fast-moving motor vehicles.

Despite CTC and NCU opposition to the uneven Western Avenue cycle
track, often crowded with pedestrians, the Ministry of Transport ordered more
cycle tracks to be built. By 1940, more than 200 miles of new arterial roads had
protected cycle tracks running beside them, with others "under construction"
and a further 300 miles planned. Britain's cycle track network was growing
(I have identified more than 80 of them so far) and, with Ministry of Transport
arm-twisting, likely to increase. The Alness Report recommended that the
building of a fully segregated national cycle network should be accelerated, with
cyclists and pedestrians given protected slices of the newly minted highways.

Cycle tracks built in the 1930s—like many of those in Britain today—were
used also by pedestrians, didn't form a usable network, and frequently required
cyclists to give way at the increasing number of side roads and residential
driveways.

Expensive cloverleaf intersections for motorists could be designed and
budgeted for at this time, but similar intersections for cyclists would be

The Neville's Cross cycle track still exists and still has its original concrete surface; the A1 has now been renumbered to A167. See bikeboom.info/cycletracks1930s

"impossible" or "too costly," town planners told the six peers on the Alness committee. (The Automobile Association submitted plans to the committee showing underpasses and other cycle path features that were similar to those built in Utrecht in 1941 but which only started to become commonplace in the Netherlands from the 1970s.) In evidence given to the committee, witness after witness—from surveyors to arch motorists—attested to the dire nature of England's cycle tracks but, apart from cyclist witnesses, most wanted cyclists to be forced to use the tracks.

When questioning witnesses, the peers on the committee—the Lords Iddesleigh, Birkenhead, Brocket, Rushcliffe, Addison, and Alness—made frequent mentions of their love of motoring, a bias not lost on interested parties. In a parliamentary debate welcoming the Alness Report, Lord Sandhurst said:

... the editor of *Cycling* finds it necessary to invent a new body of your Lordships' House, which he calls the Peers Road Council. Having invented it, he then elects four members of the Select Committee to it . . . and then, having described them as keen motorists, he says, "Let us see what this Committee recommends for cyclists." What is the idea? Obviously they are trying to get at their not too well educated public and suggest that this is such a biased Committee that no attention need be paid to their recommendations.

The motoring bias of the report is as obvious today as it was obvious then. Motoring organizations and motoring magazines were very much in favor of almost all of the report's nearly 300 recommendations. *Commercial Motor* described the report as "the finest of its sort that has ever appeared" and liked its victim-blaming approach:

The case for the fair-minded motor driver has been put forward admirably. There is little need to read between the lines to appreciate that the Committee is fully aware how the good driver is constantly "nursing" the careless pedestrian and, often, the cyclist. . . . Exception is taken to "a popular fallacy . . . that the motor driver, being in control of what is sometimes termed a lethal weapon, is usually to blame when an accident occurs." This is a destructive attitude, whilst the Report throughout is constructive. Its compilers obviously realize that progress, represented by fast road transport, is desirable, that the change of conditions following in its train must be accepted, that the mode of life of the people must be modified in accordance and adapted to the new conditions, and not that progress should be checked in order that that mode of life may remain unaltered.

There was palpable excitement from the peers at the prospect of German-style autobahns being built in Britain—free of cyclists, pedestrians, and animals—and frustration when cyclist and pedestrian groups said they weren't too keen on ordinary roads being made into "race tracks for motors." Lord Brocket, for one, didn't fancy being forced to drive at a prescribed speed: "I drive a lot and I must admit that I regard the speed [limiting] device as being very dangerous."

Soon after being built, some of the 1930s cycle tracks were narrowed to make more room for motor vehicles. Yet cycling was booming. Six million more people had taken to riding bicycles since 1928, the peers were told, a fact that "staggered" Lord Alness. Cyclists were largely "proletarian," said one lord in the debate launching the Alness Report of 1939, and so were not deemed to be as valuable to the economy—or the war effort—as motorists. (In the 1930s, the motor industry was cosseted because it was expected that car production would be shifted to military vehicle production; bicycle factories, such as the Raleigh plant, were also converted for armaments production, but Sturmey–Archer gears couldn't power tanks. And, roads, unlike the railways in the 1926 General Strike, couldn't be brought to a standstill by powerful unions.)

In evidence given to the Alness committee, CTC officials stressed that the main objection was to the *quality* of cycle tracks, and not just to the principle of being able to continue riding on the carriageway. The CTC feared that legislation would be brought in that would make it compulsory to use such tracks even before a useable network had been built, and that going by the poor provision of tracks in the previous five years, there was little likelihood that the tracks of the future would be of good quality.

Some older club cyclists might have hankered after the old days—of riding on bucolic country lanes empty of motor traffic—but many of the younger ones *preferred* to ride on the concrete arterials. The new roads—gleaming white ribbons of modernity—were smooth and built for speed.

The new arterial roads might have been busy with motor traffic on holiday weekends, but they were often quiet at other times. In effect, Britain's cyclists felt they had been provided with speedways, and they baulked at the prospect of giving them up to ride on narrow, bumpy cycle tracks where they might have to ride slowly, in single file. Writing in 1943, CTC secretary George Herbert Stancer noted that: "A young lady who overtook me on my last journey [on Western Avenue], and rode with me for a short distance, told me that she had to cover 15 miles each way on her daily trips between home and work, and that she was obliged to keep on the road in order to maintain the necessary speed. . . . Resorting to the paths would have slowed her down too seriously."

Club cyclists also wanted to do what motorists could do, and that's talk to someone beside them. The right to the road also meant the right to ride two or more abreast, chatting with companions as they rode out fast to some tearoom or other.

Ministry of Transport traffic surveys showed how cycle use on the new arterials exploded in the mid-1930s. Ministers and their mandarins, road planners, and motoring-besotted newspaper letter writers complained bitterly about being blocked by packs of cyclists, and even industry figures couldn't believe their eyes: "I was amazed when I saw the large number of club cyclists on the main roads last weekend," wrote a cycle-trade visitor from South Africa.

The smooth, fast "motoring" roads might have been deadly for cyclists, but club cyclists loved riding on them. Literary diarist and day-tour cyclist John Sowerby remarked in 1939: "It is good to be on the road . . . especially these great arterial roads and by-passes with plenty of traffic—keeps one alive. Swarms of coaches, buses, lorries and smaller-fry all around one, and if one day one of them does hit me out, well, I have enjoyed their company ever since they came into being; and the roads would be dull indeed without them. . . ."

Such opinions horrified the peers on the Alness committee. The following exchange between CTC secretary George Herbert Stancer and his aristocratic interlocutors clearly shows the antagonism between the parties, although the CTC man remained polite throughout.

> **Lord Alness:** "Your Association is . . . broad-minded enough to regard motor traffic as necessary and proper development?"
>
> **Stancer:** "Yes, my Lord. Of course, we have grown up with the motor movement and I think that during the whole of that period we have treated it with perhaps more tolerance than we have always received at the hands of the people who have been concerned with motoring."
>
> **Lord Alness:** "Is your Club in favour of the provision of separate cycle tracks for cyclists?"
>
> **Stancer:** "No, my Lord, we are not. Our feeling is that cycle paths at the side of the road do not, in the present circumstances, and never can, provide the same facilities for enjoyable cycling as are provided by our present road system."
>
> **Lord Alness:** "I should have thought personally that it would be more enjoyable to cycle on the cycle track on the Great West Road than to cycle on the highway there?"

Stancer: "Those people who are not accustomed to cycling always tell me that and I think that it must be a general view. . . . The fact of it is that the existing experiments in the construction of cycle paths are, I think, most unsatisfactory and they have created a bad impression amongst cyclists."

Lord Alness: "Assume the track was adequate in dimensions, in breadth, as in Germany, 9 feet let us say, and its surface was good, do you not approve of the experiment at least being made?"

Stancer: "On most of them even if we had a sufficient width and an excellent surface there is still the disadvantage that the track by the side of the road is constantly being interrupted and broken by the passage of other tracks coming from houses. . . . Every time there is a private house with a garage or there is a filling station or there is a . . . way into a shop . . . everything has to come across the cycle path; so that while on the carriageway you get a perfectly straight, smooth, unbroken, uninterrupted course for whatever vehicle is using it, the cyclist has always got something coming across."

Lord Alness: "But he is not submitted to the same dangers as when he is cycling on the highway on the Great West Road?"

Stancer: "No, my Lord. My suggestion is that those dangers ought to be removed."

Lord Alness: "Is that not a counsel of perfection? The removal of the dangers seems rather idealistic?"

Stancer: "The other alternative seems to be a counsel of despair: 'The law is powerless to preserve you on the road now; you must get off the road.' That is roughly what it comes to."

The six Lords were dissatisfied with the answers from Stancer so they recalled him five days after his first appearance. The Earl of Iddesleigh returned to the use of cycle tracks.

Earl of Iddesleigh: "If we could enable you to avoid the great motor roads and provide for you really satisfactory roads on which you would not have to compete with a great deal of fast-moving traffic, there would be a gain in enjoyment?"

Stancer: "If it were possible to provide facilities that are equal to those that we enjoy now, with the advantage that they would not be shared by motorists, I think that cyclists would have no objection. . . ."

Earl of Iddesleigh: "Are the two grounds upon which you are against cycle tracks these? First, because the cyclist insists on his abstract right to the use of the highway, and secondly, because it is less pleasant to use a cycle track than a highway?"

Stancer: "The second one you have mentioned is far more important. Cyclists would never insist upon their abstract rights if it were not that they are losing the chief pleasure of cycling by being forced onto the paths. If the paths are by any miracle to be made of such width and quality as to be equal to our present road system, it would not be necessary to pass any laws to compel cyclists to use them; the cyclists would use them."

The Alness Report of 1939 recommended that children of ten and under should be banned from the public highway on bicycles, and that segregation on the roads should be carried out with utmost urgency. Cyclists, said the report, should get high-quality cycle tracks and should be forced to use them. Pedestrians were also to be fined for daring to cross the road at points other than designated crossing points. Motorists, decided the motoring lords, should be treated with a light touch by the law, and should be provided with motorways and many more arterial roads. (Naturally, there were no recommendations that motorists should be restricted to motorways alone—today this would mean motorists would have access to only 2 percent of the roads in Britain.)

The House of Lords committee published its findings in March 1939; war was declared in September. The Alness Report—derided by one Labour MP as a "tale of deaths and manglings . . . and extraordinary conclusions"—was mothballed. After the war, a House of Commons select committee dusted it off. Many of

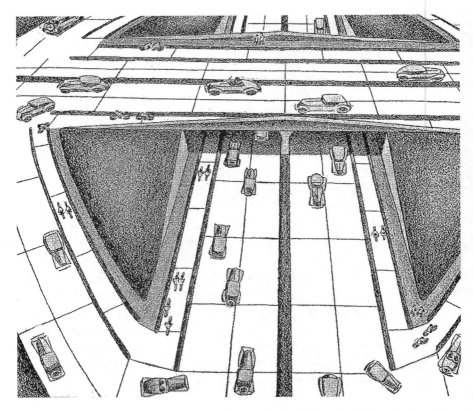

In 1936, Britain's Cement and Concrete Association
imagined a future of concrete roads and cycle tracks.

the Alness Report's recommendations were taken forward, but only the pro-motoring bits; the cycling bits were dropped.

Postwar austerity killed off putative plans for a national network of cycle tracks. Nor was there any immediate construction of "motorways"—the first wouldn't be built until 1958. The government's first priority was housing: building "homes for heroes." But while there would be no more provision of cycling infrastructure, postwar politicians were still urged by motoring organizations and newspapers to force cyclists off the roads, even though cyclists were still by far the most numerous actors on the roads—and probably *because* cyclists were still the most numerous actors on the roads.

Faced with calls to take action, politicians did what they often do best:

they did nothing. Cyclists were still a force to be reckoned with. It was easy for politicians to pick a fight with the CTC or NCU (these organizations were tiny compared to the combined might of the 51 organizations that made up the British Road Federation at the time), but to impose restrictions on all of the country's 12 million cyclists would have been folly.

(One of the witnesses to the original select committee said as much, showing how a powerful minority had no qualms about extinguishing the rights of a weak majority: "[Cyclists] ought to be forced to use [tracks]. The only reason they escape is because there are so many of them. There is a vague idea on the part of Governments that they would lose the cyclists' vote." This was the claim of Lord Newton, who repeated the claim when the report was published: "[Cyclists] form a very formidable body, of which all Party politicians are very much afraid. That is the sole reason why they have not been regulated up to now, and I hope sincerely that that state of things will come to an end.")

By not banning cyclists from the road, as many organizations demanded, politicians avoided antagonizing cyclists. By building roads with no cycle facilities on them, it was motorists who did the antagonizing. Nineteen-forty-nine was to be the peak year for cycle usage in Britain. In the 1950s, the increasing numbers of motorcars slowly forced cyclists off many roads, and not just the arterial ones.

Motorways—roads long championed by the CTC as a means of removing fast-moving traffic from the ordinary roads of Britain—started to be built at the end of the 1950s, but it was well into the 1960s before motorway-mania took hold, with many trunk roads also being built or old roads widened, straightened, and made less friendly for cyclists. None of the postwar arterial roads had cycle tracks built beside them.

The "right to the road" concept had been common among middle-class cycling officials, but it was irrelevant to the bulk of cyclists riding to and from factories and who, because of their numbers, dominated on the roads at certain times anyway. In 1958, Professor Sir Colin Buchanan, soon to become Britain's top town planner, wrote: "The meagre efforts made to separate cyclists from motor traffic have failed, tracks are inadequate, the problem of treating them at junctions and intersections is completely unsolved, and the attitude of the cyclists themselves to these admittedly unsatisfactory tracks has not been as helpful as it might have been."

Club cyclists didn't warm to the tracks *because* they were unsatisfactory. This was stressed by a Ministry of Transport report in 1944 that stated that the opposition of cyclists "does not arise from a spirit of obstinacy but is largely based on the inadequacy of the cycle tracks so far constructed and the dangers [to] which they give rise."

Some modern bicycle advocates suggest it was the opposition of cycling organizations to the cycle tracks of the 1930s that prevented the widespread rollout of these tracks. A typical claim is that if only CTC and the NCU had supported the Western Avenue track, a Dutch-style cycle network might have later evolved. This does not fit with the evidence. As has been shown, many powerful and influential organizations *did* want such a network of tracks to be built, and the Ministry of Transport was determined to provide funding for local authorities to build even more of them. Opposition from cycling organizations (the CTC only had 34,000 members in 1939) would have been of little consequence against the British Roads Federation or the Automobile Association or, for that matter, the Ministry of Transport.

The reason Britain didn't get a Dutch-style cycle network is almost all down to the war. Postwar austerity meant no new tracks were built, nor were the 200 miles of existing ones improved to the standard that CTC and NCU said would be required. (Many of the 1930s cycle tracks still exist, either incorporated into cycle networks people assume were built in the 1980s or lying dormant and unloved beside arterial roads where few of today's cyclists want to venture. Some of the wide, curb-protected 1937-vintage cycle tracks built in residential areas are today assumed to be service roads, and motorists park their cars on them, not realizing the paths, with their original concrete surfaces and which were pink when new, were built for cyclists, and are more than 80 years old.) Had the cycling organizations of the time welcomed the cycle tracks it would have made no difference. In the 1940s and 1950s, there was little appetite to provide anything at all for cyclists despite the fact they still far outnumbered motorists. Postwar politicians and planners were deeply dismissive of "proletarian" mass cycling—instead, they were attracted to the social and economic potential of motoring. It was felt that cycling was outmoded, not suited for the motor era, and most certainly not worth spending any money on.

In Britain, just as in America, people wanted to own and drive motorcars, and when they could give up their bicycles, they did.

2 | From Victory Bikes to Rail Trails *(1940–1969)*

"Do not fear to be eccentric in opinion, for every opinion now accepted was once eccentric."

—Bertrand Russell

"LAST JUNE IN DRIVING INTO PEMBROKE, CANADA, my nerves were suddenly set on edge by a cloud of cyclists leaving the gates of a factory," wrote William Pierce Randel of St. Paul, Minnesota, in 1942. "If in the United States workers take to the bicycle in increasing numbers, our city streets will present new traffic hazards," continued the professor of English, "and it seems logical that certain streets should be closed to all but bicycles, which could then be excluded from other streets."

Randel was describing the uptick in cycling that was happening over much of North America in 1942. According to a cycling trade body, the bicycle in 1942 was in a "position of importance more commensurate with its current development in other countries." Bicycling was back, but more out of necessity than choice. In the previous year, the attack on Pearl Harbor resulted in America joining the World War, which meant lifestyle changes for many, including how they traveled. Private motoring was discouraged—an Office of Price Administration poster chided Americans: "When you ride ALONE you ride with HITLER!" The Office of Price Administration's Automobile Rationing Branch urged patriots to pedal instead, issuing the report *We Need Plenty of Bicycles during the War*. This was an eight-page study spelling out the many benefits of bicycling. Author Harry

Reginald De Silva—a psychologist who, before the outbreak of war, had studied the addictive nature of driving—wrote that

> . . . there is a growing demand for home-to-work transportation far beyond that of peace time. . . . [Therefore] in view of the adequacy of the bicycle for short trips, for persons who work at irregular hours and live in out-of-the-way places, and who on account of the financial burdens of the war are unable to afford automotive transportation, and in view of the fact that the bicycle can carry light payloads, is easily reparable, requires no gasoline, is extraordinarily economical in its consumption of rubber . . . it would seem highly desirable for us to provide an adequate supply of bicycles for adults.

Relishing the obvious market opportunities, the Bicycle Manufacturers' Association of America promoted the facts that cycling didn't burn gasoline and that many bicycles could be made with the amount of rubber and steel necessary for just one automobile. Workers who cycled "would permit a saving in essential materials of . . . 480 tons per 1,000 workers" across the nation, calculated the organization.

Professor Randel's earlier call for streets to be closed to bicycle traffic was echoed elsewhere. The month after his letter in the *New York Times*, the newspaper reported on the idea that some streets should "be reserved for bicycle traffic during specified hours every day," and that these " 'bicycle streets' would be cleared of motor traffic during hours when children and laborers were pedaling to and from school and work."

And it wasn't just men and boys on bikes—the privations of war resulted in "housewives in suburban areas" taking up cycling, revealed the *Times*. "Mrs. Franklin D. Roosevelt is among those who have acquired bicycles in the last few months," added the newspaper. However, showing how far cycling had fallen from grace in the preceding years, the *Times* revealed that "She has not yet had time to learn to ride."

For most Americans at this time, bicycles had long ago been set aside for the automobile. The bicycle was a child's toy, not an adult's transportation device. The war flipped this status, with production of children's bikes being halted for the priority manufacture of adult bicycles. The Office of Price Administration commissioned bicycle manufacturers Huffman and Westfield to make the

Victory Bike. This was launched in January 1942 by OPA "price boss" Leon Henderson at a press shoot in Washington, DC. The Victory Bike was robust and had a large steel basket on the front. (Today we'd call it a cargo bike.) Henderson demonstrated its agility in front of the Capitol building, riding no-handed while chomping on an unlit cigar. Later in the shoot, he rode for some distance with his female stenographer in the basket, ahead of a "caravan of cycling [OPA] clerks."

Press reports projected that 750,000 Victory Bikes would be sold each year to "help meet [the] auto shortage." The actual number sold was far less than this—because of distribution problems and scarcity of raw materials, only 154,586 were made and sold in 1943. Nevertheless, it was significant that a government department officially promoted bicycling as a more patriotic choice than motoring. Not all Americans were convinced it was their duty to scrimp on their driving, but such skepticism was called out by the *New York Times*. In an article subtitled "Both for Business and Pleasure the Bike Is Replacing the Vanishing Motor Car," the paper remarked: "To the skeptic who says 'Bosh! The cycle will never replace the auto,' the cyclist can point to England where the cycle has always been an important factor in public transportation. Today at least 25 per cent of the British population, including some 7,000,000 war workers, pedal about." A report from Britain's Ministry of War Transport confirmed this, stating that a "considerable fillip has been given to pedal cycling as the result of wartime restrictions on travel by car."

POSTWAR AMERICA saw cycling reduced to its former status as a mode of transport for kids and cranks. When the chance came to jettison bikes and get back into cars, it was taken with gusto. Automobiles were envisaged as anti-austerity symbols of victory; bicycles were portrayed as buzz-kills, a form of rationing on two wheels. "Bicycling was not inherently patriotic," suggests historian James Longhurst. "It became so only by virtue of the rider's choice to forgo another, preferred mode of transport. As a result, postwar Americans associated the automobile with affluence and freedom, and the bicycle with exigency and sacrifice."

Cyclists quickly came to be again seen as toy-riding interlopers on roads meant for motorists. In 1948, one newspaper even called for "the regulation of the use of bicycles and other play vehicles on the public highways."

And America's existing highways were soon to be joined by many others. The Federal-Aid Highway Act of 1944 committed federal money to expansive road-building projects, which led to what would become the National System of Interstate Highways. In 1956, with the say-so of President Dwight D. Eisenhower, the Federal-Aid Highway Act of 1956 apportioned vast sums of money to start creating the world's greatest motor-only highway system. Bicycles were excluded from this network, and there was no parallel funding for bikeways, but then there was little popular demand for such dedicated infrastructure anyway. The slow but steady expansion of the freeway system led to more motoring, and in a perfect feedback loop, more motoring led to more demand for freeways. It had been natural for slow-moving bicycles to be excluded from freeways—slow-moving tractors were similarly excluded—but now all roads, even low-speed local ones, were believed to be for motorists alone, with adult cyclists seen as deviant users, deserving of abuse.

"Since adults in the United States no longer use bicycles as a means of transportation or for recreation, American machines for the past 25 years have been sold almost exclusively to boys and girls between the ages of 5 and 14," stated a 1956 publication on import tariffs. "Some 15-year-olds continue to ride, but social custom, especially strong among adolescents, taboos the bicycle after its user becomes eligible, usually at 16 years of age, for an automobile driver's license."

Adult users of bicycles were deemed by many to be losers too poor to get with the automobility program, or to be car-less thanks to a conviction for Driving Under the Influence. Cycling bombed. But in the following decade, cycling—to the surprise of many—started to revive. "There's a [downtown] lawyer . . . who is completely prepared for the Chicago of the future," wrote the *Chicago Tribune* in 1963. "He owns a bicycle!" This was clearly a shock to the newspaper, but they still named Edward Rothe their "Chicagoan of the Future." Admitting that he was often described as "some kind of nut," Rothe said that some of Chicago's streets should be "allotted to cyclists" and that this was "not an unreasonable suggestion . . . since the expressways cope with the serious traffic."

Rothe had taken to the bicycle for its speed, but also because it was "healthy." That cycling prolonged life became a key driver for bicycle sales. "The United States today is on the biggest bicycle binge in history," a cycle industry body informed newspapers in 1964, "and the bicycle craze is bigger than ever." And

After addressing an American Bike Month meeting on May 1, 1964, Dr. Paul Dudley White, second from left, and Secretary of the Interior Stuart Udall, right front, join with a group of congressmen riding to the Capitol in Washington. At left is Rep. Carton R. Sickles, with Rep. Dante B. Fascell riding between Dr. White and Udall. (Associated Press)

who did the Bicycle Institute of America thank for this explosion in interest? Dr. Paul Dudley White.

"DR. WHITE did more for bicycles than any man living or dead," the advertising manager of America's largest bicycle company, told the *New York Times* at the start of the Great American Bicycle Boom of 1970–74. Dr. Paul Dudley White's numerous promotional campaigns to get more Americans on bicycles—he advocated daily bicycle rides, and in the 1950s he was the face of American Bike Month—led to sales surges. When Dr. White "recommended cycling for those with cardiac problems bicycle sales almost immediately shot up by 33 per cent," reported a newspaper in 1957, "and are still on the rise."

White all but invented preventive cardiology, and he was a staunch advocate of exercise, especially cycling. Appointed as Dwight Eisenhower's physician following the president's heart attack in 1955, White was one of the first doctors to link lifestyle with heart health. He recommended that Eisenhower should take up regular exercise, such as cycling. The president preferred golf to bicycling, but that didn't stop the cycle industry from latching on to White's words: "Ike's Doctor writes a prescription," stated a Raleigh magazine advertisement in 1956. "Just try a bicycle ride once a day."

"Dr. Heart," as many called him, led a "five-mile bicycle safari from Cambridge to historic Boston Common . . . in a demonstration of cycling as a means of getting Americans 'back on their feet again,'" reported a newspaper in 1959. "Dr. White was joined by Shane MacCarthy, director of the President's Council on Youth Fitness, who said 'Americans must get off their pedestals of pride and onto their saddles of humility.'"

White launched a national Safe Bicycling Committee in 1957 at the Harvard Club at Harvard University in Boston. Members included Dana L. Farnsworth, medical director of the university. Said Farnsworth at the committee's launch: "We might . . . help postpone the last great traffic jam that's bound to occur when everybody decides to drive his car to Boston on the same day."

White stressed that "bicycling . . . cannot be of much use in keeping Americans fit if it cannot be done safely." Talking at a New York Heart Association conference in 1957 White said: "I'd like to put everybody on bicycles, not once in a while but regularly as a routine."

However, a US newspaper predicted that White would have an uphill battle getting Americans out of their cars: "By the time youngsters are sixteen . . . they have their eye on the family car or a car of their own." The newspaper added: "It is obvious that America's automobile-jammed streets and highways offer hazards for cyclists. There is no advantage in anyone's improving his heart condition if he is likely to get smacked by a truck while he is doing it." (White would have probably agreed. In 1973, he told *National Geographic*: "I'm in favor of bicycling, but not on the same streets as cars.")

When a town wanted a high-profile name for its community cycling club, it would contact the president's physician and he would agree to the (long-winded) use of his name. The Dr. Paul Dudley White Bicycle Club was started in Homestead, Florida, in 1962, and White visited to view the town's system of "interconnecting bicycle safety routes called Bikeways." According to the *New York Times*, Homestead soon had more transportation cyclists than anywhere else in America. Homestead's network of "bike boulevards" meant that "the sight of large family groups wheeling around town is nothing new for cycling is a major recreation here." Cycling was "so popular . . . that Homestead's nickname had become 'The City of Bicycles,'" reported the paper.

Homestead's provision for cyclists included waymarked "Bicycle Safety Routes" where motorists were encouraged to drive slowly and with care. Homestead had 25 miles of such routes, marked with 350 blue-and-white metal signs. "The routes connect residential sections with schools, shopper centers, and the downtown business district," observed a newspaper. "Some routes go through heavily populated areas, but there has not been a single bicycle accident . . . since the signs were installed and the 'Bikeways' opened."

The bikeways had been the idea of George Fichter and his wife, who "managed to get some local streets set aside primarily for bicycles." The couple thought big: they managed to persuade none other than Mae West to officially open the network. The famously curvaceous Hollywood actress cut the ribbon August 21, 1961. She was "an avid cyclist," winked a local newspaper, "claiming the activity to be part of the reason why she was able to maintain her well-known physique."

grow young together...
GET BACK ON A BIKE

A bicycle ride is a trip back to youth, the key to lighthearted new friendships with children and grandchildren. It's the ticket to togetherness with family and friends, a chance to use a never-forgotten skill, an opportunity for healthful exercise. And a bike ride is fun. That's why 57 million Americans will enjoy bicycling this year. Today's bikes are light-weight, maneuverable, easier to ride than ever, perfect for travel on or off the beaten path. Discover the fun for yourself. Just climb aboard and head for the horizon. You'll be surprised how young you are when you *get back on a bike.*

Bicycle Institute of America · 122 East 42nd Street, New York, N.Y. 10017

NEW SIGN OF COMMUNITY ACTION

Lifestyle-magazine ad from the Bicycle Institute of America, 1966.

"It was a lovely day for the dedication," recalled Ruth Campbell, then serving on the city council. "The project extended the paved portion of Eighth Street beyond Krome Avenue and it was going to be open to bicycles as well as for automobiles. It was the bicycle club that arranged for Miss West to come. We had the stage and podium set up and she actually arrived on another part of Krome in her automobile with her entourage that included two very nice-looking young men."

Later, Dr. White said: "I have urged all cities to study and follow the Homestead Program. It is the perfect example of individual initiative and municipal cooperation, and demonstrates what can be accomplished at low cost and high enthusiasm." (Today there is no evidence on the ground that the bicycle routes ever even existed.)

Dr. White remained associated with Homestead—and American Bike Month—for many years. By 1964, American Bike Month had been changed to National Bike Month. At one Bike Month event in that year, Rochester, New York, teacher David M. Thomas asked some of his ten-year-old pupils for their views on "bicycling in today's crowded traffic." Their responses—all asking for cycleways, with the children perhaps coached by Mr. Thomas—were "deemed worthy of passing on to readers and to city and county planners," wrote the editor of the Rochester *Democrat and Chronicle*. One pupil complained: "Why can't we have separate cycleways for bikes, and make bikes as useful and popular as cars?" Another suggested: "One of the ways to encourage cycling is to build cycleways. Cycleways are safer to ride on than streets and sidewalks. The adults have their roads to enjoy and young people have a right to have cycleways."

"TODAY EVERYONE who values cities is disturbed by automobiles," wrote Jane Jacobs in her seminal study, *The Death and the Life of Great American Cities*. But she pointed out that, in the pre-automobile nineteenth century, city streets were hardly wonderful places. The problem wasn't the automobile as such (cars didn't deposit manure), it was that "we went awry by replacing, in effect, each horse on the crowded city streets with half a dozen or so mechanized vehicles, instead of using each mechanized vehicle to replace half a dozen horses." One car isn't a problem; the problem is millions of them. "The mechanical vehicles, in their overabundance, work slothfully and idle much," continued Jacobs, "the powerful and speedy vehicles, choked by their own redundancy, don't move much faster than horses." But she liked trucks, which "accomplish much of what might have been hoped for from mechanical vehicles in cities." For Jacobs, "trucks are vital to cities. They mean service. They mean jobs."

Jacobs didn't want cars and trucks to be banned from cities, as her many champions sometimes claim; rather, she wanted them to be controlled. "To concentrate on riddance . . . to negatively put taboos and penalties on automobiles as children might say, 'Cars, cars, go away,' would be a policy not only doomed to defeat but rightly doomed to defeat."

She advocated that trucks should make deliveries at night, "principally a separation in time, rather than in space." She was no champion of physical separation of modes, and while she was a city cyclist herself she did not believe that an excess of bicyclists was preferable to an excess of motor vehicles:

> I am doubtful as to whether the advantages of separation are . . . very great. The conflicts between pedestrians and vehicles on city streets arise mainly from overwhelming numbers of vehicles, to which all but the most minimum pedestrian needs are gradually sacrificed. The problem of vehicular dominance . . . is not exclusively a problem involving automobiles. . . . People who have experienced an Amsterdam or New Delhi rush hour report that bicycles in massive numbers become an appalling mixture with pedestrians.

"To think of city traffic problems in oversimplified terms of pedestrian versus cars, and to fix on the segregation of each as a principal goal, is to go at the problem from the wrong end," she wrote. Jacobs might not have been in favor of segregation, but many of her contemporaries were. Quixotic New York City mayoral candidate William F. Buckley said in 1965 that, if elected, he would build an "elevated bikeway" along Second Avenue. The Conservative said the bikeway would have a fifteen-cent toll and would "ease the traffic problem and . . . provide New Yorkers with an opportunity to exercise and so to stimulate their health." He told reporters gathered at his campaign headquarters that he would ride the bikeway to City Hall "on nice days" but then added, with a prankish grin, "I suppose it's ultra-reactionary to go back to the age of the bicycle." He clearly didn't rate his chances of winning very highly; when asked what he would do if he won, he quipped: "Demand a recount."

Other cities were more serious about providing for cyclists. In 1967, Chicago Mayor Richard J. Daley asked city planners to prepare a provisional plan to get

Early 1970s bike path icon, Chicago.

people cycling in the city. Paul Rasmussen of the Department of Development and Planning produced *Guidelines for a Comprehensive Bicycle Route System*, a 28-page report featuring recommendations on how to separate cyclists from both pedestrians and motorists. It talked about linking Chicago's lakefront path to the rest of the city (which was done) and also suggested the "construction of bike paths" to add to the eighteen miles already in the city, and a "citywide system of interconnecting safety routes." The report acknowledged that this would require "substantial engineering and capital outlay, and therefore, should be developed over an extended period of time." (Very extended—Chicago's current

2020 plan calls for the completion of a 645-mile network of bike facilities.)

The report said that 30 percent of Americans rode bicycles and "if 30% of Chicago's population are bicycle riders then there must be a million cyclists in the City of Chicago." It added that already in 1967 there had been a "sudden, almost explosive increase" in cycling's popularity. Rasmussen stressed that the new bikeway system should be "linked together to form a single unified path [network]. . . . Developing this kind of continuity is important in order to obtain the greatest amount of use. . . ."

> As traffic congestion in the city increases, the need for safe places to bicycle becomes more and more apparent. The type of bicycle paths suggested in these guidelines are safer than alternative routes that the cyclist may choose for himself because they are either completely free from motor vehicles or have only limited traffic volumes. Bicycle paths that pass through areas where crime is prevalent need special attention and cooperation from the city's police department to protect both riders indigenous to these communities and those from outside it who are just passing through.

The plan was largely created to link recreational areas, but there was also a recognition that "bike paths can also serve a utilitarian function by linking schools, transportation terminals, and shopping areas. . . . A bicycle can reach the center of the city from a distance of up to five miles faster than an automobile. . . . Many people who work in Chicago's central business area have discovered this fact and are taking their bicycles to work."

IN WORLD WAR II, the Victory Bike with its heavy-duty front basket had been foisted on an unwilling public as a symbol of patriotism, with pedaling promoted as being helpful to the war effort. After the war the bikes were trashed. During the Vietnam War, it appeared that Americans were still dismissive of the luggage-carrying capacity of bicycles until this became important to the enemy side. Known in Vietnamese as "steel horses," bicycles were essential cargo carriers during the long war, with the record-holder, in 1964, hauling 925 pounds along the length of the Ho Chi Minh Trail. Most were French-made Peugeot bicycles. In 1967, a *New York Times* reporter described the effect of Vietnamese bicycle supply lines on the war effort: "I literally believe that without bikes they'd have to get out of the war," said the Hanoi-based Harry Salisbury to a Senate Foreign Relations Committee.

"Why don't we concentrate on bombing their bicycles instead of the bridges?" Senator William Fulbright demanded, adding, to laughter, "Does the Pentagon know about this?"

The Pentagon most certainly did know about it, and the military's top brass weren't laughing. "The bicycle survived the most modern weapons in the American military arsenal," explains historian and Vietnam vet Arnold Blumberg. "Although the Vietnamese used 600 Russian-made Molotova 2.5-ton trucks as well as sampans, ponies, and some 200,000 porters carrying spine-breaking loads, the mainstay of their logistical network was composed of 60,000 tough bicycle-pushing men and women."

The Pentagon commissioned a 1965 report from the Advanced Research Projects Agency (ARPA) on the use of bicycles in wartime. The introduction to Bicycle Troops noted: "Interest in the employment of bicycle troops is emerging once again, this time in Southeast Asia, where the road network is inadequate for motorized transportation, but where paths and dikes may provide an acceptable avenue for bicycle movement."

The report from the agency that later created ARPANET, which in turn led to the Internet, said bicycles had many advantages: they "require no fuel and are inexpensive to maintain . . . the silence of bicycle travel [allows] early warning of approaching planes . . . and bicycles do not create a large cloud of dust as do tanks and trucks." Furthermore, noted the report, bicycles had been used to great effect in the First World War with "active soldiers of good physique" who had "morale . . . above the average."

(Incidentally, patriotism, pedaling, fuel frugality, and cargo carrying on a Victory Bike lookalike were all wonderfully brought together in a 2003 TV advert for Miller Beer. Academy Award–winner Errol Morris filmed a chunky, middle-aged American man riding through snow, with bottles of Miller High Life clinking in his front basket. A gravelly voiceover intoned: "That's the way, patriot; let the OPECs keep their gasoline. We'll just tap into a far more efficient energy source: man power. If we all learn to pull our weight, nobody—nobody—will be able to siphon away . . . our High Life.")

"IT IS something of a tribute to Americans that they do as much cycling and walking as they do," claimed a government-sponsored report in 1962, "for very little has been done to encourage these activities, and a good bit, if inadvertently, to discourage them."

The report continued: "We are spending billions for our new highways, but few of them being constructed or planned make any provision for safe walking and cycling. And many of the suburban developments surrounding our cities do not even have sidewalks, much less cycle paths."

Published by the Outdoor Recreation Resources Review Commission (ORRRC) the report, *Outdoor Recreation for America*, looked overseas for inspiration:

> Europe, which has even greater population, has much to teach us about building recreation into the environment. Holland is constructing a national network of bicycle trails. . . . In Scandinavia, buses going from the city to the countryside have pegs on their sides on which people can hang their bicycles. Car ownership is rising all over Europe, but in the planning of their roads . . . Europeans make a special effort to provide for those who walk or cycle. Why not here? Along the broad rights-of-way of our highways—particularly those in suburban areas—simple trails could be laid out for . . . cyclists.

Led by Secretary of the Interior Stewart L. Udall (whom we shall meet again in chapter 5), ORRRC morphed into the Bureau of Outdoor Recreation, and this organization lobbied not just for recreational bike trails but also urban bikeways. In May 1964, Udall told a meeting attended by Congressmen and (the man got everywhere) Dr. White that he deplored "the tyranny of the automobile" and wanted more space devoted to bicycles. "The automobile has become . . . the great impersonalizer of our country," he complained.

One of the pioneers of the environmental movement, Udall warned in his best-selling 1963 book *The Quiet Crisis* of the conservation catastrophe to come. He highlighted the dangers of pollution and overuse of natural resources. Along with Rachel Carson's *Silent Spring*, Udall's book was required reading for budding

Dr. WHITE'S
Message to Nation:

RIDE A BIKE
FOR HEALTH, FUN
AND ECONOMY

Paul Dudley White, M.D.
Famed Heart Specialist

Some of the happiest days of my life have been spent riding a bicycle. It has kept me young in mind and body. As a physician I have recommended cycling to many of my patients as a way of keeping fit, provided their condition is suitable for that exercise and provided they can cycle safely. I advise bicycling for healthy people to help keep them healthy. For our nation, I know of no better activity than the two-wheeler for all around health, pleasure and economy.

That's why I'm pleased to serve as the 1964 Chairman of American Bike Month, dedicated to the welfare of our country's bike riders. The zest for cycling shows steady growth. Today America has more than 30 million bicycles in action—pedalled by youngsters and adults, and, in many cases, by entire family groups.

We live in a highly mechanized age, which tends to reduce human activity. The bicycle with its self-propelling, body-building power, helps offset the harm of inactivity. The government's physical fitness program recognizes the need for recreation. Communities, increasingly aware of the problem, are building more bikeways and paths to make it safer and easier for cyclists to get to work, schools, shopping areas, and outside city limits to enjoy nature's wonders.

American Bike Month throughout May, sponsored by a responsible minded industry, has become an important annual event. It spurs bicycle festivities and activities throughout the country. During May special safety parades, bike games, races and rodeos, bike tours and celebrations will be held in hundreds of cities. I hope you will participate in them and enjoy their benefits.

In these pages, you'll find bicycle games, valuable riding tips, safety rules and a bike inspection chart to make your own bicycle activity safer and more pleasurable. I hope you'll read and study these, and then put your own bicycle know-how against the test we've devised. Enjoy riding your bike in May—and throughout your entire life.

HOW TO RIDE YOUR BIKE PROPERLY AND GET MORE FUN OUT OF IT

1. Check saddle position. Adjust it—up or down—so that your knee is slightly bent at the down position of the pedal. Determine this by placing the heel of one foot on the pedal in down position. If leg is perfectly straight, it will have the proper bend when the ball of your foot is placed on the pedal, as it should be when you ride.

Correct position of feet and leg.

2. With the saddle thus adjusted, sit comfortably. Adjust the handlebars, if necessary, to permit the body to lean forward slightly as you assume the riding position. Leaning forward too much will place undue strain on the arms.

Correct tilt to saddle.

3. Pedal evenly and rhythmically. Put weight of the body on pedals as they pass the top of the stroke, particularly when going upgrade. This increases driving power of the muscles.

Too far forward.

4. Correct riding position permits you to apply brakes easier. Avoid "jamming" the brake, unless in an emergency. If pressure is applied gradually you will get safer and better braking action over a longer period of time.

Too far to the rear.

HERE ARE 12 BIKE RULES FOR SAFE RIDING

1. Observe all Traffic Regulations—red and green lights, one-way streets, stop signs.

2. Keep to the Right and ride in a straight line. Always ride in single file.

3. Have White Light on Front and danger signal on rear for night riding.

4. Have Satisfactory Signaling Device to warn of approach.

5. Give Pedestrians the Right of Way. Avoid sidewalks—otherwise use extra care.

6. Look Out for Cars Pulling Out Into Traffic. Keep sharp look-out for sudden opening of auto doors.

7. Never Hitch on Other Vehicles, "stunt" or race in traffic.

8. Never Carry Other Riders—carry no packages that obstruct vision or prevent proper control of cycle.

9. Be Sure Your Brakes Are Operating Efficiently and keep your bicycle in perfect running condition.

10. Slow Down At All Street Intersections and look to right and left before crossing.

11. Always Use Proper Hand Signals for turning and stopping.

12. Don't Weave In Or Out of Traffic or swerve from side to side.

BE ALERT • WATCH TRAFFIC SIGNS • USE HAND SIGNALS

BIKE INSPECTION CARE CHART

A HANDLE GRIPS: Replace worn handle grips. Cement them on tightly.

B SADDLE: Adjust to body and tighten all nuts.

C WHEELS: Eliminate wobble. Tighten wheel nuts and oil bearings.

D REFLECTOR: Must be visible for 300 feet.

E COASTER BRAKE: Does it brake evenly? Unless you're an expert, have it adjusted by a serviceman.

F CHAIN: Check for damaged links. Secure snug fit. Clean and lubricate frequently.

G PEDALS: Lubricate and tighten pedal bearings and spindle. Replace worn pedal treads.

H CRANK HANGAR: Keep clean and greased. If it wobbles, have serviceman make adjustments.

I WARNING DEVICE: Be sure it works properly.

J HANDLE BARS: Adjust to body. Tighten and keep stem well down in fork.

K FORK BEARINGS: Lubricate.

L LIGHT: Must be visible for 500 feet.

M SPOKES: Replace broken ones promptly.

N TIRES: Inflate to correct air pressure. Remove embedded metal, glass, cinders, etc.

O TIRE VALVE: Inspect often for leaks.

Dr. Paul Dudley White was the face of 1964's American Bike Month. He was also the event's chairman. The Bike Month event was staged by what Dr. White called the "responsible-minded" bicycle industry.

environmentalists, of whom there was a small but growing number in the early 1960s. A decade later, in a 1972 article for *Atlantic Monthly*, "The Last Traffic Jam," Udall was one of the first to write about what became known as "peak oil," and he also talked of "livable cities" and said the "end of automania would . . . contribute greatly to ending suburban sprawl." This, Udall wrote, "would lead to the building of more compact, sensitively planned communities in the future— and it would prompt many cities to build quick, quiet, and convenient modes of transportation ranging from bicycle paths to mass transit systems."

The Udall-commissioned *Trails for America* report called for new hiking trails and bikeways. "To avoid crossing motor vehicle traffic," said the report, "bikeways would be located along landscaped shoulder areas on frontage roads next to freeways and expressways, along shorelines, and on abandoned railroad rights-of-way" or "along quiet back streets and alleys." The National Trails System Act of 1968, which Udall helped to enact, established a national program to build rural bike trails. (Today, the Rails-to-Trails Conservancy reports there are more than 21,000 miles of such trails in the United States, many of which extend into urban areas and are used for transportation.)

While significant, Udall's contribution to the National Trails System Act didn't extend to pledging sufficient funding. "We would encourage the States . . . and the cities . . . to spend more money on this type of project," said Udall in a congressional hearing. Encouraging is always easier than delivering, and Udall's urban bikeway plans were, for now, left largely unfunded. This was partly because both the US House of Representatives and the Senate were packed with politicians who had little to no interest in cycling. One of the few who did pedal was Congressman Robert C. Eckhardt. In a 1968 letter to the Texas congressman, President Lyndon Johnson wrote that "as far as we know you're the first to show up [to Congress] on a bicycle." Eckhardt rode from his home in Georgetown to Congress in every kind of weather, and always in his trademark three-piece suit, bow tie, and Panama hat. "You see things from a bike you don't notice in a car," he told the *Washington Post*. "This is a great city for bicycling. The terrain is ideal, but the traffic is terrible."

ECKHARDT WAS considered an eccentric for using a bicycle as transportation, but interest in recreational cycling had been growing throughout the 1960s. "Autumn Brings Bicycle Traffic Jams on Central Park Paths," enthused the *New York Times* in October 1968. Ten thousand or more cyclists were flocking to the park every weekend, reported the newspaper. And some of those on bicycles were celebrities. "One Sunday I saw Harry Belafonte, Kirk Douglas, and Douglas Fairbanks Jr.," disclosed a "middle-aged secretary from Brooklyn who comes to the park every sunny Sunday to pedal with the stars," adding "my friend [has] seen Cary Grant—the actual, real Cary Grant—Sidney Poitier and Sandy Dennis." The newspaper added that "hundreds of other well-known New Yorkers—politicians, actors, and businessmen—are cyclists." A "pretty nurse" told the *Times*: "I'm not much for exercise. But there are so many men riding bikes that I grit my teeth and pedal after them."

Many of those who cycled in Central Park were not using their own bikes. People walked or drove or took public transit to the park, and then hired bicycles from the rental stations at the entrance gates. The rental bikes were not meant to be taken out of the park, but plenty of folks ignored that and started to explore New York City on two wheels. Amenities for cyclists in 1968 were not very ambitious, merely the provision of "Bike Route" signs on fifty miles of lightly traveled roads. "It would be minimal expenditure," said Alfred Shapiro, director of planning for the parks department, when discussing the installation of the signs. "That's the beauty of it," he enthused. Park Commissioner Hechscher added, "this makes use of what we have—the streets and peoples' sense of adventure." Cyclists, hoped the commissioner, would be "propelled from one sign to the next . . . like a trail through the woods."

Such lackluster provision was normal for New York, but on the other side of the country a small West Coast city was demonstrating how, in 1967, America *could* build for bicycles. By 1976, Stanford University law professors described this city as "a bicyclist's utopia," and it's to Davis, California, that we travel next.

3 | Davis: The Bicycle Capital of America

"Never doubt that a small group of thoughtful, committed citizens can change the world."

—American anthropologist Margaret Mead

TASTELESS TOMATOES? Blame Davis. Or, more specifically, the food science faculty at the University of California, Davis. Founded as an agricultural research station in 1907, UC Davis was where, in the mid-1960s, plant breeder Jack Hanna and engineer Coby Lorenzen created "vf-145," a tomato bred tough to survive mechanical harvesting. Tough, but bland. The development revolutionized the ketchup industry and put UC Davis on the map. Unlike Sacramento, twelve miles to the west, the flat and sleepy town of Davis still had a cycling culture in the early 1960s, but with a growing influx of students, and their cars, this culture came under threat.

University chancellor Emil Mrak realized that a plan to increase the student population from 2,000 to 10,000 would, if enough of the baby boomers brought cars, destroy the ambience of the town. The bicycle-loving chancellor directed architects to "plan for a bicycle-riding, tree-lined campus." Prospective students were told to bring bicycles, not cars. Faculty members Frank and Eva Childs had spent a sabbatical in the Netherlands, and in 1963 they formed a small but persistent activist group to press for Mrak's vision to be seen through by the city. A melodramatic letter from Frank Childs to the local newspaper warned of the consequences of pandering to the motorcar, waxed lyrical about the separated

Cycling was popular in Davis many years before the installation of curb-protected bikeways in 1967. (City of Davis)

cycleways in the Netherlands, and chided the civic authorities with a biblical barb: "Where the leaders have no vision, the people perish."

Car use was restricted on campus, with traffic barriers and a ban on car ownership. Bicycle routes were striped on the roads to the 37-square-block downtown core. Further chivvying from the activist group led to the creation, in 1967, of bicycle paths separated from motorcars by concrete curbing, normal for the Netherlands but a first for America. A 1972 bicycle study stated:

> In speaking of Davis the word most commonly used is "unique," perhaps the only accurate portrayal . . . as regards its most outstanding characteristic—the bicycle. "Davis" and "bicycle" are synonymous. . . . In Davis, the bike is far more than a recreational toy or exercise vehicle. It is a vital element of the transportation system.

On an early-1970s cycle map, a tagline was added by the city's business leaders: "Davis: The Bicycle Capital of America."

Today in Davis, if you squint, you could be in the Netherlands: people get around on bikes. School kids. Students. Professors. Bank managers. There are bike paths on the campus and in the city, the civic symbol of which is a penny-farthing. Cycling in Davis is not cultish—it's ordinary, no special clothing required. In most American cities, the modal-share for cycling struggles to reach 2 percent; in Davis, it's 20 percent.

The campus—cheek-by-jowl with the city—is car-free. There are excellent rail connections to Sacramento, San Jose, and San Francisco, and with a free bus service for students and university staff it's easy to live without a car in Davis. It's even easier when all of your urban travel can be done swiftly and safely on a standard bicycle.

In the 1960s and 1970s, when the rest of America was building only for automobiles, Davis built for bicycles. A heady mix of factors—pancake-flat topography, dogged citizen activism, full political buy-in—created a culture, especially on campus, in which bicycle use was nearly as high as in Dutch cities such as Groningen, where half of the population still rides bicycles for everyday use. Davis didn't measure bicycle use in the 1960s or 1970s, but with a share of 30 percent in 1980 it would be safe to assume the modal-share was far higher in the preceding two decades. A 1966 photo series by the legendary landscape photographer Ansel Adams showed that the Davis campus once hummed with people on bikes. One of his black-and-white photographs shows a cycle parking area packed with hundreds of bicycles, and students riding to and fro on either side. It's perhaps one of the most un-American photographs imaginable.

This image of very high cycle use in Davis was taken *before* the curb-protected bikeways were installed. While elsewhere in America adults stopped riding bicycles in the 1950s and 1960s, they carried on in Davis. The city's 1952 General Plan favored bicycling. At this time Davis had more bicycles per capita than any other city in the United States. In 1964, Senator Pierre Salinger visited the campus and the local newspaper reported that he rode "the students' usual form of transportation, the bicycle. . . ."

There was a town-and-gown split between the city of Davis and the campus, but even so the use of bicycles in downtown Davis was still far higher than anywhere else in America. When the first cycle advocacy group met on the campus in the mid-1960s, it did so knowing that cycling was an important transport mode in Davis—the activists weren't setting out to *create* a cycling culture, they were aiming to *protect* it.

Writing in the *Davis Enterprise* in 2003, Dale Lott, one of the members of the original advocacy committee, remembered that

> We liked to do our daily travel around town by bike, and wanted
> to preserve that feature of life in Davis. We dubbed ourselves the
> Bicycle Safety Committee. Membership was always open, but no

one else ever came, so at most meetings you could count us on the digits of one hand. But the press releases that followed our every meeting didn't report how many were there—just what they said. The press releases were about providing a safe environment for the Davis bicycling tradition amid growing population and traffic.

News stories duly appeared in the local newspaper, and members of the Bicycle Safety Committee also made presentations to the city council. Demands for protected bikeways went unheeded at first, so, in the run-up to the 1966 council election, the committee lobbied prospective councilors. "Two seats were open and bike paths were the big issue," said Lott. "Norman Woodbury and Maynard Skinner pledged themselves to bike paths and sought our endorsement."

The pro-bicycle candidates won, and this tipped the balance toward bikeways. "I was on the edge of my seat at the first [council] meeting," said Lott, an animal behaviorist.

The council members eyed each other uneasily in . . . silence and my heart began to sink. Then Maynard got up, pointed to Third Street on a map of the city and said, "I move that bike lanes be established on Third from B to L." The motion passed. So did the motions he made for bike lanes . . . on nearly all the other streets in our petition. At the end of the meeting, city staff was directed to meet with our committee and design bike lanes. We danced out of City Hall.

Engineers were allocated to put the bikeway plans into action. Davis became a test bed for bikeway designs, with engineers traveling from other parts of California and the rest of the United States to see how Dutch-style infrastructure could be accommodated in an American setting.

A small number of short, curb-protected bikeways were trialed in other cities in California. Thanks to Google Street View they can still be spotted today. In Oxnard there's a sidewalk-integrated bikeway—all 0.12 miles of it—and there's a bidirectional curb-protected bikeway on 0.1 miles of Via Real in Carpinteria. Both were constructed in 1970. The Oxnard bikeway offers protection off to the side of Ventura Road, but then the curbing swerves and cyclists are deposited back onto the same stretch of road. No attempt was made with either of these trials to protect cyclists at intersections. In Davis, however, there was a 1976 plan

Experimental protected bikeway in Oxnard,
California, 1970. (Google Street View)

for just such a protected intersection—but it never got further than the drawing board. Described by the Federal Highway Administration as an "offset crossing," this plan suggested that bicyclists should be "channeled onto the sidewalk area and to crossings of the intersecting streets just outside . . . the normal pedestrian crosswalk area. In effect, a bikeway ring around the intersection is created."

The design was dropped "primarily due to the problems with bicyclist acceptance," said a 1976 FHWA report. "Although this treatment has been successfully employed in Europe, it essentially involves treatment of bicyclists as pedestrians. All observational experience of US cyclists would indicate certain rejection and disuse of such a facility by the vast majority."

As well as observing how cyclists in Davis negotiated trial bikeways, the FHWA reported that "vocally active cyclists"—in other words, "vehicular cyclists" (see chapter 6)—had lobbied against the trials, but that "it is important to realize that the most vocal element is not necessarily representative of the general cycling population."

An animation of a protected intersection overlaid onto film of a US road went viral in 2014. Produced by Nick Falbo of Alta Planning + Design, the video has had 764,000 views on Vimeo.com, and his design went on to influence American planners who have now installed a number of these so-called Dutch intersections including one—at last!—in Davis. While they are not as good as Dutch examples, they are a "very good first step for America," said David Hembrow, writer of an influential Dutch infrastructure blog.

THE BIKEWAYS of Davis "were not intended to provide a means of recreation, but to develop a community transport system in which the bicycle would have an assured and important role," Bob Sommer told *Bicycling* in 1972. Sommer, one of the early members of the Bicycle Safety Committee, added that

> Bicycles . . . are as dependent upon effective environmental support as are fish in water. . . . In areas where automobile traffic is heavy . . . a separate area of the street is set aside for the exclusive use of bicycles. . . . Bicycle riders want the route they travel to be convenient and direct, the shortest possible distance between where they are and where they want to be. . . . It is tempting to think that bicyclists ought to be content with a winding route along some side streets, but the fact is they will not be. Bicyclists will not go inordinately far out of their way to use bike paths. . . . The present city government is solidly committed to bicycling.

Historian Bruce Epperson has said the Dutch-influenced infrastructure of Davis "resulted from unique circumstances that could not be transferred to other locations, were of limited duration, and often were implemented for reasons that had little to do with their actual contribution to their long-term transportation needs"; what's more, they "died out with amazing rapidity."

The Federal Highway Administration's *Bikeways—State of the Art* (1974) reported that bikeways

> . . . which employ barriers to protect the lanes make it difficult for cyclists to cross the street at mid-block. . . . As a result they tend to produce bi-directional use with the problems of . . . bike conflicts in the lane and conflicts at intersections. . . . Because of these problems, employment of the protected lane concept is becoming less frequent.

The Davis campus overflows with
bicycles in parking stands.

Nevertheless, Davis still has a bikeway network, and much of it has been expanded since the 1970s, including underpasses beneath a freeway. Most of the main streets in Davis have some form of bicycle provision. Cycle use is highest on the campus, with 50 percent modal-share (lecture rooms are distant, class scheduling is tight). When 7,000 or so new students arrive each October, many struggle to cope during their freshman induction days—upperclassmen students gather at campus intersections and cheer as newbies wobble into each other on the bicycle-specific traffic circles.

But for all its spacious and separated bikeways, its bike parking corrals with free air and use of tools, and its continued self-proclamation as the "Bicycle Capital of America," Davis is becoming less and less of a paradise for pedaling. In 2003, Sommer wrote an op-ed for the local paper asking, "Where have all the cyclists gone?" He reminded readers that "at one time, Davis was unquestionably

The City of Bicycles," but that distinction was gone. "Today, I don't know how many bikes are stored in garages and backyards, but there seem to be a lot fewer ridden by adults on the streets."

> In the 1970s I gave illustrated lectures about bike paths in schools of architecture and planning. One of my favorite pictures showed the half-empty auto parking lot at Davis High on a school morning. I announced with pride that this was probably the only high school parking lot in California not filled to capacity. . . . That is history. The masses of cyclists are gone from the intersections and from campus. The first-in-the-world bike traffic circles, introduced on campus to handle peak loads during class changes, are no longer crowded. I feel like a bird who has lost his flock. . . .

The UC Davis psychology professor stressed that "The reduction in transportation cycling . . . cannot be blamed on an external threat. There has been no Detroit conspiracy to replace bikes with SUVs. Autos have not taken over the bike lanes."

Cycling's modal-share in the city of Davis dropped to as low as 14 percent in 2007. A graph from an academic study showed that cycle use was on a precipitous decline, and that car use, and riding on the free city buses, was on the rise. When, in 2009, the US Bicycling Hall of Fame wanted to relocate from Somerville, New Jersey, it chose Davis, but securing this honor did not arrest cycling's slide in Davis or on the campus.

In the Hall of Fame's basement museum I met with David Takemoto-Weerts, the bicycle coordinator at UC Davis since 1987. He's a cycling enthusiast, and was attracted to the city because of its bicycling lifestyle. It pains him to see cycling's decline and he's not entirely sure why a small, warm, and flat city with such a well-connected and safe bicycle network should have halved its cycling modal-share since the 1970s, especially considering the fact that cycling is now blossoming elsewhere in the United States, with Boulder in Colorado likely to soon overtake Davis as the "Bicycle Capital of America." (Boulder has 160 miles of bikeways, and—rubbing salt in Davis's wounds—it hired Dave "DK" Kemp, the former bicycle coordinator for the city of Davis, an expert at raising state funds for cycling projects.)

Takemoto-Weerts said Davis is too "timid" when planning for cycling,

Davis has cycle-specific traffic circles. Buses
also access this circle, but infrequently.

guilty of resting on its laurels, while many other American cities have created ambitious bicycle programs that have increased their modal-shares of cycling in recent years.

Takemoto-Weerts, like other Davis bicycling experts I talked to for this book, credits the "golden age" of bicycling in Davis to Dave Pelz, who became the public works director for the city in 1968. It was Pelz, with a remit from pro-bicycling politicians, who kept cycling on the city's agenda, who built bikeways, and who created educational programs such as "Mr. Smartspokes," a talking bicycle that toured the city's elementary schools. When Pelz (and Mr. Smartspokes) retired in 1999, much of the fizz went out of the city's provision for cycling.

"The city backed away from its commitment to bicycling that it had exhibited under Pelz," agreed Takemoto-Weerts. "It may never return to the 'golden age' we enjoyed under Dave and his crew."

This opinion is shared by Ted Buehler, author of the only rigorous study into the history of cycling in Davis. He told me that bicycling had been the norm for almost every student and university staffer in the 1970s, but since then lackluster promotion of the bicycle—and the provision of a free bus service—have dented cycling's popularity in Davis. "A lot of students stopped riding bikes, and now ride the bus or drive a car," complained Buehler, who moved to become a bicycle advocate in Portland, Oregon. Pulling on his beard, he added: "Even though Davis appears to be a magical place, it doesn't create a strong culture of people who are excited about riding their bikes."

Davis needs to recreate this culture with every new academic intake. "Many students come from towns where bikes aren't part of their lives," explained Timothy Bustos, the current UC Davis bicycle coordinator (Takemoto-Weerts retired in 2016). Chinese students are often the hardest to convince, noted Bustos. "It's considered old-fashioned [for them] to ride a bike. A car shows 'you've made it' in many cultures."

Bustos has to work hard to keep or get people on bikes: he organizes monthly "slow rides" and encourages the "cool factor" of cycling by staging events such as the Davis Tweed Run, an event, started in London in 2009, in which dapper gents and stylish ladies "take to the streets in our well-pressed best." It might surprise many bicycle advocates that Davis—a city with a dense network of high-quality bikeways—has to stage these sorts of promotional events and yet still cannot guarantee that people will choose to cycle.

Davis is a stick-in-the-front-wheel to those that argue the only thing that gets people on bikes is safe, well-connected cycling infrastructure.

4 | Cycling in Britain—From Swarms to Sustrans (1942–1979)

"There is a great future for the bicycle provided you make the conditions right. If you make them wrong there isn't any future."

—Ernest Marples, UK Transport Minister, 1959–64

THE TWEED RUN IS A DANDY'S DELIGHT—Brylcreem and bow ties for the gentlemen; capes and cycling skirts for the ladies. This gloriously eccentric bicycling bricolage matches top hats with Harris tweeds, and conflates Steampunk romanticism with verifiable vintage. A typical outfit consists of 1890s-style waistcoat and breeches coupled with a 1920s-era working man's flat cloth cap. A typical bicycle is a 1930s-style roadster with "mustache" handlebars. It all makes for a strong look but, like many of the chic ensembles on these now-international rolling fashion parades, it's an amalgam of faux nostalgia. Harking back to a presumed golden age of cycling is great fun, and a peloton of tweedy riders is visually arresting, but one mustn't get too misty-eyed about the indeterminate period that is being evoked. Once motorcars muscled their way onto the real scene, the golden age was a goner.

The early motorists forced riders from their bicycles, as attested by this report from a cycling club newsletter in 1912: "Sal turned up to tea, cursing motors in general and with great particularity those which had driven him into the gutter." Into the 1920s and the 1930s, cyclists were mistreated, maimed, and killed, driven from the road by the fear and danger posed by seemingly uncaring motorists. Cyclists became an endangered species. The protective cycling tracks provided by the powers-that-be were of no great help, for they were often narrow and pitted, as well as few and far between. As was shown in chapter 1, the British government in the 1930s held cyclists in scant regard, and a series of road safety reports from the 1940s through into the 1970s demonstrated that if cycling were to die out completely that would have been of no great concern to officialdom.

A 1942 report from the Ministry of War Transport recommended that British cyclists should be provided with cycle tracks, but the report's author, Sir Herbert Alker Tripp, acknowledged the defects in existing tracks:

> The use of cycle tracks, as in Holland and Denmark, is regarded by many people as the main hope. Unfortunately, cycle tracks break off at all junctions, which are just the spots where accidents are most frequent and protection is most needed. Nor are the cycle tracks themselves as good as they sound. At the entry of every minor road the cyclist finds he has to bump over the gutter and camber of the minor road; motor vehicles trying to emerge from these roads pull athwart his track . . . mothers and nursemaids with perambulators use the ramps at the road junctions and thus obstruct the cyclists. . . .

Tripp was a police officer, town planner, and poster artist (all at the same time—twenty of his bucolic watercolors were reproduced as posters for railway companies). As assistant commissioner of the Metropolitan Police in the 1930s, he was responsible for London's traffic. According to the *Oxford Dictionary of National Biography*, Tripp was a "passionate motorist and cyclist," and was especially interested in reducing the death toll on Britain's roads. This, he felt, would be best achieved by training cyclists and pedestrians in the new road order: motorists now came first. When nonmotorized road users bristled at his suggestions, he came to believe that physical persuasion would have to be employed instead—pedestrians should be penned in at road crossings, and cyclists should be corralled on tracks. Gentlemen of education and position in their fast motorcars would be less likely to be dastardly and caddish if they were given free rein on roads, he felt. And for that to happen the only solution would be for a separation of transport modes. Perhaps instructively, Tripp preferred the word *segregation*.

Tripp developed his ideas in his 1942 study, *Town Planning and Road Traffic*, recommending car-free, pedestrian-only shopping precincts, and bridges and underpasses in town centers to keep pedestrians and cyclists apart from motorists. Critics complained that this would mean drivers would get ground-level access to the streets, but all other users would have to climb into the sky or creep underground. Such plans were broadly welcomed by the establishment of the day—Tripp was especially popular in America—and the ideas were later adopted by architect and town planner Colin Buchanan in his team's internationally influential 1963 report, *Traffic in Towns.*

Tripp was not one of the town planners appointed to a 1943 Ministry of War Transport committee looking to reconstruct postwar Britain, but his segregationist influence can be seen throughout the committee's report, published in 1946. *Design & Layout of Roads in Built-up Areas* recommended segregated provision for the growing number of cyclists, worrying that "conditions obtaining in early postwar years will tend still further to popularize the cycling habit." The team led by Sir Frederick C. Cook believed there was a strong case for the "necessity of making ample road provision for pedal cyclists."

Wartime casualty figures led the report's authors to the "inevitable conclusion that by far the best preventative of accidents to pedal cyclists lies in their segregation from motor traffic, for it is clearly unsound that a running surface should be used at one and the same time by heavy motor-driven vehicles capable of developing high speed and by light and unstable vehicles such as pedal cycles."

The report discussed the merits of "motor ways," "pedestrian ways," and "cycle ways." These cycleways were to be "well-surfaced" and "for the exclusive use of pedal cyclists, separate from the general road system and of width sufficient for two-way traffic." The width of tracks should be 9 feet, stated the report, separated from adjacent footways by a low curb and from the carriageway by a 6-foot verge.

"Segregation . . . should be the key-note of modern road design," stressed *Design & Layout.* "Police supervision would be necessary to ensure that . . . cycle ways are not used by other classes of traffic or otherwise abused" and such "segregated tracks for cyclists" should be provided "as a matter of course on arterial, through- and local-through routes. . . ."

Taking a dig at the Cyclists' Touring Club—one of the organizations consulted for the report—the authors snarked: "we regard it as unfortunate that attempts should be made in any quarter to discourage cyclists from using [cycle tracks]." However, echoing the similar complaints voiced in the 1930s, the authors also revealed why cyclists of the time didn't always use the tracks: they could be inferior to the road. "Objections to cycle tracks have been stimulated by the indifferent surfaces with which some of the early tracks were laid," admitted the report, and this didn't allow for an uninterrupted ride, a design flaw that had to be remedied. "The profile of tracks should be unbroken across intersecting vehicular entrances, and they should approach side roads with an easy ramp," advised the report, which also suggested that "the surface is best formed by materials of pleasingly distinctive colour." (Some of the prewar cycle tracks had red and pink concrete surfaces.)

National government policy might have called for the provision of separated cycle tracks, but it was up to local authorities to include them at the design stage of new roads. However, British cyclists were only ever provided with perhaps 200 or so miles of such tracks while there were 200,000 miles of roads, including 500 miles of freshly minted bypass and arterial roads. As was shown in chapter 1, the halting of the proposed cycle-track building bonanza had almost nothing to do with opposition from cycling organizations, and everything to do with a blind desire to provide only for the motoring classes which, at this time, were mostly the likes of leading police officials, architects, town planners, and, of course, politicians.

EVEN WITHOUT miles and miles of protective infrastructure, and despite the maimings and the killings, cycling remained popular in Britain during and just after the war. Cycling levels peaked in 1949 when 15 billion miles were ridden by cyclists, representing 37 percent of all journeys (which is higher than the cycling levels in the Netherlands today). Cycle use was so high in some English cities that one town planner described cyclists as "locusts." Thomas Sharp, the author of *Town Planning*, a Pelican Book that sold 250,000 copies in 1940, was describing postwar Oxford, but his comment that "the bicycle . . . is one of the main causes of traffic congestion" would have been true of the war years, too, when cycling was both commonplace and necessary.

We may consider the bicycle to be benign; Sharp did not. He called it "the new and dangerous invention of the [eighteen-] eighties. . . ." He went on: "Bicycles came in hordes, like locusts, upon the university towns. . . . The bicycle . . . is one of the main causes of traffic congestion. . . . [They] cannot be lightly dismissed as mere bicycles. A few locusts are of little importance. A swarm is a plague."

Sharp, like many of his fellow urban thinkers, wanted to cleanse towns of such plagues. The future was to be motorized, and archaic bicycles had no place in such popular visions of modernity. Urban planners such as Sharp and others measured existing car use and extrapolated into the future, making heady predictions that the use of cars would rise (predictions they helped to facilitate). Few felt there was any point in measuring cycle use; cycling might still have been a significant form of transport, but it was in decline.

"Trips by pedal cyclists and pedestrians . . . have not been included in most of the major urban transportation studies in America, or in this country," complained M. A. Taylor in 1968, "and this should be borne in mind in making any comparison of results."

Taylor studied three English towns—Gloucester, Northampton, and Reading—for the Ministry of Transport's Road Research Laboratory, and he carried out in-depth travel surveys in each. These surveys were far more detailed than national census reports, and they show how majority transport modes were overlooked in favor of a minority one. In Gloucester, Taylor and his team of researchers found that the use of bicycles was about equal to the use of public transit—21 percent for bikes compared to 22 percent for buses—but the greatest transport mode was walking, which accounted for nearly 30 percent of all journeys. Fifteen percent of journeys were made by people driving (with these motorists sharing with passengers, which accounted for nearly 8 percent of journeys).

The numbers in cars were dwarfed by the numbers not in cars, yet over the following decades Gloucester devoted resources to the 23 percent and not the 72 percent. In terms of numerical and social fairness this was deeply illogical, but at the time it was not considered to be so. British planners and politicians were blinded to the actual numbers of cyclists and pedestrians at this time, and did everything in their power to hand control of the roads to their favored mode of transport: the motorcar.

IN 1948, Britain's Minister for Transport Alfred Barnes introduced the Special Roads Bill. This would—eventually—lead to the creation of Britain's motorway network. But the bill also promised "special roads for cyclists." The bill became the Special Roads Act in 1949. Special roads for cars—motorways—could now be constructed. The first wasn't started until 1958, but they came thick and fast in the 1960s. Back in 1948, newspapers reported that the Special Roads Bill would see the building of cycleways, too. And just as cyclists would be fined for riding on motorways, the transport minister promised that pedestrians would be fined for straying onto cycleways. Introducing his bill, Barnes stressed that "everybody" benefited from motorization:

> It will be a mistake for anyone to assume that the Bill is promoted to satisfy the selfish interests of the private motorist. It is nothing of the kind. It is often overlooked that nowadays we are all motorists, whether or not we drive a private car. Everybody travels on buses or coaches and the greater proportion of our domestic and personal needs are delivered by motor van.

He believed national highway authorities should be in charge of major motoring roads, but "special roads for pedestrians and cyclists" should be provided by local highway authorities. And these "special roads" were clearly deemed to be recreational, rather than for practical, everyday travel:

> I should emphasise . . . under the powers given to them to construct a special road, highway authorities could determine that the only classes of traffic using that road should be motor vehicles. These same powers can . . . be used by county highway authorities for the construction of special roads for pedestrians and for cyclists—across, for instance, a national park, along a river bank, across mountain, moor, or the coast line. [This] responsibility will rest upon local highway authorities, who ought to meet the cost of special roads.

Because bicycle infrastructure was classified as "local" it had a lesser status and was more likely to be provided on a whim—in other words, rarely. However, one of the few "special roads" to be provided was actually world-class. This was the Tyne Pedestrian and Cyclist Tunnel, a wonderful piece of protected infrastructure, still in use today. It's a 900-foot, two-tunnel tube lying 40 feet below the River Tyne between Jarrow and Wallsend, near Newcastle in the northeast of England. The tunnel was opened in 1951, sixteen years before the

Tyne Tunnel for motor vehicles. At its peak, 20,000 users—mainly shipyard workers—rode or walked through the tunnel each day.

This hugely expensive project was an outlier. Apart from the cycleways of Stevenage, to be discussed in chapter 7, and the cycle tracks on the Briton Ferry bridge, built in 1955, little else was built for British cyclists in this period, although there were suggestions of provision such as the sniff of an idea in 1957 from H. J. Longstaff, the county surveyor for Cambridgeshire, who proposed that cyclists should be provided with cycleways alongside the proposed Huntingdon bypass. This was eventually built, but not until 1973, and the final version dispensed with the cycleways altogether.

THE SHIPYARD workers descending under the River Tyne would have identified with Arthur Seaton, the hard-drinking working-class antihero of Alan Sillitoe's *Saturday Night and Sunday Morning,* a gritty 1958 novel set in another northern city and famous for the refrain "Don't let the bastards grind you down." The bastards in question were the foremen at Raleigh's Nottingham plant, a bicycle factory "smelling of oil-suds, machinery and shaved steel that surrounded you with air in which pimples grew and prospered on your face." As a fourteen-year-old, Sillitoe—pimples and all—had worked in this factory, and he gave his character the same job: capstan lathe operator. The novel was a best seller, but it was the 1960 movie of the same name that propelled Arthur Seaton to fame. Played by Albert Finney in his first movie role, Seaton was shown churning out bicycle parts, hating on his supervisors and, as each shift ended, riding his bicycle home, along with tens of other workers—and not a car in sight. *Saturday Night and Sunday Morning* the movie was an unexpected box-office smash for the executive producer Harry Saltzman. In 1961, the Canadian used the profits he made from his hit production to buy the film rights to Ian Fleming's James Bond. That's right, a film about working-class cyclists making Sturmey–Archer gears led to the third highest-grossing movie franchise of all time.

But working-class transportation cycling was already dying out. Also at a low ebb was cycling for leisure, which had been madly popular before the war. Bicycling's decline had started in 1949. Within a few short years, a Raleigh worker would arrive at work not on a bicycle but in a car. New cars would have

A 1946 transport plan for England's second city of Birmingham envisaged cycleways next to the main roads. The main roads were built; the cycleways were not.

been out of the reach of most blue-collar workers at the time, but there was a roaring secondhand market and buying in instalments on the "never never" was becoming socially acceptable. Many people were desperate to drive rather than cycle. To ride a bike was seen as a telltale sign of poverty of aspiration as well as means. Bicycles and cloth caps were—literally and figuratively—thrown on the scrap heap.

Roadster bicycles, that is. In 1962 a new style of bicycle appeared, and it soon appealed to an up-market clientele. This was the year when Dr. Alex Moulton, the designer of the suspension on the Mini motorcar, morphed into a bicycle manufacturer. He created the small-wheel Moulton with its innovative front-and-rear suspension, and it was soon billed as the "bicycle of the future."

Along with the Mini, the Moulton became one of the design icons of the "Swinging Sixties." It was ridden by the high-profile Lords Snowden, Rothschild, and Montagu. "At the very time that Rolls Royce moved a bit down to the masses . . . England's establishment was turning a bicycle into a lordly conveyance," wrote *Newsweek*. The leading "Moultoneer" of the 1960s (and right through to the 1980s) was influential architecture and design critic Peter Reyner Banham.

He believed that the Moulton would inspire a new generation of middle-class cyclists who would come to rely on bicycles for transportation. "Conceivably, with the disappearance of the proletarian cyclists, the Moulton may bring on a new breed of cyclists who are middle-class urban executive radicals," he imagined. These riders would create a "cultural, as well as technical revolution," putting a "new class of men in the saddle, most of them ignorant of the cloth-cap and racing-pigeon culture of which cycling is (or was) an integral part."

In the 1960s, Banham was part of the "progressive" middle class but "the working class is where I come from," he wrote. "I come from a cycling community . . . I was a bob-ender [i.e., cheap-seats user in the cinema] in the days when a bob-ender meant a certain class of person." Describing his formative years in a working-class area of a rural East Anglian city he added, "Anyone who knows Norwich knows that the cyclist was king of the road there, and all other traffic has to stand aside when the cyclists get loose." But cycling was not one of "those long-term permanent working-class things," observed Banham. "The working class don't ride bicycles anymore . . . the working class have got Populars and Cortinas and Minis . . . radicals like me ride bicycles."

BUT RADICALS can't hold back the tide, and as Banham himself promoted, the actual future was one of concrete and gasoline. Banham idolized the freeways of California. His classic 1971 book *Los Angeles: The Architecture of Four Ecologies* is a love letter to mass motorization. And it was mass motorization—a seemingly unstoppable force—that was behind the steady decline in cycling's popularity. *Traffic in Towns*, the 1963 report mentioned earlier, featured cycling only in passing; lead author Colin Buchanan clearly believed that urban cycling would wither to nothing:

> . . . it is a moot point how many cyclists there will be in 2010. . . . [This] does affect the kind of roads to be provided. On this point we have no doubt at all that cyclists should not be admitted to primary networks, for obvious reasons of safety and the free flow of vehicular traffic. . . . It would be very expensive, and probably impracticable, to build a completely separate system of tracks for cyclists.

Traffic in Towns was commissioned by Transport Minister Ernest Marples. He also commissioned *The Reshaping of British Railways*, a now infamous 1963 report by Dr. Richard Beeching on Britain's railway network, which resulted in its decimation. In 1960, Marples told delegates at the Tory party conference that "we have to rebuild our cities. We have to come to terms with the car." And it was this accommodation that he tasked Professor Buchanan with finding. Marples was far from a disinterested party. He owned two-thirds of Marples, Ridgway, and Partners, a Westminster-based civil engineering firm that built roads, and would later be handed the contracts for the style of motorways and flyovers illustrated in *Traffic in Towns*. In 1975, Marples, who had by then been made a baron, fled the country, not because of his hushed-up proclivity for prostitutes, his introduction to Britain of traffic wardens and parking-is-prohibited double yellow lines, or the conflict of interest in building motorways at the same time as cutting Britain's rail network, but because of tax evasion.

He may have gutted the railways and promoted, instead, the use of motorways, but Marples was also a cyclist. He was a member of the Cyclists' Touring Club, the first member to rise to the role of minister for transport. When staying at his French chateau—which he did rather a lot of after absconding from Britain in disgrace—he toured by bicycle. Marples, naturally, rode a Moulton.

Earlier, in 1967, Marples had been chairman of a meeting of the Royal Society of Arts in London. Dr. Alex Moulton was in the audience, but the speaker was Eric Claxton, the designer of a cycleways system, whom we shall meet again in chapter 7. Claxton extolled the virtues of cycleways not just for small towns but also for major cities, such as London. He proposed that every fourth street should be turned over to bicycles alone:

> There is no means of releasing existing towns from the thraldom of traffic congestion without a radical appraisal of modes of transportation. . . . The bicycle . . . is the only door-to-door transport that remains available to us except the chauffeur-driven car. Cycleways alone can free the bicycle from the dangers of mixed traffic. . . . I foresee the beginning of a new era of greater convenience and safety in which the bicycle plays a major part.

In his speech of thanks to Claxton, Marples admitted: "I don't use [my bicycle] in London anymore, because . . . if you try and go round Hyde Park

Corner on a cycle you are signing your own death warrant. . . . I am quite certain that we will never get the pedal cycle back on any scale unless it is segregated from ordinary forms of traffic."

Cycle Trader editor Harold Briercliffe gave short shrift to this answer: "I am going to attack [Mr. Marples] for advocating that we cyclists should give up until we get segregation. This is going to cost an infinite amount of money. . . . [We need to be] making use of the existing road. . . . The dangers have been exaggerated. . . ."

And Leslie Warner, secretary of the Cyclists' Touring Club, blamed Marples for the danger on the roads: "If [Mr. Marples] finds Hyde Park Corner so dangerous it is really partly his fault, because Ministers of Transport have been so obsessed with keeping the traffic moving as fast as possible at the expense of everything else on the road."

Marples dismissed them both, saying he believed in segregation because motorists were not to be trusted: "Man is conditioned by original sin, and once you put him in a motorcar you multiply that original sin by the number of horses underneath the bonnet! If you put an 18-year-old in a Jaguar you have given him more power than he is capable of using wisely."

THE CTC's views on segregation in the 1960s were much changed from those of the 1930s, when it had bitterly opposed the United Kingdom's putative cycling tracks. "What is the CTC's present attitude to cycle paths?" the CTC asked itself in a 1963 pamphlet. "Should we welcome (or even demand) exclusive cycling routes?" The answer was yes, but to Claxton-style cycleways rather than the inferior cycle paths of the 1930s.

"Our objections to those [1930s] paths are based on logical argument and not on an outdated feeling that we might lose our right to the road," wrote John Hunt, the chairman of CTC's Rights and Privileges Committee. Reheating policy lines first used in the 1930s, Hunt added that the CTC's objection had long been to the sort of cycle path where the cyclist is "pitched into the maelstrom of traffic at the most dangerous point." Instead, he stressed that the CTC wanted to see a "distinction drawn between this 'old bogey' of cycle *paths* alongside the carriageway, and the new cycle*ways* which we have seen . . . in Stevenage New

Town, where an entirely new set of roads, divorced from the carriageway, has been constructed especially for cyclists."

In 1968, the CTC published a policy pamphlet that welcomed Dutch infrastructure, calling the Netherlands "a country with extensive cycle paths, whereon cyclists are given priority over motor traffic at all intersections with minor roads." The policy document added that "encouragement should . . . be given to the construction of cycleways, as pioneered at Stevenage and now being adopted in other new towns and areas of redevelopment." And just so there could be no doubt, elsewhere the document stated: "We welcome the modern cycleway systems, quite separate from the carriageway. . . ."

The CTC remained opposed to the "old type of cycle path introduced in the 1930s" which was defective because—and this is an argument used later by "vehicular cyclists" (see chapter 6)—"there is little danger to cyclists from traffic following the same direction." The danger is at junctions, "and it is just there that cycle paths cease to exist."

Instead, the CTC in 1968 highlighted "the system adopted in Holland, a country with extensive cycle paths, whereon cyclists are given priority over motor traffic at all intersections with minor roads. . . ."

CTC may have been in favor of such superlative cycleways, but they were not provided, and one of the reasons was officialdom's reluctance to do anything at all for cycling. "It is not good enough to treat cyclists' organisations in this way," complained Liverpool's Labour MP Eric Heffer in a 1968 parliamentary debate. "Cyclists are badly treated here. Elsewhere in Europe the cyclist is somebody of importance. . . . But not here; in Britain the cyclist is somebody we do not care much about."

MOST POLITICIANS of the time thought the same as town planners such as Buchanan: cycling was in its death throes. Workers had abandoned it, and the handful of middle-class Moulton riders didn't register nationally. Sales were depressed. "Ten years ago, most people in the industry felt doubts about its future," fretted Tom Barnsley, chairman and managing director of Raleigh, in October 1973. "There was despondency. A group of experts had done a study for Raleigh on the future of the cycle industry. The outlook was poor, they said."

Barnsley was addressing his fellow industry leaders at the first meeting of the Bicycle Association, which in the summer had split from the Cycle and Motor Cycle Association. One of the reasons for the split was the relative health of the two industries. Sales of mopeds and motorbikes in the run-up to 1972 had been dire; sales of bicycles had been excellent. "Nowadays, the cycle industry [is] a growth business," confirmed Barnsley. Some 572,000 bicycles had been sold in 1969; 800,000 were sold in 1973.

Raleigh—which at this time had a 65 percent domestic market share—was buoyant because of hearty sales of the Chopper hi-rise bicycle and its spin-offs, and even the Shopper, a small-wheel unisex bicycle mainly aimed at women, was selling well.

To the surprise of Raleigh and other companies, bicycling started to be promoted from outside the industry. British environmentalists latched on to what their equivalents in America had already discovered: the bicycle, they claimed, was going to save the world!

The CTC members' magazine *Cycletouring* was intrigued by this new radical breed of eco-activism, and described for its readers the formation of a bicycle protest group linked to the Young Liberals:

> Commitment is the name of a new group whose activities have gained press recognition in the past few months as a result of "bike-in" demonstrations in London. One newspaper described how supporters had swept down Oxford street, wearing slogans like "bike power," and had delivered a letter to the Greater London Council demanding a network of car-free cycleways. "We will concentrate on bikeways for commuters, not only within central London but through arterial routes to the suburbs," says a Commitment spokesman. "Bikeways for pleasure, linking parks, theatres, concert halls and railways stations, are also planned. We believe we are fighting not only cars on the road, but cars in the head."

The call for cycleways may have fallen on deaf ears in most British cities, but in 1971 Oxford constructed the sort of cycleway that was becoming common in the Netherlands at the time. Seen from above in the satellite option of Google Maps, Marston Ferry Road looks like a standard dual-carriageway. However, you can drop Street View's stickman onto the road to reveal that one of the

BRITISH CYCLING BUREAU

THE NATIONAL PLAN FOR CYCLING

The BCB have prepared a handbook, which will be presented at a lunch in the House of Commons and distributed to all local councils, designed to encourage town planners and politicians to:

1 Extend and improve existing cycle paths.

2 Create separate cycleways in towns.

3 Provide safe crossings for cyclists at road junctions.

4 Allow cyclists to ride in recreational areas i.e. public parks, disused railway tracks, Forestry Commission land.

WE NEED YOUR SUPPORT IN ORGANISING PRESSURE GROUPS TO INFLUENCE YOUR LOCAL COUNCIL TO ACT FOR THE BENEFIT OF CYCLISTS.

Contact: Angela Owen/Nicholas Cole
British Cycling Bureau
Greater London House Hampstead Road London NW1
01-387-6868

(Opposite) Advert for British Cycling
Bureau's National Plan for Cycling, 1972.

carriageways is, in fact, a cycleway. This is so wide that it's more of a road than a standard-issue British cycleway.

The road crossed the River Cherwell and made obsolete the line-ferry from whence came the road's name. The ferry had been a favorite haunt of poet laureate—and bicyclist—John Betjeman, who studied in Oxford in the 1920s. In his blank-verse autobiography, *Summoned by Bells*, Betjeman wrote:

> Take me, my Centaur bike, down Linton Road . . .
>
> And, with the Sturmey–Archer three-speed gear
> Safely in bottom, resting from the race
> We pedalled round the new-mown meadow-grass
> By Marston Ferry with its punt and chain.

While the Marston Ferry Road cycleway is good, it's unusual for Oxford: the city has very little cycle infrastructure. Despite this, cycling's average modal-share in Oxford is 17 percent—15 percent higher than the national average—but some areas of the city have cycling levels of up to 30 percent. Cherwell School, beside the Marston Ferry Road cycleway, has 1,900 pupils, 1,300 of whom cycle in for lessons each day.

BICYCLE INDUSTRY organizations wanted to see Britain build more cycleways. The representative bodies for bicycle retailers and bicycle manufacturers jointly raised a levy on all sales which funded a PR body, the British Cycling Bureau. This had been created in 1965 in an attempt to lift flagging sales. The Bureau was, in fact, a front for Planned Public Relations of London. In 1972, it launched a "National Plan for Cycling." George Shallcross, national director of the retailers' organization, said that this plan would "press for traffic-free cycleways and to make the authorities, national and local, recognise the bicycle as an asset to the environment, as it is noiseless and fumeless, and takes up so much less room in parking and riding than motorcars." Trade-magazine editor Harold Briercliffe said the plan was "the most hopeful outline of what we must all do that has been seen in Britain for many a long day."

The National Plan was promoted to national and local government via a handbook, *Before the Traffic Grinds to a Halt*. A launch press release said the Bureau had sent a copy of this pamphlet to MPs and every local authority in the UK, and wanted

> . . . to see Local Authorities:
> 1. Create separate cycleways in towns and cities.
> 2. Provide safe crossing for cyclists at road junctions.
> 3. Extend and improve cycling facilities in recreational areas.

The Bureau's figurehead and lead consultant was Eric Claxton, the original designer of Stevenage's extensive cycleway network. Promoting the plan, he guided MPs around these cycleways. "All the MPs were very impressed," said Claxton. The National Plan highlighted the fact that Stevenage was "a place where segregated traffic—motorists and pedestrians and cyclists—has led to increased convenience all round."

As part of the plan, the Bureau approached the Friends of the Earth (FoE) "suggesting that its campaign was in line with the Friends' own objectives." This approach was "enthusiastically received" and the organizations agreed to work on a "manual for action groups around the country with advice on how to pressurise local councils to institute a cycleway system."

The Friends of the Earth had only been founded two years previously and was, at this time, a radical campaigning group rather than the membership organization it would become. The FoE was, in part, inspired by the Paris-based Amis de la Terre (French for "Friends of the Earth"), which had co-organized "velorution" demonstrations protesting against the building of a four-lane highway along the left bank of the Seine. In the first edition of *Richard's Bicycle Book*, Richard Ballantine described how a "massive bike-in" attracted 10,000 cyclists to the center of Paris in 1972 but the "beautiful" campaigners were charged by "helmeted troops on motorcycles" who fired tear gas, and "used the shelter of the woods to smash up bicycles with their nightsticks." Ballantine clearly welcomed such direct action by the protestors; he wrote that "the French experience points the way to real victories." He joked (I *think* he was joking): "If we are lucky, there will be a major smog disaster in which thousands of people will suddenly die all at once, instead of piecemeal as they do now." But he warned, "the power of vested interests in maintaining a motor age is such that there will probably be a long, drawn-out struggle and concessions will not be won without a fight."

The politicization of the bicycle as a "symbol of ecological awareness" was a "challenge to the almost universally accepted economic priorities of the motorist," wrote a Dutch-born American, Rob Van Der Plas, in the 1980s.

Talk of social change and political battles rattled the prim and proper Cyclists' Touring Club. CTC officials called 1972 "the year of bicycle demonstrations," and sniffed that these had been organized "completely independent of the recognized cycling bodies." Nevertheless, the officials were glad they were "no longer the only voice in the wilderness" but cautioned that "encouraging though these signs may be . . . cycling still gains little favour in the eyes of the highways authorities."

A cycling-themed issue of *Design* in 1973 agreed with this analysis. "Bicycles have not been given the facilities they deserve and need," editorialized the opinion-forming magazine. "For all our sakes, planners must be persuaded to provide them. . . . Segregated road space may be the only ultimate solution."

Design pointed out that cycling was far from dead: "The car's popularity is not half as overwhelming as its priority planning rating suggests; and even if it were, planners should recognise that their purpose is not solely to follow real or imagined traffic trends. The bicycle offers a golden chance to anticipate and encourage a traffic revolution: more cycling means greater freedom of movement for everyone."

The magazine contrasted Britain's dire efforts at planning for cycling with that of the Netherlands: "Efforts led by the British Cycling Bureau and its consultant engineer, Eric Claxton, to persuade inner London boroughs to adopt 'canalised' networks of priority cycle routes on minor roads have so far failed. Yet it is quite natural for the Netherlands authorities to superimpose a cycle priority system on the ancient street pattern of Utrecht."

Changes that *Design* wished to see in the UK included separation of transport modes, by time and with curbs: "Cyclists in Holland have their own traffic lights, giving them a five-second advantage. Cycle tracks are a natural part of Dutch street systems for old and new developments alike. . . . Many European cities automatically build facilities for [cyclists] into their urban schemes . . . but Britain does virtually nothing and a hopelessly small pittance is spent on promoting bicycles. The situation demands to be changed."

THE CYCLE industry also desired change, knowing that more facilities for urban cycling would generate sales. And to bring about change the previously conservative bicycle industry worked closely with Friends of the Earth. In effect, FoE became the lead British organization lobbying for cycling infrastructure. Because it had allied itself with an environmental organization, the bicycle industry believed it was well placed during the OPEC oil crisis, which started in October 1973. The crisis was caused by an embargo issued by the Arab members of the Organization of Petroleum Exporting Countries protesting against the West's support of Israel in the Yom Kippur war. The price of oil skyrocketed and motorists were asked to economize in their use of fuel. Instead, and predictably, long lines formed at filling stations. In November, British motorists were issued ration books. In February 1974, the chairman of the Transport 2000 campaign group argued that "if the energy crisis means anything it means a complete change in transport priorities, with less emphasis on private motoring." But even though gas prices went through the roof, neither the industry nor FoE were able to land many punches on mass motorization. The British government's National Economic Development Office noted that between November 1973 and February 1974 the average price of petrol had increased by 43 percent, and that this "would suggest a steep fall in consumption." It added: "A further effect will be a reduction in the rate of growth of car ownership." Neither happened: motoring in the UK weathered rationing, and, after the crisis had abated, fuel consumption and the purchasing of cars both increased. (This was not the case in the Netherlands, where the oil embargo had a far greater impact on the nation's transport modes; see chapter 8.)

The oil crisis resulted in a greater number of cycle-campaigning recruits. In the coming years, these more militant advocates would push aggressively for cycling as transportation. The baton had been passed on to a new style of campaigner: young, bright, eager, and passionate about the planet-saving potential of bicycling. The environmentalist Philip Brachi exemplified this new breed. He wrote for magazines such as *Ecologist* and was commissioned to write green-leaning pamphlets for the British Cycling Bureau. Brachi was heavily influenced by Ivan Illich, author of 1974's *Energy and Equity*. Explicitly anti-car, Illich was a Marx-inspired philosopher and critical of the automobile's high energy demands and its speed:

> A true choice among practical policies and of desirable social relations is possible only where speed is restrained. Participatory democracy demands low-energy technology, and free people must travel the road to productive social relations at the speed of a bicycle.

The Austrian former priest wrote that "Man on a bicycle can go three or four times faster than the pedestrian, but uses five times less energy in the process. . . . Equipped with this tool, man outstrips the efficiency of not only all machines but all other animals as well." Illich believed that

> The bicycle also uses little space. Eighteen bikes can be parked in the place of one car, thirty of them can move along in the space devoured by a single automobile. . . . Bicycles let people move with greater speed without taking up significant amounts of scarce space, energy, or time. [Cyclists] can get the benefit of technological breakthroughs without putting undue claims on the schedules, energy, or space of others. They become masters of their own movements without blocking those of their fellows. . . .

Pointedly, Illich complained that "the advantages of modern self-powered traffic are obvious, and ignored." The British Cycling Bureau was determined to change that and, in 1974, ordered one thousand copies of *Energy and Equity* for free distribution to MPs, local authorities, leading civil servants, and the media.

Channeling Illich, Brachi wrote that the bicycle was "the most efficient means of transport known" and that there are

> . . . reasons aplenty for preferring pedal power. Enjoyment, exercise, and an unrivalled economy and convenience are the ones most often mentioned. In another age, another culture perhaps, one might hope that the case for the bicycle might not require numerical proof.

> A source of pleasure and mobility perfectly suited to the human
> scale, neither endangering others nor bruising their freedoms;
> comprehensible, with a transparent honesty of form and operation;
> ecologically meek; such a device should need no defence.

The efficiency of the bicycle was one of the core themes at MAUDEP conferences staged from 1972 to 1979. MAUDEP (the Metropolitan Association of Urban Designers and Environmental Planners, an offshoot of the American Society of Civil Engineers) was a US organization founded to educate urban planners on the benefits of both cycling and walking. The organization's conferences were held in cities such as New York and San Francisco, or locations such as Walt Disney World in Florida, but in 1974 MAUDEP organized its first international conference, decamping to London for the "Cycleway Seminar." Fifty delegates from around the world were welcomed by the British Cycling Bureau's Eric Claxton. Other speakers included Stevenage's then–chief engineer Roy Lenthall, who spoke on "Segregation: The Dynamic Solution," and Mrs. Evelyn Denington, the chair of Greater London Council's transport committee as well as chair for Stevenage Development Corporation. The following year, and still in partnership with the Bureau, MAUDEP staged a cycle planning conference in Amsterdam. This was opened by the Dutch Minister of Transport.

IN 1975, Richard Feilden, fresh out of architecture school, wrote *Give Way: A Report on Cycling in Britain* for Friends of the Earth. This chided the government for not doing more for cycling, and for suggesting that cycling was a dying activity and, as such, local authorities should no longer cater for cycle traffic in towns and cities.

"Cycling has been seen as an unattractive form of transport with an unfashionable image," argued Feilden's polemic. "The discomforts and dangers in sharing road space with increasingly heavy traffic, accidents, and near misses . . . all serve to discourage cycling." Nevertheless, his report noted that "sales have been soaring"—a million bicycles were sold in 1974, he said. *Give Way* believed the solution to road dangers was to mark out "cycle priority routes" where cyclists had right-of-way and motorists would be allowed on sufferance.

These bicycle icons would become known as "sharrows" in the USA in the 1990s. They were used here in Portsmouth, England, in 1975.

This was a reference to a short-lived "Cycle Route" trial in the south-coast city of Portsmouth. Friends of the Earth and the British Cycling Bureau had been the lead protagonists in pushing for this trial, which was a UK version of what was later known in the US as a "bicycle boulevard." Petitioning the local authority to authorize the trial, Friends of the Earth campaigners in Portsmouth quoted extracts from the Bureau's *Before the Traffic Grinds to a Halt.*

"The Portsmouth scheme represents nothing short of a revolution," argued *New Scientist*:

> It will be the first in Britain to introduce cycling facilities into a mature urban area. . . . Traditional provisions for the bicycle— separate cycleways or reserved cycle lanes—are difficult to provide in already developed urban areas. . . . Rather than creating new space for bicycles, the use of existing road space is being altered. A network of existing residential streets is to be restricted for the use of cyclists.

There was no segregation on the four miles of roads chosen for the trial; the cycle routes were marked with painted cycle icons (these would later become known in the United States as "sharrows"), but—critically—49 of the 54 junctions en route gave priority to cyclists. Residents were informed about the trial via leaflets sent to 10,000 homes. "How motorists will gain," explained the leaflet. "It is hoped that the scheme will result in fewer cycles using the main roads and that you therefore enjoy easier journeys on these roads." Cyclists were told that "The Cycle Routes are designed to make your journey quicker, safer, and more pleasant than those on main roads, where the traffic is heavy."

The scheme was radical for the time, and aimed at improving cycling conditions for less-confident cyclists. According to Portsmouth FoE, the trial was "not designed to please current cyclists, but to encourage the far more numerous timid citizens and children who would like to cycle but are deterred by today's terrifying road conditions."

The scheme was monitored by the government's Transport and Road Research Laboratory. Portsmouth had been chosen because it was "geographically ideal for cycling," said a TRRL report. It was flat and compact, had mild weather, and journeys to work were relatively short ("less than 2 kms on average"). The city had an existing cycling modal-share of 11 percent.

"Considerable interest has been shown recently in Britain in cycling as a means of transport," said the TRRL report, describing how it would carry out the trial:

> A number of schemes were considered, beginning with segregated tracks, which were difficult to site, because of the many routes which cyclists use, and expensive to construct, as it would have been necessary to acquire land and/or properties. Segregated cycle routes were considered to be only practicable in areas which were not built-up, implying routes more for leisure use than for work, school, and shopping trips. . . . It was decided that use must be made of the existing highway network, and to avoid using major (and often congested) roads, attention was focused on the use of parallel residential roads which were quieter and carried much less traffic.

Claxton, representing the Bureau, described the trial as "the first cycle priority route network in Europe." It opened on November 19, 1975; news of the scheme appeared that day in national newspapers, radio news programs such as BBC Radio Four's *Today Show*, and on local and national TV, including the main BBC1 evening news, BBC2's *News Extra*, and ITN's *News at Ten*.

The route was in operation until June the following year. TRRL found that motor traffic during the trial was reduced by two-fifths, mainly because cars couldn't use the cycle-route streets to bypass busy roads. "Cycle flows rose by about one-third," reported TRRL. But it noted that the city's docks and naval base had not been linked to the routes, probably reducing its usefulness.

TRRL also discovered that motorists were not very good at sticking to the rules: it was found that 41 percent of motorists did not turn left when instructed to do so by signage. "Some motorists were prepared to make potentially dangerous illegal manoeuvres to avoid the restrictions," said a later report. "Substantial proportions of motorists did not obey the restrictions imposed on movements by the special junctions, one-way streets, and prohibitions of entry to certain streets." (Such streets in the Netherlands work well today, and Dutch motorists can be observed waiting patiently behind cyclists.)

Twenty-five percent of cyclists reported taking a different and longer route in order to get to the cycle route, and between 2 and 6 percent of those using the route had been encouraged to take up cycling because of the trial. However, the road priority changes had not been welcomed by local retailers. Half of the 39 shopkeepers on the cycle routes claimed that they had lost business. "All the shops on the Cycle Route are small and, given the economic conditions prevailing in 1976, it may well be that trade was already declining and that the cycle routes were used . . . as a rationale for this," speculated TRRL.

Claxton said that retailers and residents "rebelled against the experiment and agitated for the abolition of the scheme," and he complained that now that the scheme had been "terminated . . . inevitably the advantages to cycling have gone and no doubt the environment generally will have slid back . . . because of the tacit encouragement for motorists to use the route as a rat run."

IN 1975, Friends of the Earth fronted "All Change to Bikes," a multi-agency national campaign to push for cycleways. The partners included the Cyclists' Touring Club, the Council for the Protection of Rural England, the Civic Trust, and the British Cycling Federation. The aims of the campaign included the desire to "reallocate existing road space to create priority routes by local authorities for cyclists and pedestrians" and to establish a "network of priority routes linking all destinations (e.g., schools, shops, offices, factories, and places of entertainment) and access to the countryside." All Change to Bikes was bankrolled by the British Cycling Bureau.

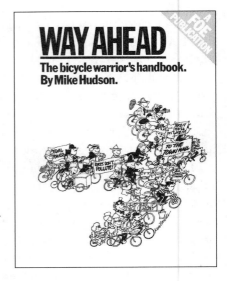

The following year, the Friends of the Earth launched an "FoE Cycleways Campaign" due to the "increasing interest in cycling and the ever-increasing knots in our transport system." The emphasis would be on promoting separated cycleways, said the first issue of the organization's *Bicycles Bulletin*, edited by Mike Hudson, FoE's administrative director who would go on to write *Way Ahead: The Bicycle Warrior's Handbook* for the lobbying group, and later to edit the more sober and serious *Bicycle Planning*, a detailed cycle-infra design guide published by the Architectural Press of London.

"The Bicycles Campaign aims to demonstrate the advantages of cycling as a means of transport and persuade local authorities to provide carefully designed, clearly marked, and well publicised cycleways and cycle parking facilities," wrote Hudson in the first bulletin. He stated that the FoE wanted to organize "simultaneous demonstrations in all the major cities demanding improved facilities for cycling."

Protests were staged in London, but few elsewhere. Instead there were pamphlets, including "Why Cycleways?" which were distributed to FoE groups around the country. *Bicycles Bulletin* conveyed instructions such as "prepare briefing document on Cycleways and Structure Plans," "How to campaign for cycleways," and "How to draw up cycleway plans." The first *Bicycles Bulletin* of 1977 included news about the "Cycleways Manual" that Hudson had written to distribute at a "local group co-ordinators meeting," first discussed with the Bureau back in 1972, and he stressed that FoE would "encourage, assist, and support all local groups working on cycleways."

Despite others thinking otherwise, the CTC still believed itself to be the leading cycle-campaign organization in the UK, and although it was an enrolled member of All Change to Bikes, CTC remained conflicted about how hard it should push to improve conditions for urban cycling. "Perhaps the interesting question which now needs to be faced is that of the extent to which the CTC is to be involved in the campaigning for urban facilities and their detailed planning," voiced an editorial in the CTC members' magazine, "particularly in the context of continuing to be regarded as the principal spokesman . . . on matters affecting cyclists in the use of the roads." The editorial continued:

> . . . the club has assumed throughout its long history a traditional role of the "cyclists' champion." But where do we stand now in light of the apparent success of bodies such as the British Cycling Bureau, Friends of the Earth, and the "All Change to Bikes" groups—all of whom have been so active in pressing for the special treatment of cyclists in towns and their segregation from motor traffic? . . . Should we now leave it to the more demonstrative pressure groups so that we can concentrate on our first love—cycling for recreation in the countryside? Or is there a need to co-ordinate all the currently fragmented effort and weld it into an authoritative "common front"—with its own official and representative spokesman?

Such a "common front" was suggested by the race-focused British Cycling Federation, which theorized that the CTC could join with it and the Road Time Trials Council to form a single, national representative cycling body. Both CTC and RTTC rejected the overture, and far from joining together, British cycling advocacy in the 1970s was notable for the spawning of even more organizations. This was partly caused by the FoE losing interest in cycling (its last major event was a "National Bike Rally" in London's Trafalgar Square in 1979, but this was more of a general "Reclaim the Road" protest than a bicycle advocacy event). The withdrawal was surprising, and led some of the FoE's cycle advocates to leave the organization and start campaigning on a local level. FoE's Feilden created the Lambeth Campaign for Safe Cycling in 1975, and other borough-based cycle advocacy groups were created at around the same time. These groups were later absorbed by the London Cycling Campaign, which was launched in September 1978 at the Cheshire Cheese pub on Fleet Street. "LCC started as an idea in a dingy basement at Number Nine Poland Street," recalls one of the founding members, Nick Lester. "We had poor lighting, no ventilation and no smoking ban—we'd try to finish quickly and get out into the fresh air." Number Nine Poland Street was owned by the Joseph Rowntree Reform Trust and also housed a number of other left-leaning campaign groups including, ironically, the Friends of the Earth.

IT WOULD be some years before the nascent campaign groups could influence government thinking on transport. A 1975 parliamentary debate initiated by Sir George Young—he would later become known as the "bicycling baronet"—clearly shows how far cycle advocacy still had to travel. "Although the Government have not lifted one finger to help the cyclist, there has been a dramatic growth in cycling since 1971," Sir George stated, optimistically.

> I raise this subject . . . on behalf of the 80,000 Londoners who cycle regularly to work every day and also on behalf of the 18 million cyclists in this country. As an example of the potential if adequate provision is made, in Stevenage where a grade-separated system of bicycle routes has been constructed, between one-third and one-half of all journeys are made by bicycle. Therefore, the potential exists and is a prize worth grasping.

He suggested that if the government's attitude to cycling were to change from "cautious indifference to one of positive encouragement, the benefit to society in terms of energy saving, of a better environment and of the improved health of the British public would be enormous."

He added:

> Up to 1971 bicycle usage declined mainly because the conditions were wrong and the planners assumed that the car would ultimately displace other forms of personal transport. They were misguided, but unfortunately their prophecies were fulfilled because inadequate provision for the cyclist was made in the transport plans drawn

up during that period. The bicycle is pollution-free and the least offensive of all transport modes. On behalf of cyclists I have drawn up a short shopping list, or cyclists' charter, to put to the Minister. . . .

Sir George's charter included a request for a cycle-specific unit in the Department for Transport; he wanted this unit to look at the "positive measures taken overseas to help the cyclist."

By this Sir George meant the cycling facilities being installed in the Netherlands. In an era when Britain was spending billions on motorways, some of them slicing through cities at huge expense, almost nothing was being spent on facilities for cyclists. In his speech, Sir George remarked that parking a car in a railway station cost 22p a day. The much smaller bicycle ought to cost 1p a day, he reckoned. It actually cost 17p a day (yes, there was a time when cyclists had to pay for bicycle parking at rail stations).

Sir George then turned to the separation of cyclists from motorized traffic:

> The major deterrent to the cyclist . . . is the risk of an accident. . . . The segregation of the cycle from the car, would overcome the worst fears. . . . Provision should be made not just to cater for today's bicyclist but to encourage the bicyclist of tomorrow by separating his journey from the motorist and seeing that there is adequate parking provision. . . . We all look to the Government to give a lead.

No such lead was forthcoming. Denis Howell, the Labour minister for the environment, replied:

> There is something to be said for traffic lanes. I believe that these can be provided better in new towns like Stevenage where they are starting from scratch. It is difficult to provide separate traffic lanes in the middle of Birmingham, Manchester or London. . . . I cannot accede to the request that my Department should set up a separate cycling advisory unit. We are being asked to cut down on the numbers of civil servants. We already have a traffic advisory unit.

The government insisted—as it had done since 1948—that cycling was a local matter, not one of national import: "The need for the provision of a separate cycle network rather than the use of the urban road network is a matter for local authorities to decide . . . ," and similarly a transport "Green Paper" in 1976 dismissed "suggestions . . . that special roads should be constructed . . . for pedal bicycles" because providing for this form of personal mobility "could hardly be justified unless large numbers of people, who would otherwise have used the general road system, could be attracted to use the cycleway system. . . ." (However, in the same document, in opposition to those calling for an end to the preferential treatment meted out to motorists the government said car use "*should* increase, for personal mobility is what people want, and those who already have it should not try to pull the ladder up behind them.") The Green Paper concluded that provision would not be forthcoming because "encouragement of [cycle] use for journeys in crowded city centres would need to be accompanied by extensive and sometimes costly segregation measures."

The Cyclists' Touring Club and the British Cycling Bureau responded to the Green Paper by insisting that "cyclists are not such a small section of the community as often supposed" and that the number of cyclists "are increasing rapidly." The response added that 467,000 bicycles had been sold in 1970, but this had more than doubled to 1 million by 1975. "In no other form of transport are usage and vehicle numbers increasing so rapidly, with adult sales increasing by 30 percent p.a. [per annum], passenger miles increasing by 15 percent p.a.," argued the campaigners. "Yet in no other field of transport is investment or provision of facilities so low. If there was this rate of growth in any other form of transport there would be talk of crisis measures to deal with it. This implies that a much more positive attitude should be taken towards cycling."

In 1977, the Department for Transport issued a design guide that demonstrated it only ever expected build-it-and-they-will-come to work for motoring infrastructure. "DB32" said weakly that the "provision of comparatively short lengths of segregated cycle routes may be sensible . . . provided the use of cycles is sufficient to warrant such provision."

Some local authorities *were* willing to spend on cycling. Bedford, sixty miles north of London, is one of the few British cities to have invested in cycling, if somewhat sporadically. With the construction of four crosstown cycle tracks in 1953, it has done so for as long as Stevenage. The key reason for the building of these tracks was that cycle use in Bedford was high—in fact, far higher than most other English towns—and was approaching Dutch levels of use. A 1945 traffic census found that "for ten minutes in one midday period cyclists passed

The derelict Bristol-to-Bath railway line was transformed into a cycle trail by Cyclebag/Sustrans. (Sustrans)

the census-takers at the rate to three thousand an hour." There were some improvements to the town's "network" in the 1960s, and then there was a slightly more ambitious expansion in the 1970s. Not that this was welcomed by all. "Don't waste cash on racetrack, say angry residents," screamed a 1977 headline in the *Bedfordshire Times*.

This was in response to plans put forward in the Bedford Urban Transportation Study of 1976. Bedford's council planned to install a number of striped, protected, and off-carriageway routes from suburban areas into town, mostly away from arterial roads. Two reasonably good routes were installed, but the rest were spiked because of protests from residents.

Elsewhere there were one-off schemes of relatively high quality, including a short curb-protected lane in Middlesbrough, a chemicals-manufacturing city on England's northeast coast. The "Middlesbrough Cycleway" scheme had ambitious intent (officials had consulted with the Bureau and with Claxton) and was to form a backbone of routes that could, in time, have led to a granular network, but only a few stretches were built in 1978 to the "innovatory" standard that had been envisaged, and the would-be network failed to attract cyclists in sufficient numbers for the trial to be rolled out further.

FOLLOWING THE 1963 publication of Dr. Beeching's report mentioned earlier, the motor-centric government of the day wielded the "Beeching Axe" and ripped out more than 5,000 miles of track from Britain's historic and world-famous rail network. The steel rails may have been removed but the track beds remained and, in time, some of these rights-of-way were transformed into cycle trails. The UK's current "National Cycle Network"—14,000 miles of traffic-free and quiet routes administered by a charity called Sustrans, founded by a visionary called John Grimshaw—sprang from one fifteen-mile stretch of former railway line.

Grimshaw wasn't the first to lobby for the cycle-conversion of Britain's (not at all) Permanent Way. That distinction goes to Michael Dower, a conservationist who, in 1992, became director general of Britain's Countryside Commission. In 1963, writing in *Architectural Review*, Dower proposed that the track beds left after the Beeching cuts should form a national system of "greenways," and that it would be cyclists who would be the greatest beneficiaries of them. The idea lay fallow until a 1970 government report picked up on the suggestion. Written by J. H. Appleton for, as it happens, the Countryside Commission, *Disused Railways in the Countryside of England and Wales* suggested that the track beds might also be used as refuse dumps, shooting ranges, nature reserves, linear campsites, running tracks, and—in Cambridgeshire—as an access road to a radio telescope.

But cycle-trail use was one of the leading contenders, for Appleton said: "Increasing traffic has made conditions on many roads less attractive and less safe for cyclists, and the ability to move freely through the countryside . . . would open up greatly the possibilities . . . [for cycling]." He admitted that "cycling is a declining activity" but said this was a decline that the "disused railways might be able to relieve."

Appleton revealed that the Ramblers' Association, the British Horse Society, and the Cyclists' Touring Club were "pooling their interests" in order to "secure facilities which they would be unlikely to achieve for any one of them alone." He

John Grimshaw of Cyclebag/Sustrans was one of the laborers to work
on the transformation of the Bristol-to-Bath railway line. (Sustrans)

explained that "this common interest of users" was motivated by "the desire for
segregation from road traffic as an issue of safety."

The British Cycling Bureau also took an interest in the potential in the
grubbed-up lines, contributing to a 1972 episode of BBC1's *Tomorrow's World*
that broadcast a four-and-a-half-minute piece on the future for rail-trails in the
UK, focusing on the derelict former railway lines in Stoke-on-Trent. Two years
later, cycle campaigner Philip Ashbourn noted in his PhD thesis that cycling
could be encouraged by the "creation of cycle routes along disused railway lines."

In July 1977, a group of Bristol-based environmental campaigners formed
Cyclebag, a cycling advocacy group that would put these ideas into action.
Cyclebag—an acronym for Conserve Your Calf and Leg Energy Bristol Action
Group—would later transform into Sustrans. The group's founders included civil
engineer John Grimshaw (who would become CEO of Sustrans and who would
create the National Cycle Network concept); journalist Alistair Sawday (who
would go on to create a travel-guide empire and sustainable-holiday company);

cinematographer David Sproxton (co-creator of the Oscar-winning studio Aardman Animations, maker of *Wallace and Gromit*); and architect George Ferguson (who, in 2012, became the first elected mayor of Bristol).

"Cyclebag emerged as a constructive protest against the domination of the motor lobby in our politics and our roads," stated Ferguson. In 1979, the campaign group—led by Grimshaw—leased a stretch of the former Midland Railway and, with volunteer labor (including Grimshaw's own), created a five-mile cycling and walking trail between Bath and Bitton; it was later extended to became the station-to-station Bristol-to-Bath trail. This was not the first rail trail in the UK—the Manifold Railway Path in the Peak District of northern England was created in the 1930s—but it was the springboard from which Sustrans, founded in 1983, pushed for the formation of the ambitious National Cycle Network. Sustrans—short for *sus*tainable *trans*port—is today criticized by some cycle advocates for focusing on traffic-free paths that are mainly used for leisure journeys.

"I've always seen it as critical to have a positive strategy to start people cycling again," Grimshaw said in 2006, "and you don't start with the journey to work. The way into cycling, that first journey, will almost certainly be a leisure journey."

The following year, academic John Parkin countered that "it cannot be assumed that use of the bicycle for recreational purposes will follow through into use for utilitarian purposes," but it's unavoidable that the National Cycle Network, imperfect though it may be (which is not always the fault of Sustrans), is the nearest thing Britain has ever had to, well, a national cycle network.

5 | The Great American Bike Boom *(1970–1974)*

"Bicycles have come back and cyclists again want their share of the road."

— *Lubbock Avalanche-Journal*, 1972

BEFORE THE BLACK FRIDAY MALL STAMPEDES and before the Cabbage Patch Doll riots of 1983, there was the Great American Bike Boom. "Crowds press into Chicago's Turin Bicycle Co-op hunting for new models," reported *Life* in July 1971. Under the headline "The Bicycle Madness," *Life's* article featured a double-page photograph of a diverse crowd waiting to buy bikes: men and women, black and white, young and old. "So far this year, Turin has sold over 3,000 bicycles and could have sold several thousand more if supplies had been available," continued the magazine. Today, the retail madness that is Black Friday lasts just a day. The Cabbage Patch Kids craze was over within weeks. The bike boom lasted for the best part of four years.

Bike sales in 1970 rose so fast that *Time* claimed that it was the "bicycle's biggest wave of popularity in its 154-year history." This was not pleasing to all: Peter Flanigan, a Wall Street investment banker and one of President Richard Nixon's most trusted aides, chided that: "The United States is not going back to the cold, the dark, and the bicycle." He was soon proved wrong—about the bicycle, at least—and even some of President Nixon's closest confidantes fell under cycling's spell.

COMMUTING AND shopping by bike, cycling while pregnant, riding with musical instruments: it all sounds very Dutch but, as *Time* explained, in 1970 it was becoming normal for Americans, too.

> Harvard English professor Joel Porte . . . sold his car four years ago, and hasn't "even been tempted" to own one since. Instead, Porte, 36, and his wife Ilana, 31, get by on three-speed English bicycles; he makes the trip from . . . a Boston suburb, to the Cambridge campus in 17 minutes flat. Last week, just before her first baby was due, Mrs. Porte was still running errands by bike. Actress Doris Day regularly bikes into Beverly Hills to shop and expects to keep it up "even when I'm 80." Doctors and professors at Case Western Reserve University . . . frequently commute by bike, as do some members of the Cleveland orchestra—with piccolos, flutes, violins, and violas strapped to their backs.

Bicycling broke through into the mainstream during the boom years of 1970–74. "Some 64 million fellow travelers are taking regularly to bikes these days, more than ever before," gushed *Time*, "and more than ever [they are] convinced that two wheels are better than four."

A Bank of America report said bicycle sales had been "rolling along" at 6 million a year "until the boom began." In 1971, sales increased 22 percent to 9 million and hit 14 million in 1972. In the following year, this climbed further to 15.3 million. And, said the bank, most of the increase was due to the sale of adult bikes. Only 12 percent of the bikes sold in 1969 were for adults; by the peak of the boom, almost 60 percent of bikes were destined for adults. These were mostly ten-speed bikes, with a derailleur mechanism at the back instead of a clunky "coaster" hub. Some of the lighter, costlier, more-exotic ten-speeds were imports from England and Italy.

The boom was rural and recreational, but it was also urban and practical.

Highly placed politicians—a few of whom were cyclists—told planners to get on with building miles and miles of urban bikeways. "Both national and local governments have recognized the phenomenal growth of bicycling," reported *Time*, "and the Department of the Interior has plans for nearly 100,000 miles of bicycle paths to be constructed in the next ten years."

In 1973, 252 bicycle-oriented bills were introduced in 42 states; 60 were passed into law, half of them were bikeway bills. The Federal-Aid Highway Act of the same year provided $120 million for bikeways over the following three years.

The reemergence of the bicycle had taken most observers by surprise. What had been an "exiled device, to be used somewhere between kindergarten and acne," claimed *Time*, became a transport mode to be reckoned with. "It might have remained a thing of beauty and a toy forever," continued the magazine's essayist Stefan Kanfer,

> But . . . the agent of its obscurity was also the cause of its revival. For too long, the combustion engine befouled the atmosphere and lulled Americans into a dangerous sloth. But today, the new conservation and the high incidence of circulatory and cardiac diseases have caused the natural life to be reappraised. The bicycle no longer seems juvenile; indeed, it offers transportation, romance, and exercise. . . .

"Bikes are back," claimed *National Geographic* staff writer Noel Grove in the magazine's May 1973 edition. "Glutted roadways, ecological concern, the quest for healthful recreation, and the sophistication of geared machines have all contributed to a flood of cycling activity," explained Grove, adding that "legislators are beginning to think bikeway as well as highway." His twelve-page feature concluded that "with bikeway construction and ecological concern marching hand in hand, America's bicycling boom could harbinger a whole new era in transportation."

Ecological concern was one of the drivers of the boom. During 1967's "Summer of Love," the Haight-Ashbury district of San Francisco reeked of patchouli oil, weed, and incense. With flowers in their hair and buzzed with "acid," some of the area's self-styled "freaks" protested against not just war but also waste. This concern deepened for many, and for those "hippies" who became environmental protestors the automobile became a potent symbol of everything that was wrong with the "military-industrial complex." In February 1970,

Masked Nancy Pearlman, and friends, Los Angeles, Earth Day, 1970.
(Los Angeles Times Photographic Archive, Charles E. Young Research Library, UCLA)

nineteen ecologically aware humanities students at the San Jose State College bought a brand-new Ford Maverick and, with the blessing of their professor, buried it in a twelve-foot-deep hole dug in front of the campus's cafeteria. This crowd-funded destruction of the hated motorcar made news around the world.

With six students riding on the roof of the car, "it was pushed through downtown San Jose in a parade led by three ministers, the college band, and a group of comely coeds wearing green shroud-like gowns," reported the *San Francisco Chronicle*. "As the local citizenry looked on from the sidewalks the students marched by at a slow funeral pace set by the band which played a selection of songs in dirge styles."

The burial was one of the events staged in the run-up to the first Earth Day on April 22, 1970. For many event organizers, the automobile was public enemy number one. An event guide published by Friends of the Earth included a chapter titled "Warning: The Automobile Is Dangerous to Earth, Air, Fire, Water, Mind, and Body." And if the automobile was the problem, the bicycle was the solution. The Earth Day coordination team suggested forty ideas for Earth Day events; one of them was "Encourage people to walk or ride bicycles instead of driving cars on April 22." Twenty million Americans took part in a variety of events on the day itself and in the months beforehand, many of them held at colleges, schools, and universities, galvanizing the young and melding together the first "green" generation. Environmental broadcaster Nancy Pearlman, coordinator of the Earth Day events in Southern California, went on to found Concerned Bicycle Riders for the Environment and lobbied to get bikeways for Los Angeles by riding with a World War II–era gas mask.

"Bicycles are small, inexpensive, require little maintenance, pleasurable to use, and smogless," stated the Whole Earth Catalog for 1970, adding: "If America traded in all their [cars] for bikes, a lot of problems would be solved." By 1974, the right-on publication included four bike-related pages: "Not only is bicycle travel human-scaled, healthful, and non-polluting, but it turns out to be more efficient than jetplanes, salmon, or seagulls." This was a reference to an article on bicycle technology that had appeared in *Scientific American* the previous year and which encouraged many people to learn more about cycling.

The long article was by S. S. Wilson, a lecturer in engineering at Oxford University. He wrote that the purpose of a bicycle was to "make it easier for an individual to move about, and this the bicycle achieves in a way that quite outdoes natural evolution."

> When one compares the energy consumed in moving a certain distance as a function of body weight for a variety of animals and machines, one finds that an unaided walking man does fairly well . . . but he is not as efficient as a horse, a salmon, or a jet transport. With the aid of a bicycle, however, the man's energy consumption is reduced to about a fifth. . . . Therefore, apart from increasing his unaided speed, the cyclist improves his efficiency rating to No. 1 among moving creatures and machines.

(This extract, and the graph that accompanied it, went on to inspire many others, including Steve Jobs of Apple, who used it in a 1980 presentation to explain the efficiency of the personal computer: "What a computer is to me is it's the most remarkable tool that we've ever come up with, and it's the equivalent of a bicycle for our minds.")

Wilson continued, "For those of us in the overdeveloped world the bicycle offers a real alternative to the automobile."

> The possible inducements are many: cycleways to reduce the danger to cyclists of automobile traffic, bicycle parking stations, facilities for the transportation of bicycles by rail and bus, and public bicycles for "park and pedal" service. Already bicycling is often the best way to get around quickly in city centers.

The simplicity of the bicycle chimed with E. F. Schumacher's 1973 best seller *Small Is Beautiful*. This was one of the key eco-polemics of the 1970s—it theorized that capitalism was inherently bad for the planet because, like a Ponzi scheme, it can only survive by growing, unsustainably. What was required instead, believed Schumacher, were small-scale "appropriate technologies." The bicycle, believed the bike activists ("biketivists"), was more of an appropriate technology for city use than the smelly, dangerous, gas-guzzling, space-hungry automobile. Jane Jacobs's *The Death and Life of Great American Cities* was the second non-cycling philosophical tome on the bookshelf of every card-carrying cycle activist of the 1970s, with the third being Ivan Illich's *Energy and Equity* of 1974.

CHICAGO-BASED Edward Aramaic explicitly linked cycling with environmentalism when he founded Bicycle Ecology and organized a "pedal-in" in October 1970. This was the era of "-in" demonstrations, which had started in the 1960s with "sit-ins" protesting against racial segregation at American colleges and universities. Later, there were "teach-ins," "be-ins," "love-ins," and, in 1969, the famous "bed-in" with Yoko Ono and John Lennon, who espoused world peace from a bed in the presidential suite of Amsterdam's Hilton Hotel, and who were gifted a White Bicycle by the city's Provo anarchist group.

"Bicycle Ecology is a group . . . who want to ban trucks, buses, and automobiles from [downtown] and replace them with bikes," reported the *Chicago Tribune*. "1,500 to 2,000 enthusiastic riders of all ages . . . braved a stiff north wind and temperatures in the 40s to wheel down major arteries to the Civic Center, where speeches extolled the bicycle as good for the individual and for the environment."

An anti-car, pro-bicycle protest in Stockholm, Sweden, attended by New York urban planner David Gurin, inspired him to join with other activists to form a Triple-A with a difference. Action Against Automobiles organized a demo in November 1972 calling for an end to highway spending, and for motorcars to be barred from downtown Manhattan. Riders met in Central Park and rolled past the Greater New York Automobile Show, chanting "Cars must go! Cars must go!" Speaking to a crowd of cyclists, Gurin applauded the radical bicycle activism of the Provo anarchists, and he urged New Yorkers to adopt similar "eco-tactics." One of the posters he designed to promote the AAA protest rides suggested the provision of Provo-style "FREE BICYCLES" and promised there would be "MASSIVE DEMONSTRATIONS . . . UNTIL THE STREETS ARE CLEARED OF THE AUTO GANGRENE." (In 1978, Gurin, who had been writing anti-car polemics in the *Village Voice* since the mid-1960s and who was a friend of Jane Jacobs, became New York City's deputy commissioner for transport, a post he held for twelve years. In the late 1980s, the city banned not automobiles but bicycles—see epilogue.)

The other cofounders of Action Against Automobiles included Charlie McCorkell, who went on to own New York City's Bicycle Habitat bike-shop chain which opened as a single store in 1978, and Barry Benepe, founder of the Greenmarket farmers' markets. The biketivists decided that the Triple-A name was too provocative, so they changed it to Transportation Alternatives. The founding event for this multimodal action group was a protest ride in 1973, again routed via an automobile show. The Ride and Rally for a New York Bicycle Lane Network demo was promoted with a leaflet that included a graphic by renowned pop artist Red Grooms, and attracted 400 riders. They were treated to an impromptu concert by folk singer Pete Seeger, the civil rights activist responsible for popularizing the spiritual anthem, "We Shall Overcome." The following year a bike-in parade staged by Transportation Alternatives on Broadway attracted 10,000 riders. Placards and balloons demanded, "Bike Lanes Now!"

Congressman Ed Koch—who would become New York City's mayor in

1977—rode in some of the early 1970s New York protest bike rides, and in 1971 he stressed: "The only way to ensure safety for the many thousands of New Yorkers who want to bicycle is to designate official and exclusive bike lanes." (Koch installed bikeways when he became mayor of New York; but he also ripped them out again—see epilogue.)

While Koch wanted cyclists to be safely integrated into New York's traffic, many in the bicycle advocacy movement elsewhere in America were fiercely anti-car. Sam Oakland, a Portland State University professor, told the Associated Press in 1971 that "We want to redesign Portland [Oregon] to make it a city for people . . . instead of what it now is, a giant, smelly parking garage for commuters." Oakland headed a university-based campaign group that wanted to "abolish the automobile." His group, founded in 1968, became known as the Bicycle Lobby. In 1971, Oakland, a poet and author, led a fifty-mile ride from Portland to Salem to lobby the Oregon Legislature to apportion highway funds to improve conditions for cyclists and pedestrians. The lobbying worked: the Oregon Bicycle Bill was passed in the same year. This set aside 1 percent of state transportation spending for bike-specific facilities and was the first designated state funding for cycling in the United States. Governor Tom McCall signed the bill into law using a Schwinn Paramount ten-speed bike as a makeshift table.

One of those who joined the many Bicycle Lobby rides in the early 1970s was Portland City Commissioner Neal Goldschmidt, who would go on to become mayor—the first of several mayors and city commissioners who cycled. Portland planned for the construction of 75 miles of recreational trails, and more than 100 miles of bikeways on city streets. A citizen Bicycle Path Task Force was appointed to oversee the city's bikeway program, and Oakland was appointed as chair. The Task Force met with resistance from the city's engineers—they had little interest in the use of bicycles for transportation and instead wanted to use the money from the highway pot to build recreational trails. "As long as the bicycle continues to be considered a toy for recreational use only, we're not going to get anywhere with paths in the city," complained Oakland. In April 1973, after many struggles with city officials, the Task Force was able to push through *Bicycle Facilities for Portland: A Comprehensive Plan*. By the following year, 60 miles of bikeways had been striped statewide, with another 50 miles under construction and 70 miles to be delivered. Mighty oaks from little acorns grow—Portland, Oregon, is now one of America's most cycle-friendly cities, thanks in part to it being one of America's most ecologically aware cities.

STEWART L. UDALL, introduced in chapter 2, was one of the greenest US politicians of the 1960s—during his stint as interior secretary he commissioned a study that resulted in the *Trails for America* report, which promoted hiking trails in national parks but also bikeways in cities: "To avoid crossing motor vehicle traffic, bikeways would be located along landscaped shoulder areas on frontage roads next to freeways and expressways, along shorelines, and on abandoned railroad rights-of-way," imagined the 1966 report. Once out of office, he was even more explicitly pro-bicycle. In 1973, he advised President Nixon and Congress to aim for smaller and fewer automobiles, fewer airline flights—but more bicycles and urban bikeways. "We've got to get away from the pretense that there is some easy painless way that we can save energy," Udall told the *New York Times*. "We're at the final stages of the climax of the automobile era. . . . We've gone as far as we can go." Give people choice, he said, build more bikeways. "People cling to their cars because there is no alternative." Hundreds of articles in the mainstream press demonstrated that there *was* an alternative. If *National Geographic* were to publish a spread today similar to the one from 1973, it would likely have glossy adverts from the likes of Cannondale, Specialized, and Trek, America's leading home-grown bicycle brands. The three were all founded during the boom years.

Cannondale was born in 1971 above a rural pickle shop in Wilton, Connecticut. It made backpacking gear as well as the Bugger, a backpack-on-wheels for towing behind bicycles. In the foyer at Specialized's high-tech headquarters in Morgan Hill, California, there's a replica of the Volkswagen campervan that founder Mike Sinyard sold to fund the European bike tour that would lead to the foundation of his business. Sinyard started in 1972 by selling hard-to-get European bicycle parts to US bike shops. Famously, he schlepped the first parts in a bicycle trailer: a Cannondale Bugger. Trek was started in 1975 from a red barn, a former carpet warehouse in Waterloo, Wisconsin. The firm made 900 steel touring-bike frames in its first year.

Much of Specialized is owned by Merida, which also owes its beginnings to the boom. The Taiwanese company was founded in 1972 by Ike Tseng to produce Raleigh bikes for the voracious North American market—he modeled his fledgling factory on Raleigh's plant in Nottingham, England. The world's largest specialty bike maker is Giant Bicycles of Taiwan. The company was spawned in 1972 after a typhoon wiped out King Liu's fish farm. Eel breeding's loss was bicycling's gain—Liu's factories in Taiwan and China now make many of the bicycles for the world's high-end brands, including Trek of Wisconsin.

The industry-promoting Bicycle Institute of America was one of many organizations frequently quoted in the mainstream media during the early 1970s—thanks in part to its bikeways-boosting newsletter, *Boom in Bikeways*, which it had been sending to the media since the late 1960s. The BIA—which also placed lifestyle advertisements in the press—crowed about the seemingly never-ending rise of the bicycle market. The good times were here to stay, thought many, including authors who penned zeitgeist-tapping best sellers.

Sex had Dr. Alex Comfort; cycling had Richard Ballantine. *Richard's Bicycle Book* was a 1970s publishing sensation—it sold more than a million copies. Ballantine plugged into the politics of eco-activism which had encouraged many onto bicycles, but he also enthused about the physicality of riding. "Look at what happens to you on a bicycle," he wrote:

> It's immediate and direct. *You* pedal. *You* make decisions. *You* experience the tang of the air and the surge of power as you bite into the road. You're vitalized. As you hum along, you fully and gloriously experience the day, the sunshine, the clouds, the breezes. You're alive! You are going someplace, and it is *you* who is doing it.

"Most active stores are able to sell out a shipment of bikes within two to three weeks," wrote Ballantine of the boom. The same could have been said for his book. It was published in October 1972 and had to be reprinted within weeks. There was a third printing in March 1973 and a fourth just three months later.

Richard's Bicycle Book wasn't the only best seller of the time. Eugene Sloane's *Complete Book of Cycling* predated it. The instant success of the book—selling 100,000 copies in its first year—allowed Sloane to quit his job as the public relations director for the Midwest Stock Exchange to become a full-time bicycling writer. There was a rush of other books, too. The authors of *The Bicycle—That Curious Invention* ended their 1973 book by writing that "bicycles offer . . . a means of mobility that is quiet, clean, healthy, space saving and economical. . . . The next move is to get the politicians to *think cycleways!*" But it was Ballantine's book that most fired up its readers, first in the United States and then, in 1973, in Britain when Ballantine moved to live in London.

On the face of it, the book—subtitled *A Manual of Bicycle Maintenance and Enjoyment*—was about fixing bicycles and "zestful riding," but Ballantine also made a bold case for assertive urban cycling: "If it is unsafe for you to let [motorists] pass, don't hesitate to take full possession of your lane so that they *can't* pass. . . ." Some motorists, he said, were "authentic maniacs," but nevertheless he encouraged riders to "*integrate* yourself with the traffic." He also suggested readers who witnessed an attack on a cyclist from a car should "beat the assailant up black and blue" and, despite being an animal lover, he also had some sage but brutal advice for a cyclist attacked by a dog: "Ram your entire arm down his throat. He will choke and die."

Ballantine's book imagined a utopian future of bikeways, but he didn't think this would be sufficient to get more people cycling. "Bikeways are not enough," he wrote. "What is needed is the elimination of polluting transportation. . . . The absolute elimination of internal combustion engines from urban areas is the practical solution which benefits everybody."

Ballantine was the only child of publishers Ian and Betty Ballantine, creators of the New York paperback publishing house Bantam, which popularized the likes of Tolkien, Arthur C. Clarke, and Isaac Asimov. His aunt was a radical political author. Ballantine grew up in a fog of intellectual New Leftism. "A better deal for cyclists," he asserted, "is a better deal for society."

When he argued that bicycles could change the world he meant it, but he also told his readers that there would be a "long drawn-out struggle," for they were up against "the power of vested interests in maintaining a motor age." *Richard's Bicycle Book* warned readers not to be "too surprised if you are beaned at a bike-in by a club-swinging cop who calls you a dirty communist, and don't back off because of it. You have a right to live—it is your birthright—but you will have to fight for it."

As other writers pointed out, the biggest fight would be with "motordom." Illustrated with a cartoon of two staid cyclists being chased by a yapping, toothy dog and a yapping, toothy car, the *New York Times* in 1972 said cyclists were growing in number "despite the curses of their motorized oppressors." Miraculously, the paper added, "the bikers are even managing to seize slivers of their tormentors' territory."

According to correspondent Roy Bongartz, there were 15,000 miles of bikeways in the United States "and the total mileage is increasing," as were the numbers of cyclists, "61 million of them at the last estimate, braving the perils of highway and byway to make cycling America's No. 1 outdoor pastime." Nevertheless, Bongartz stressed that "it cannot be exactly said that the establishment of bikeways is threatening the dominance of the automobile in our society . . . [but] what can be said is that bikeways are starting to command from motorists a degree of recognition that may lead to the beginnings of driver respect for all the people who pedal away on their puny two-wheelers."

The new bikeways weren't on main roads but on "little-trafficked secondary streets and highways parallel to main arteries. . . ." In his accounting of the total number of bikeways—which was contradicted by other sources—Bongartz also counted the long-distance rail trails that had been opening since the mid-1960s. "The [bikeways] idea has spread all over the country, to hundreds of towns and cities, and even to large cities such as Baltimore, Chicago, Cleveland, Denver, Fort Worth, Dayton, Milwaukee, Minneapolis-St. Paul, San Diego, San Francisco, Seattle, and New York." And, marveled Bongartz, "The Coconut Grove National Bank in Florida has a pedal-in window."

IN 1972, University of Montana students could choose from geology, psychology, biology, or—new for that year—bikeology. "And for a full credit, too," one newspaper stated, adding that this was "just another example of America's love affair with the bicycle. . . ." Students could even dress the part, for "special bikewear for both sexes is found in the smart shops of every college town." At the University of Iowa at Ames, the "three most popular subjects on campus were social change, bicycling, and sex, in that order." These university courses— and there were others at the Universities of Texas, Utah, and Oregon—studied the creation of bikeway masterplans, including "how to get bikeway legislation passed" and "how to integrate bikeway systems into urban planning."

The term *bikeology* wasn't coined in the 1970s—it dates to the 1940s as a school subject and was used even earlier than that by itinerant singer-songwriters— but the counter-cultural ecological awakening in the 1960s and 1970s gave currency to the word with its fortuitous mix of *bike* and *ecology*. It was used by city planner and landscape architect Ken Kolsbun, who said he wanted "massive funding for bikeways, traffic control, and cycle-storage facilities." He founded Friends of Bikeology in 1971 from his home in the Santa Barbara foothills. Forty

Ride to work, fast, on a Raleigh. Advertising poster, 1932.
It might also be a good idea to have hands near the brakes?

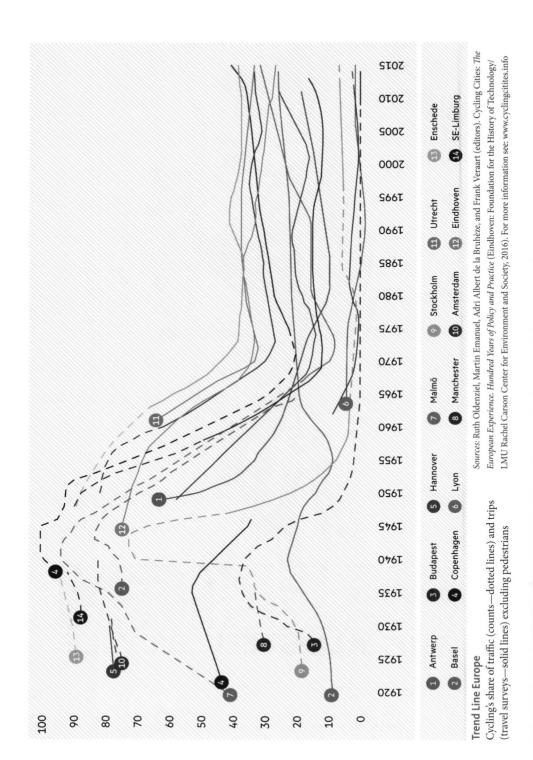

Trend Line Europe

Cycling's share of traffic (counts—dotted lines) and trips (travel surveys—solid lines) excluding pedestrians

Legend:
1 Antwerp
2 Basel
3 Budapest
4 Copenhagen
5 Hannover
6 Lyon
7 Malmö
8 Manchester
9 Stockholm
10 Amsterdam
11 Utrecht
12 Eindhoven
13 Enschede
14 SE-Limburg

Sources: Ruth Oldenziel, Martin Emanuel, Adri Albert de la Bruhèze, and Frank Veraart (editors). Cycling Cities: *The European Experience. Hundred Years of Policy and Practice* (Eindhoven: Foundation for the History of Technology/ LMU Rachel Carson Center for Environment and Society, 2016). For more information see: www.cyclingcitites.info

"CYCLISTS ONLY." Cycle track icon, England, 1937. The icon changed little in the next thirty years. Here's the one from 1967, as used in the body of this book:

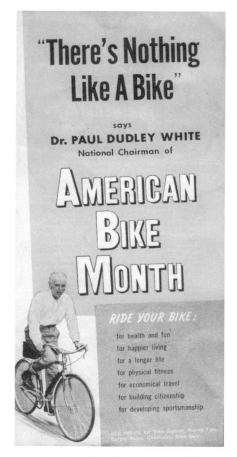

American Bike Month leaflet, 1964.

"COO, LOOK—THERE'S A CYCLIST!"

English cartoonist Fougasse satirizes those cyclists who
preferred to ride on roads with cars rather than ride on the
adjoining cycle track. *Punch*, 1938.

Dutch streets look as though they have always been
people-friendly. In fact, in the 1970s streets such as these
would have been choked with cars.

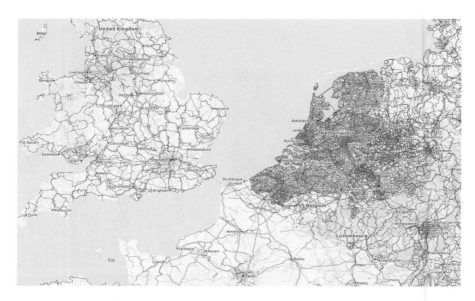

Above: Booms do not respect borders? The Netherlands has a dense network of cycleways. (Google Maps). **Right:** Cyclists in Stevenage do not have to cycle along main roads; there are cycleways for that. **Below:** The cycleways beneath the Seven Hills roundabout in Stevenage have here been recently resurfaced; cycle use in Stevenage remains low.

"Bikes Have Equal Rights." Poster by Lou Stovall,
Department of Motor Vehicles, Washington, DC, 1971.

Bikeology poster, 1972 (note the alternative spelling).

volunteers, including his wife Jannice, organized events across the United States and distributed the members' magazine, *Serendipity*.

Mrs. Martha Newlon, president of the Friends of Bikeology, was one of 32 folks appointed by the state transportation secretary to research a bikeways plan for Delaware. Also on this task force—and somewhat less enthusiastic about cycling—were heads of the police, planning, and state parks departments.

In the spring of 1973, the Friends of Bikeology paid for full-page national magazine and community newspaper ads asking: "Where are the Bikeways?" The ads rather optimistically claimed there were 80 million cyclists in the United States, only 10 million fewer than the number of motorists. (Kolsbun's group was the most strident of the 1970s bikeway-championing groups, and it advocated for what we today would consider Dutch-style cycle infrastructure. However, Friends of Bikeology was a spent force by 1975, and Kolsbun—as well as most other environmentalists—moved on to other forms of eco-activism.)

"WHEN CLAY GUBRIC opened [Washington, DC's] Towpath Cycle Shop in 1966, he counted three or four bicyclists pedaling home from work," wrote a *Washington Post* staffer in 1970. "One day last week," continued the journalist, "more than 50 commuting cyclists, most of them dressed in business suits or skirts, passed by his shop in Georgetown during the evening rush hour."

The staff journalist was Carl Bernstein, one half of the famous Woodward-and-Bernstein Pulitzer Prize–winning partnership, the investigative reporters who helped reveal the full extent of the 1972 Watergate scandal which, two years later, led to President Nixon falling on his sword. Bernstein was the *Washington Post's* "office hippie," noted *All the President's Men*, the pair's book on the scandal that gave the world the *-gate* suffix. Before they teamed up to work on what, at first blush, had been thought to be a minor burglary at the Watergate hotel and office complex, Woodward prejudged Bernstein to be a "long-haired freak who rode a bicycle. . . ."

This wasn't any old bicycle. Bernstein, just a few months into his reporter's job at the *Post*, had put himself up for the 1970 bike boom story because he was a DC cycle commuter himself. Bernstein rode to and from work—and between assignments at the White House—on one of two ten-speed racers, either his Raleigh or his Holdsworth, both of them venerable English brands. The theft of Bernstein's Raleigh became part of the Watergate story:

> Back at the office, Woodward went to the rear of the newsroom to call Deep Throat. Bernstein wished he had a source like that. The only source he knew who had such comprehensive knowledge in any field was Mike Schwering, who owned Georgetown Cycle Sport Shop. There was nothing about bikes—and, more important, bike thieves—that Schwering didn't know. Bernstein knew something about bike thieves: the night of the Watergate indictments, somebody

had stolen his ten-speed Raleigh from a parking garage. That was the difference between him and Woodward. Woodward went into a garage to find a source who could tell him what Nixon's men were up to. Bernstein walked into a garage to find an eight-pound chain cut neatly in two and his bike gone.

("Bicycle theft has become America's fastest-growing crime," reported *Time* in the mid-1970s. To foil such shenanigans, in 1971 Stan Kaplan, a bike-shop mechanic working in Bicycle Revival in Cambridgeport, Massachusetts, created the now-famous Kryptonite shackle lock, yet another brand founded thanks to the bike boom.)

As a bike-riding hippie, Bernstein could have been stating his own views when, in his 1970 *Post* piece, he wrote that "many cyclists harbor fierce antipathy for what they regard as an automobile culture that is choking the nation with fumes, speed, noise, and concrete." He added that there was a "growing group of cyclists who regard pedaling as an almost political act and inevitably flash the two-finger peace symbol upon encountering another person on a bike." Bernstein was therefore devastated when, two years after writing the commuter cycling piece, he discovered that one of the Watergate conspirators was also a "bike freak." While nosing around a bike shop for a replacement for his "beloved Raleigh," Bernstein thought of Jeb Stuart Magruder, deputy director of Richard Nixon's Committee to Re-Elect the President (known as CREEP):

> [Bernstein] had picked up a . . . disturbing piece of information that day: Magruder was a bike freak. Bernstein had trouble swallowing the information that a bicycle nut could be a Watergate bugger. And Magruder really was a card-carrying bicycle freak who had even ridden his ten-speed to the White House every day.

The facilities for cycle commuters in Washington, DC, had been poor in the late 1960s but had improved by the early 1970s, partly because of John A. Volpe, President Nixon's secretary of transportation. In 1969, Volpe—who routinely rode a bicycle that "can be folded up and carried to his tenth-floor office"—told Gilbert Hahn, the District's council chairman, to build bikeways for Washington's growing number of cyclists who, like him, were not all long-haired hippies. In fact, as Bernstein wrote in the *Post*, bike-boom bicyclists were just as likely to be "stock brokers and congressmen, secretaries and lawyers, students and government clerks, librarians and teachers, youngsters and oldsters."

Hahn handed the task of improving the cyclists' lot to Carl Bergman, clerk to the council's transportation committee. Bergman was another enthusiastic cyclist. Nineteen-seventies cycle activist Marchant "Lucky" Wentworth told me by e-mail that, at times, Bergman went beyond his brief, such as when he strong-armed DC's Department of Motor Vehicles into publishing and promoting a "Bikes Have Equal Rights" poster. A striking example of cognitive dissonance, this poster (see color plates) was produced by Lou Stovall, then an up-and-coming African American community-art activist churning out environmental posters. (He's now a world-renowned silkscreen printmaker.)

"The DMV weren't big fans of bikes," remembered Wentworth, "but the [council] chairman controlled their budget and had them by the short ones." The poster features a ten-speed bicycle floating above a lava-lamp-inspired sunset, with the orange sun dipping into a blue Potomac River and in the process deforming, hippie-style, the "Bikes Have" text. The non-deformed "Equal Rights" is above "D.C. Department of Motor Vehicles." If you didn't know it was an official poster, it would be easy to assume it was a satirical dig at motor-centrism. "I revered that poster for all it symbolized," recalled Wentworth, who at the time worked for the Washington Ecology Center, one of a national network of direct-action organizations (only the Ann Arbor Ecology Center is still going strong).

Transport Secretary Volpe used to ride his folding bike from his home to Capitol Hill. At a meeting in 1971, he encouraged all "to use our legs that the dear Lord gave us . . . [and to] show what can be done with bicycles." Volpe warned that cities had to make "radical changes in their commuting patterns" to meet clean-air standards, and suggested that bicycling would be a "valuable addition to urban transportation systems." Optimistically, Volpe told the *New York Times* that the Department of Transportation would "make every effort to establish exclusive bicycle lanes in our nation's cities and along the freeways and turnpikes between cities."

In 1971, the District's council commissioned fifteen miles of commuter bikeways and also ordered curbs to be cut so riders—and folks in wheelchairs—could easily move on and off sidewalks. The city also sought out cyclists, soliciting their opinions. A commuter to Georgetown University, one of more than 400 to be surveyed, griped: "I have been run into the curb by autos and buses. Another favorite is to sneak into the bicyclist's lane and run him into a line of parked cars.

Motorists can't stand to have a bicycle act like a car."

The provision of bikeways—and signs erected by the National Park Service along a narrow road through Rock Creek Park stating that "All persons have equal right when driving cars or riding bikes"—were thought to be a way of reducing the growing hostility between cyclists and motorists. Along with "150 dedicated bicyclists," Volpe rode in Rock Creek Park in May 1971, telling a reporter along for the ride that cycling was "both a means of exercise and a mode of transportation." Volpe added that his department intended "to make Washington a model city for bicycles."

The nation's transport secretary was mightily in favor of a 1971 plan from the National Park Service to close a lane on the Rock Creek Park Road. Built in 1897 as a nine-mile "pleasure drive" for upper-crust cyclists and horse-drawn carriages, Beach Drive—part of the Rock Creek and Potomac Parkway—has been used as a commuter cut-through by motorists since the 1920s. The winding park road—it exits at the Watergate complex, which still has a 1970s-era bikeway in front of it—allows commuters from Maryland to reach Georgetown, "avoiding the many intersections and traffic congestion that plague motorists on the regular street routes," wrote a newspaper in 1935. "There is, perhaps, no city in the world offering so much beauty for those going to work," editorialized the *Evening Star*, calling the park a "fairyland" for motorists. All pretense about the beauties of the park—and the "pleasure drive" aspects of its road—were jettisoned in 1936 when the city's traffic director declared: "This new driveway is going to be a wonderful outlet for Connecticut Avenue traffic. . . . It means a straight shot at the heart of the city."

Postwar plans for Beach Drive to become part of a six-lane expressway were snuffed out in 1957 after a long battle, but by the late 1960s the National Park Service had to deal with pressures from an altogether different kind of commuter. Hundreds of bicyclists staged a "bike-in" on Beach Drive in 1971, demanding more space.

"At the first bike-in I burned someone's driver's license on network TV," said Wentworth. "Heady times," he reminisced, wistfully.

And violent times too, as Bernstein wrote in his 1970 piece: "some members of the bicycling minority are becoming more militant." He described how one rider was forced off the Rock Creek Parkway by the driver of a Buick Riviera who "drove off laughing." The rider caught up with the smirking motorist and, "dismounting from his trusty ten-speed steed, the rider . . . proceeded to kick a good-sized dent in the rear fender." Bernstein added—perhaps with more personal knowledge of the incident than he admitted in the news report—that the motorist "watched helplessly as the pedal-power advocate remounted his bike, clenched his fist, and headed off into the opposite direction with the words 'Ride On.'"

According to a newspaper, (an unlikely) 5,000 cyclists commuted along Beach Drive each day. The conversion, in September 1971, of one of Rock Creek Parkway's two lanes to a bicyclist-only commuter lane was "well publicized and enjoyed a good response from cyclists," said a later report from the National Park Service, "but its positive aspects were overshadowed by massive traffic tie-ups with severe inconvenience to the great majority of parkway users unable or unwilling to shift to bicycles."

Wentworth disagrees that the one-week conversion was "well publicized." He told me: "The Park Service did not advertise it very well; we were forced to recruit folks to get on the lane at the last minute." He recalls that the trial came to a sooner-than-expected conclusion, at least partly because of a congressman's complaint against eco-warriors. Wayne Aspinall, the chair of the House Interior and Insular Affairs Committee from 1959 to 1973, was an opponent of the bicycle-friendly Stewart Udall, and no fan of environmentalists, calling them "over-indulged zealots" and "aristocrats" to whom "balance means nothing." On one of the first lane-closure days, the congressman from Colorado was caught in a traffic snarl-up caused not just by the space given over to cyclists, but by flooding from a water main. Wentworth takes up the story:

> When Aspinall finally got to the office, he called Russ Dickinson, then National Capital Parks director and told him to get those cyclists off the road. "I need somewhere to put them," said Dickinson. "All I have is a bridle path, but need the money to pave it." "How much do you need?" asked Aspinall. "$33,783," said Dickinson. "You've got it," shouted the chairman. The path . . . was put in within the week.

"Of course," added Wentworth, this bike path "was not very high quality." The NPS report added: "The political impossibility of continuing the lane closure— the goal of the bicycle lobby—was quickly apparent." What the report didn't mention was that the "political impossibility" had involved a called-in complaint from an influential congressman, so influential he could override the wishes of the nation's transportation secretary.

The failure of the bicycle-lane trial fired up activists. "I learned about the closure, and used [the lane] to bicycle to my office," said Cary Shaw, who rode his yellow Schwinn to a computer-programming job at the National Planning Association. "I decided to form an organization."

On May 1, 1972, Shaw unveiled the Washington Area Bicyclist Association. WABA wasn't the first US cycle advocacy group—the San Francisco Bicycle Coalition had been founded in 1970—but it became the model for other groups which also sprang up in 1972. "If there was a legacy from the turbulent 1960s, it was the feeling that the individual could make a difference," states a WABA history. "And if the individual could cause change, so much more so could a group of individuals."

WABA was a city campaign group but in America's capital city. *Ride On!!*— the association's two-exclamation-mark journal—discussed not just issues important to locals, such as the need to cover wheel-swallowing city grates, but also national issues. WABA urged federal officials to review Environmental Impact Statements for their effect on cycling. The organization also criticized the Office of Management and Budget for dismissing bicycle facilities as "cosmetic effects." *Ride On!!* also covered the progress of the Federal-Aid Highway Act of 1973, which authorized funds for cycling facilities. The first issue of *Ride On!!* proclaimed: "We whole-heartedly endorse the idea of bike lanes. . . ."

When DC planners proposed a scheme that WABA thought dangerous, council members were each sent a detailed analysis of the proposals. The parking and bike path provisions were passed, but the routes opposed by WABA were defeated. An article in *Ride On!!* cheered: "genuine progress on safer commuter biking in the District can come only when WABA and the Highway Department agree on plans." It was a bold claim, but the accompanying saber rattling—that "proposals opposed by WABA will fail"—did not pan out.

In 1974, WABA sued the District for "flagrantly and deliberately violating a federal order to build a pilot bikeway." This had been commissioned by the US Environmental Protection Agency, part of a national Clean Air Act plan that required metropolitan governments to build 180 miles of bikeways by the summer of 1976. The DC bikeway would have been the nation's flagship route, a safe cycling facility that would, it was hoped, influence other cities to cater similarly to cyclists. The planned bikeway would have extended through much of Washington, including past the White House and the Capitol building.

The president of WABA believed this bikeway would act as a catalyst: "the implementing of EPA's plan could do for the region's cyclists what Sputnik did for the space effort."

Under the EPA requirement, the bikeway was to be completed by May 1974, but the DC Highway Department dragged its heels. WABA's suit in defense of the bikeway plans was thrown out, as was a later appeal. In response, DC cyclists started to take direct action to improve streets that clearly weren't going to improve themselves. In 1974, Cary Shaw installed his own asphalt bike ramp. The DC Highway Department had refused his request to build a curb cut in a particular location, so he took matters into his own hands. When a container of asphalt appeared on his street for a road-mending task, he decided to "borrow" some. In broad daylight, he "grabbed a whole bunch of it." Dressed in overalls, he dragged the asphalt to where he felt a cycle-friendly lip was needed.

> I plopped it down and I made this big, fat, wide, smooth ramp up to the sidewalk. And I also got some yellow paint and I painted a big traffic stripe leading to the ramp. When it was finished, I turned around, and almost immediately, someone was wheeling her baby carriage up the ramp. The woman said, "I was watching you from the window. Thank you." And a couple of minutes after that, someone whizzed along on a bicycle, saw the thing, zipped up on the ramp, and away he went.

The ramp that Shaw built was later adopted by the city—and it's still there. Direct action worked. Sometimes.

WASHINGTON, DC, "was a very different city from the one we see today," Tedson Meyers told a people-first planning organization in 2012. Meyers served on the City Council in 1973 and helped to thwart the building of a freeway through downtown DC. "We had a highway director, Tom Arris, who was an awfully good man and very professional, but he'd never met a blade of grass he didn't want to pave," said Meyers. "He had the very bright idea of bringing I-66, which ends at the Theodore Roosevelt Bridge, into DC and . . . down the National

Mall as a covered trench: a four-lane highway parallel to Ohio Drive on the river side of the Mall with a grilled trench on top. Then it would dive under the Tidal Basin and the Potomac River, come up on the other side, and join I-295."

What would have been I-695 DC never got built, thanks to Meyers and moonlighting activists working for other organizations, including Katie Moran, Bill Wilkinson, and Noel Grove (Moran worked for the National Highway Traffic Safety Administration; Wilkinson was with the Department of Transportation, and Grove was author of the 1973 article in the *National Geographic*).

After being voted off the council in 1975, Meyers "called together the crew that was helping me before" and formed the Bicycle Federation of America (this later morphed into the still-extant National Center for Bicycling and Walking). "We needed an executive director, and [Moran, Wilkinson, and Grove] suggested Dan Burden, who'd just led the Bike Centennial ride from the Pacific to the Atlantic. We met at the Golden Temple Restaurant on Connecticut Avenue in DC, and there was born the Bicycle Federation of America." This organization intended to become an umbrella body for the many cycle advocacy groups that were born in the bike boom years to encourage the use of bicycles. Those bicycles that had been bought so far, that is—during the boom years, entering a bike shop was like going into a bank: you had to wait patiently in line.

"The nation faces a serious bicycle shortage," warned *Time* in 1971:

> Sales in many bicycle shops are racing 200% ahead of last year's level, and delivery dates for new merchandise are uncertain. Complains Gano Thomas of San Francisco's Nomad Cyclery: "The factories aren't making bicycles fast enough. If we order 100 bikes, we're lucky to get 25." Adds Henry Devilmorin, a Los Angeles two-wheeler dealer: "I can sell every bike I can get my hands on."

Today, almost every household owns at least one adult bicycle; many "non-cycling" households own several. This wasn't the case in the early 1970s, especially in America. Bikes were meant for kids, not adults; adults drove cars. This all changed when baby boomers started doing the buying. At the beginning of the 1970s, the post–World War II birth-rate spike resulted in a glut of teens and twenty-somethings—many had cash, were eager for novelty, wanted independent mobility, and were desperate to throw off the shackles of their elders.

In newspaper interviews at the height of the bike boom, industry leaders suggested all sorts of reasons for the doubling of market size, but the most obvious one—"the cry of the baby was heard across the land," as historian Landon Jones described the trend—eluded them. "No one could have predicted [the boom]," said the president of a chain-store bicycle supplier in 1971. "We're not clairvoyant."

It's true, bicycle-industry execs could not have known the expanded demographic would settle upon cycling, but the signs of the pig-in-a-python demographic bulge had been building for some time. *Life* magazine, in 1958, cover-headlined an issue: "Kids: Built-in Recession Cure" and, referring to the retail potential of the rising number of American newborns, added: "How 4,000,000 a Year Make Billions in Business." Presciently, the magazine said the four-year-olds on its cover represented a "backlog of business orders that will take two decades to fulfil."

More than 4 million babies were born every year from 1954 until 1964 (today's birthrate is still surprisingly high). By the 1970s, there were over 70 million baby boomers in the United States, accounting for almost 40 percent of the nation's population. Diapers had been the first product to spike; then postwar parents used their newfangled credit cards and charge accounts to buy family-size refrigerators, televisions, and, of course, automobiles.

Car registrations rose along with the birthrate: from 26 million in 1945 to 60 million by the end of the 1950s. Station wagons, the SUVs of their day, proliferated. "A suburban mother's role is to deliver children obstetrically once," wrote comic novelist Peter De Vries, "and by car forever after." The baby boomer generation was the first to be driven rather than to walk.

These consumerist kids, who came of age at the end of the 1960s, kept on buying, and despite the bulge predicted in the 1950s, the bike industry was caught off guard when the demographic alighted on their products. It was a perfect storm, with drop-out baby boomers attracted to cycling for its anti-motoring environmentalism; suburban-conformist baby boomers latched on to cycling because it was healthy and "outdoorsy"; and pre-motoring teens upgraded to lightweight ten-speed bikes after having been attracted to cycling because of "high-rise" bicycles such as the "cool" Schwinn Stingray of the 1960s. By 1971, 86 percent of Schwinn's sales were of full-size bikes, including the Varsity, a robust forty-pound drop-handlebar bike with a derailleur and ten gears.

"Environmentalists are turning to the bike as a pollution solution; physical-fitness fans like the bike as a heart preserver," wrote *Time* in 1971. "Groups of workers in some traffic-choked cities have been staging rush-hour races among car, bus, and bicycle, with the bike usually triumphant."

Industry consultant—and data-freak—Jay Townley was a Schwinn executive in the 1970s, and he remembered that the bike industry had been surprised by the sales spike. Domestic production couldn't keep up with demand, so the industry resorted to importing an increasing number of bicycles, many of which were subpar. With the boom in full swing there was no time to worry about *where* the demand was coming from, but following the inevitable crash—when the market halved within two years—Schwinn attempted to analyze where the sales had originally come from. A three-volume strategic plan from 1978, kept by Townley, spelt it out: "This dramatic increase in adult-style 26- and 27-inch wheel multi-speed bicycles is attributable in large part to youth riders in the thirteen- to seventeen-year-old segment of the population, graduating from the hi-rise bicycle to the sophisticated derailleur-equipped lightweight bicycle." Schwinn's analysis chimed with that of safety consultant Dr. Kenneth Cross who, writing for a motoring organization in 1978, concluded, rather blandly: "The so-called 'bike boom' that commenced in 1969 was due principally to a dramatic increase in the use of bicycles by the teenage and adult populations."

Thanks to the 45 million bicycles sold at the height of the boom, bicycle ownership was now higher than ever. What wasn't stated much by period news sources is that many of the bike purchases were due to contagion: people bought bikes because others were seen buying bikes. A great many of the bike boom ten-speeds gathered dust, either hidden in garages or, as sitcom star Jerry Seinfeld expressed the same concept two decades later, "I don't ride it. It's just for show."

IN THE early 1970s, some cyclists started using "Safety Spacers," a fiberglass arm with a red flag on the end. With such a device "the biker creates his own bikeway as he moves," claimed Harriet Green, director of the BIKE for a Better City of New York. With her architect husband Barry Fishman, Green had created the campaign group in 1970. It lobbied for lanes and did so via a Bike to Work Ride that attracted a thousand or so New Yorkers each time it was staged. The *New Yorker* attended at least two of these rolling demos, sending Hendrik Hertzberg in 1970 and, in the following year, columnist Calvin Trillin. Both had their own bikes: Hertzberg rode a "battered English racer"; Trillin owned an upmarket Moulton, also from England. Not all of the riders on these demonstrations were baby boomers. Hertzberg was struck by the "variety of the people on [the ride], and by the fact that the majority of the cyclists seemed to be over thirty." Some were even older, including David Dubinsky, the president emeritus of the International Ladies Garment Workers Union. "I've been riding for seventy years," the 78-year-old told Hertzberg. "Look, here's Abe," said Dubinsky, pointing to the equally antique A. H. Raskin, assistant editor of the *New York Times*. "I often ride with him on Sundays in the park."

John V. Lindsay, the mayor of New York, rode at the head of the pack, as did Jerome Kretchmer, the city's Environmental Protection Administrator, "who was resplendently dressed in a cream-colored suit and a chocolate-brown shirt and tie . . . [and who rode a] shiny wine-red Raleigh." (Not everybody was on standard bicycles; there was also a "Rasputin-like hippie . . . on a contraption that resembled a schematic model of the atom.") "A knot of pedestrians gaped at the extraordinary procession," wrote Hertzberg, "and Mr. Kretchmer yelled at them, 'Don't just stand there! Ride bicycles!'"

Officialdom's championing of cycling was parodied in *Richard's Bicycle Book*. "Hardly a Sunday goes by without some politician hopping on the ecological bandwagon and puffing his way through the opening of a special 'Bikeway,'" noted Ballantine. "A classic example was provided by John V. Lindsay, mayor of New York, who led a parade of cyclists for 14 blocks before returning to his limousine."

Other advocates weren't so cynical, believing that the Bike to Work Ride would result in change. "When my husband and I first thought of this," wrote Harriet Green,

> . . . we had in mind thirty or forty people making a quiet statement by riding together. Only lately did we realize we were going to get such a tremendous response. It makes me hopeful that we'll really be able to get some bike lanes. . . . I think people will realize that bikes really can make it a better city without tearing it down and building it up again.

Despite the numbers attracted by the ride, precious little was done in 1970 to change what Hertzberg's article had called "Car City." In September 1971, the

New Yorker sent Trillin on the same ride, and he admired that people, despite the lack of safe conditions, were "using bikes as serious transportation around the city." Riding down Manhattan's Fifth Avenue with hundreds of others, Trillin wrote that "most people who looked at us smiled." One young man "walked over to me while we were stopped at a red light and . . . informed me that bicycling was groovy."

Trillin mused on the "change in atmosphere that could come from having thousands of people use a means of transportation that made them cheerful instead of sullen." He reported that it was "very, very likely" that New York would soon install an "experimental bike lane."

NEW YORK'S rolling demonstrations radicalized some riders. One of those on the ride with the mayor of New York in 1970 was John Dowlin who, in 1972, cofounded the Philadelphia Bike Coalition, the Bicycle Parking Foundation, and an advocacy-focused news-clipping service called the Bicycle Network. One of the correspondents to this network was future US president George H. W. Bush. He wrote to Dowlin while serving as the American ambassador to China in the 1970s, when he and the later First Lady Barbara Bush became avid cyclists: "The more I think about our US domestic transportation problems from this vantage point of halfway around the world, the more I see an increased role for the bicycle in American life," mused the future US president. "Obviously, some terrains make it more difficult, obviously some climates make it more difficult, but I am convinced after riding bikes an enormous amount here in China, that it is a sensible, economical, clean form of transportation and makes enormous good sense."

The riding of bicycles, especially in cities, certainly *did* make good sense. Bicycles are one-person, single-track vehicles that take up little urban real estate compared with cars, which also tend to carry just one person. The space inefficiency of motor vehicles led former New York taxi driver Sam Schwartz to help spread the word *gridlock*, a word that gained common currency during an eleven-day 1980 transit strike that crippled the city. Schwartz is now known as "Gridlock" Sam, but he doesn't take full credit for the word, believing he heard it first used at New York's Department of Transportation sometime after he joined as a planner in 1971, during the Lindsay administration. Schwartz's first task was to stand on street corners, counting motor vehicles to gather data for a clean-air proposal known as the "Red Zone." Within this downtown zone—the idea of transportation engineer Brian Ketcham—private cars would be banned during the day. The impossible dream of Action Against Automobiles looked like it was going to come true: bikes, it seemed, would soon take over the city. But then Mayor Lindsay, who had initially championed the plan, got cold feet, and New York City's "transportation control plan" was spiked; the bikeways were canned at the same time.

In 1978, "Gridlock" Sam was appointed as New York City's assistant transportation commissioner by David Gurin, one of the founders of Action Against Automobiles. Ostensibly, he was in a position of power, but the transportation department's engineers still wanted to "pump as many cars into Manhattan as possible," said Schwartz in his 2015 book, *Street Smart*. The book's subtitle is *The Rise of Cities and the Fall of Cars*, but, as Schwartz explains, it was tough in the 1970s and 1980s to even attempt to design cities for anything else but cars—getting rid of on-street car-parking spaces was especially controversial. (In *Street Smart* he writes that he was jealous of the people-friendly changes made to New York by Janette Sadik-Khan after her appointment as transport commissioner in 2007.)

Car-centrism wasn't Schwartz's only problem—New York wasn't able to push through a radical transport plan because, throughout the 1970s and early 1980s, the city was in dire financial straits. All but bankrupt, the city was also plagued with crime, including murders and muggings. With the city administration occupied elsewhere, it's little surprise that provision of bikeways came low down the list of priorities, but in other cities—and nationally—bicycling was taken more seriously, mostly because the market growth had resulted in more people cycling. In 1973, the US Department of Transportation sponsored a major conference on cycling.

"IT IS incumbent upon us to get past the stage of talking about the revival of the bike as if we were trying to convince ourselves that it really is a viable mode of transportation," exhorted John E. Hirten, assistant secretary of transportation at the 1973 opening of Bicycles USA, a federally sponsored conference that he said would help cyclists find their "rightful place in the multi-modal mix." Journalist Robert Reinhold wrote that "[the message came] through loud and clear at [the conference] . . . that [cycling] was a possible solution to a whole galaxy of urban ills—congestion, pollution, fuel shortage, and flabby muscles, to name a few."

Bicycles USA was cosponsored by the Departments of Transportation and Interior and staged at the Transportation Systems Center in Cambridge, Massachusetts. Attracting 250 state highway planners, bicycle advocates, and government and police officials, as well as "several very happy bicycle manufacturers," the two-day conference had started with a group ride on a Boston riverside bikeway (which was later extended and named for cardiologist Dr. Paul Dudley White). According to Reinhold's newspaper report, "a growing number of cities are beginning to regard the bicycle . . . as an important factor in commuting patterns." And this new status for the bicycle "has found an echo in Washington where marked awareness of bicycles has developed within recent months at the Department of Transportation," claimed Marie Birnbaum, chair of the conference and head of the department's cycling (and pedestrian) division.

There was a clash of ideologies among the cyclists at the conference, with the bikeway advocates up against "vehicular cyclists." Martha Newlon, president of the Friends of Bikeology, was opposed to "just white lines along the road's edge, which do little more than lull both cyclists and motorists into a false sense of security." Writing for the *Chicago Tribune*, Rodale Press founder Robert Rodale noticed that "some of the more dedicated cyclists aren't happy about the thought of being segregated on special paths, though. They see nothing wrong with regular roads as conduits for bicycles . . . and think that motorists should be forced to reduce speed and otherwise accommodate the growing bicycle traffic."

"We must make the roads and streets safe for bikes," said Bill Wilkinson of the National Parks Service (the same Bill Wilkinson who later helped to create the Bicycle Institute of America). "We must move to infringe on motorists." Wilkinson's talk was on "bicycle trails, their construction and use," and he disagreed with those who advocated that cyclists should keep away from cars:

> I strongly disagree with those who suggest that biking be limited to exclusive bike trails and bike lanes. So much more can be done for so many more bikers through the development of procedures for creating safe bike routes along urban streets. I think that trails should

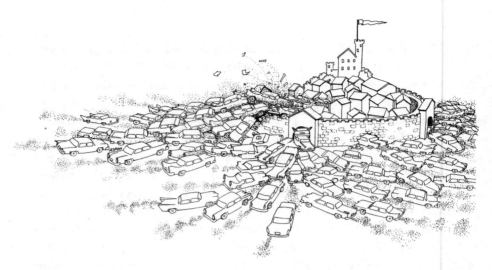

Europe's old cities can't take any more cars.
Cartoon by Richard Hedman, 1970.

be provided under two conditions only: (1) as the only alternative for safe bicycling in an area either parallel to a major highway or connecting two or more major points; or, (2) to provide a unique recreational facility.

Wrapping up the conference Hirten said, "I hope we can make the bicycle a reverse status symbol, the opposite of a big car."

David Rowlands, writing for Britain's influential *Design* magazine, had clearly not yet visited the Netherlands, but he was impressed that a conference on cycling had attracted such high-level support from the US Department of Transportation:

What emerged from Bicycles USA was a far more comprehensive response to an expanding population of cyclists than any other country at present offers [and] deserves much wider imitation.

In fact, the Department of Transportation was about to do its own imitating. Or, at least, it would send a transport engineer to Europe to find out whether the United States could learn any lessons from what was happening in cycling countries such as the Netherlands.

The DOT's Julie Anna Fee was dispatched to Europe in May 1974, and wrote a report on how pedestrians and cyclists were treated in some European countries. (When Fee married, she became Mrs. Cirillo and was later the first woman to become a regional administrator for the Federal Highway Administration.)

European Experience in Pedestrian and Bicycle Facilities reported that "Europeans [were] returning residential areas to residents and restricting the through movement of automobiles in these areas." Remarking on campaigns such as Stop de Kindermoord (see chapter 8), she said such restrictions in the Netherlands were the "result of the safety problem with young children and the need to reinforce community life in cities. . . . This concept of environmental planning is to impede the motor vehicle by changes in the highway environment."

She highlighted the fact that growing automobile use had forced some people from bicycles but that "most planners in [Europe] hope to effect a resurgence of bicycle transportation by the installation of separate bicycle facilities."

Amsterdam, she wrote,

> . . . is investigating ideas and techniques to encourage bicycling. . . . It is interesting to note that in the "city of bicycles" the method to be used to stimulate a rebirth of bicycling is to institute an extensive system of separated bike lanes. . . . There is generally not enough room on the street to provide a bicycle lane. Thus, in many cases, entire streets will be closed to motor vehicle traffic and designated for use by bicyclists and mopeds only.

She was also impressed with the English New Town of Stevenage, which offered "the ultimate in separation of modes. 23 miles of separate bicycle facilities exist and it is possible for many residents of Stevenage to travel from their home to work without ever coming into contact with a motor vehicle."

The redesign of Delft was a "stunning example of the Dutch commitment to environmental changes for . . . bicycle safety," she wrote. Interestingly, she added that the growth of cycling in the United States suggested the nation should accelerate its provision for cyclists: "Bicycle activity in Europe is far more extensive than in the United States. However, the trend of bicycle usage is decreasing, as opposed to the increase in the United States. Most of the countries visited have plans for extensive bicycle routes and have made provisions for separate bicycle paths." Fee concluded that Europe offered "interesting concepts" for providing for cyclists and that "their potential application to the United States would be an interesting undertaking."

A report from the US Environmental Protection Agency, also published in 1974, came to the same conclusion. *Bicycle Transportation* praised the facilities in Europe, and said: "America is experiencing an unprecedented boom in bicycle sales and uses. In 1972, bicycles outsold automobiles by 2 million. . . . The Government is beginning to recognize bicycles as a viable form of transportation."

The EPA report remarked that "40 percent of all urban work trips made by automobile are 4 miles or less. These short trips could easily be made by a bicycle at 13 mph in less than 20 minutes." What would get more people on bikes? asked the report. The answer seemed obvious: "38 percent of the bike owners said they would commute by bicycle if safe bikeways and secure parking were available. Of the non-bike-owners, 17 percent said they would buy a bike for commuting if there were bikeways and bike parking."

Significantly, the EPA also said, "there would be a greater number of auto commuters converting to bicycling if there were more stringent restrictions placed on the auto." Spending had to be increased on cycling because the "construction of bikeways and better law enforcement are public goods requiring governmental involvement."

> The commuter cyclist will advocate a route that is functional, while the recreational cyclist will support one that is isolated and scenic. There is, however, a unifying bond between both cyclists—a plea for protection from the automobile. The ideal plan would be bike routes, separated as much as possible from automobile traffic, which would serve the needs of both commuters and recreationists.

That year, 1974, was the peak for governmental interest in cycling because, as well as the EPA report and the European experience report, there was the publication of the first-ever Department of Transportation cycle-infra style-guide. *Bikeways: State of the Art 1974* was produced for DOT by an outside contractor and published in the summer. The 97-page report was "intended . . . as a first reference source for communities undertaking bikeway programs." A cartoon on the cover portrayed snarled traffic on a raised highway with separated cycleways snaking beneath, and a ten-speed bicycle was chiseled out of rock by a man in a suit.

The Department of Transportation's *Bikeways—State of the Art* design guide of 1974 featured a ten-speed bicycle being chiseled out of stone.

The report included information on "protected lanes which . . . provide a positive physical separation between bicycles and motor vehicles rather than a simple marking delineation," and praised the sort of rough-and-ready infrastructure provision now known as "tactical urbanism." For example: "In Sausalito, California, planter boxes have been deployed as the lane delineation buffer." *Bikeways* also consulted "European reference material," including Dutch studies, to work out the best surfaces to use on bikeways, the right widths, optimum capacity, and the best cornering angles. Although grade separations—such as underpasses beneath busy junctions—were already being constructed in the Netherlands, *Bikeways* was less ambitious, stating that, in America, "opportunities to employ them are limited by cost and the constraints of the existing development."

In the same period, there were no qualms about spending big bucks on facilities for motorists. One of the regions that spent the most on pandering

Anti-automobilism.
Cartoon by Richard Hedman, 1970.

to King Car was most definitely the County of Los Angeles. Nevertheless, the bike boom also touched the city that English novelist Aldous Huxley wrote was "nineteen suburbs in search of a metropolis." The county unveiled a *Plan of Bikeways* as part of the Los Angeles County General Plan. Nearly 150 bikeways were included in the plan. "In this era of energy shortages, air and noise pollution, and rising costs, the bicycle offers a quiet, economical, non-polluting alternative to the automobile," stated the plan. "But just as the automobile has needed support programs from its years of early development to its present stage of maturation, the bicycle needs them now."

The Bikeway Plan wanted to create a 1,501-mile "network of facilities, one that will be available to anyone who chooses to use it," and stressed "separation from vehicular traffic." "Intersections are a big problem," recognized the plan. "Operators of turning vehicles may not see the cyclist or may not choose to honor his right of way. This is a problem with all types of bicycle facilities including a separate bicycle path. . . . Even costly grade separations have not proven effective in some areas since bicyclists will circumvent them if not convenient."

Convenience was key: "Bikeways must be located where bicyclists want to go, readily accessible, and convenient for the user. . . . A bikeway should be located where it will afford the . . . greatest degree of protection. . . . [And] the bikeway system must be continuous . . . and provide access connections to bikeways in adjacent communities."

THE LOS ANGELES bikeway plan was ambitious, but it was too late. It was published in 1975, the year when the boom imploded. Bicycle sales in the US fell by a full half within months. Despite the obvious fillip to cycling in America from the 1973 OPEC oil crisis—when fuel was in short supply and getting around by car became expensive and, because of oil-saving speed restrictions, slower—cycling hadn't changed the world. The bikeway-friendly John Volpe left the Department of Transportation to become the US ambassador to Italy. State highway planners reined back what had been grandiose bikeway plans. Bike shop lines thinned out to nothing. Bicycle manufacturers canceled overseas orders. The bike boom—and the nation's interest in bicycles—was over. "The boom has turned into a bust," the chairman of the Bicycle Manufacturing Association of America admitted to the Senate Finance Committee in 1976. The assistant secretary of transportation who had opened the Bicycles USA conference in 1973 had seen this coming. John Hirten, an urban planner before being appointed to his DOT role, had warned that the Great American Bike Boom, groovy though it may be, could fizzle out: "The danger is that the bike may turn into the hoola hoop of the 1970s."

Former Schwinn executive Jay Townley believes that if the bike boom had continued—if annual sales of adult bikes had stayed at 15 million for perhaps another one or two years—some of the bikeway dreams of many cycle advocates could have come true: "If the bike boom had continued, the US might look very different today," he told me by e-mail. Perhaps, but it would have still been a long shot. Despite the high hopes of the time, there was little chance any meaningful cash was ever going to be directed cycling's way, for bikeways or otherwise: bills copying Oregon's 1971 Bicycle Bill failed nationwide. There may have been a modicum of political support at the highest levels, but one or two individuals would never have been able to turn around the tanker that is the US highways program. Federal, state, and city governments may have commissioned bikeway plans, and sponsored trips to the Netherlands for transport engineers, but it's doubtful that America in the 1970s could have ever gone fully Dutch.

At the height of the boom, a memo to members from the Bicycle Manufacturers' Association fretted: "Unless safer bike riding facilities are developed, adults could become disenchanted with the bicycle." The bike industry executives added, "We need local ordinances creating bikeways and bike paths . . . a bike lobby is needed at every level if we are to attain our objective of bike path legislation and funding." The BMA fudged, and did not fund a bikeways lobby.

"Most of the bikeway thinking to date has been directed towards finding ways to separate bicycles from the normal flow of vehicular traffic," Harold C. Munn, a California Department of Transportation engineer, told a 1974 meeting of the American Society of Civil Engineers. But, he added:

> There is simply no way to create separate bikeway systems to any significant extent in twentieth-century urban America. . . . Until very recently, reserving space on the road for bicycles was the last thing on anyone's mind. . . . Can traffic engineers and public officials . . . persuade the motoring public to accept some minimum provision for bicycle use of the public roads?

He answered his own question: "The possibilities at present are very limited." He concluded that "bicyclists will have no choice but to mix with motorized traffic . . . [and should] operate their bicycles as they do their automobiles."

Munn was the first to refer to what became known as "vehicular cycling," an ideological concept that is the polar opposite of the separated-bikeway system, and which is the controversial subject of the next chapter.

6 | The Rise and Fall of Vehicular Cycling

"I want to ride my bicycle / I want to ride it where I like."

—Freddie Mercury

IN THE EARLY 1970S, the imagined compulsory use of a bicycle route system in the cycle-friendly California university town that spawned the hippie movement led a high-speed cyclist to codify and popularize the concept that cyclists "fare best when they act and are treated as drivers of vehicles." The town was Palo Alto, the cyclist was John Forester, and the concept was "vehicular cycling."

Palo Alto is a suburb of San Francisco, home to Stanford University, the birthplace of the 1960s countercultural revolution that reverberated around the world after students, who were paid to take it, thought LSD should be available to all. Today the town is better known as the beating heart of Silicon Valley, famed for tech companies such as Xerox, Hewlett-Packard, and, latterly, Tesla Motors. It's also the home city of Apple's Steve Jobs, as well as the founders of Google, Sergey Brin and Larry Page. Mostly white, highly educated, decidedly middle-class and hyper–environmentally aware, many of Palo Alto's residents are cyclists, and the town is home to major cycling figures such as mountain-bike pioneer Tom Ritchey and also Jobst Brandt, author of *The Bicycle Wheel*. Nearly 10 percent of those living in the town today cycle to work, bested only by the bikeway-dense cities of Davis, California, and Boulder, Colorado.

Davis, 100 miles to the northeast, was scoped out for its cycling credentials

Palo Alto's traffic engineer Ted Noguchi had to face angry retailers in 1972—they were unhappy at losing parking spots.

in January 1972 by Palo Alto's traffic engineer and "active bicyclist" Ted Noguchi. Informed by what he had seen, he announced that "Palo Alto . . . will soon have 74 miles of bikeways on its 172 miles of streets." By May of that year—and three "uproarious" meetings with residents and retailers later—this had been reduced to 67 miles. When construction started in October, the plan had been chopped again to 42 miles. "It was obvious that the bike route system had become a major political issue," stated the May issue of *Bicycling* magazine. Palo Alto had had a 27-mile signed cycle route network since 1967, but as it followed "streets least used by auto traffic and therefore requiring no special lanes or other bicycle accommodations," Noguchi had recommended in 1970 that "the city dump its bike route system because it just wasn't being used." Instead, the city council charged Noguchi with creating what eventually became Palo Alto's "bicycle boulevard" system. The council was responding to demand: cycle use was growing, fueled by the bike boom. "The number of bicycles had increased by 500 percent in the past six years," reported *Bicycling*.

But Palo Alto was plagued with on-street parking, and the town's motorists were in no mood to lose these spaces, or to devote any travel lanes to bicyclists, boom or no boom. Instead, space was taken from pedestrians, with bicyclists allowed to share five-foot-wide sidewalks, many of which had been retrofitted with ramp-and-cut cement lips at junctions to enable use by cyclists hesitant to use the same roads that cars used. The suburban sidewalks featured signage that appeared to make it mandatory for the town's burgeoning number of cyclists to use these low-speed and truncated shared-use paths.

To the industrial engineer and resident John Forester, this smacked of authoritarianism and an attack on cyclists' right to the road. Born in England, Forester was a keen reader of G. H. Stancer, the obstreperous secretary of Britain's Cyclists' Touring Club, who had opposed mandatory use of poor-quality cycle facilities in the 1930s. Opposition to the supposedly mandatory aspect of Palo Alto's early bikeway system led Forester to deliberately ride on the road in front of a police officer, seeking to be fined for not riding on the shared-use path. This sanction catapulted Forester into the world of bicycle advocacy. A month after his one-man protest on Middlefield Road, he started his long, self-appointed career as savior of cyclists' road rights by penning a February 1973 article for a Californian bicycle magazine: "I was driving to work one morning and I saw along my route to work they had put up a whole lot of little signs . . . every several hundred feet along the road. They said bicycles must use the sidewalk . . . I wasn't going to ride on the sidewalk and risk myself. And I persuaded them to give me a ticket." In fact, the signs suggested that sidewalk-riding cyclists must not ride in both directions, and once the "must" was changed to "should" the mandatory aspect was no longer applicable.

Forester is the son of English writer C. S. Forester, author of *The African Queen* and the Horatio Hornblower novels, and without whom there might never have been a *Charlie and the Chocolate Factory*: Cecil Scott Forester encouraged British air ace and later intelligence officer Roald Dahl to become an author.

Forester Jr., an American citizen since 1951, is famously abrasive, inflexible, and supercilious. "He can't argue without being rude," Forester Sr. wrote of his then-nineteen-year-old son.

Noguchi, battered by motorists for doing anything at all for the bike boomers, now had a vociferous critic from the cycling side. Forester urged that the traffic engineer should remove the imposition that seemed to rule that cyclists should ride on sidewalks, and to uninstall bike lanes that, he said, went from nowhere to nowhere. Forester initially liked what became known as "bicycle boulevards." This was an adaptation that made certain roads into cyclist-friendly routes by restricting through-use by motorists via what later became known as "filtered permeability," allowing full use of a street by pedestrians and cyclists, but putting barriers in the way of motorists. Residents could access and park their cars on "bicycle boulevards," but they couldn't treat the streets as through roads. (Homestead, Florida, had "bike boulevards" in the 1960s.)

"Cyclists like boulevards," wrote Forester, because . . . "despite the traffic . . . they go to desired locations, are wide enough for all, are protected by stop signs against side street traffic, have traffic signals adjusted in their favor, and aren't impeded by the residential thicket of stop signs. . . . If you give cyclists streets with all the characteristics of a boulevard, they'll use it for sure." Despite these uncharacteristically warm words, by 1976 Forester had rejected the "bicycle boulevard" system—it found no favor in his *Effective Cycling* cycle-training course—but the concept nevertheless became popular with Palo Alto's cycle commuters. Noguchi, with the help of cycle advocate and council member Ellen Fletcher, converted more roads along the same lines. (Palo Alto's main bicycle boulevard on Bryant Street is now known as Ellen Fletcher Boulevard.)

THERE ARE two "D" words that make Forester flinch: "Davis" and "Dutch." Despite never having ridden on any, he's no fan of Dutch cycleways, and I should imagine he comes out in hives when the California city of Davis is mentioned in his presence. As was discussed in chapter 3, Davis was a test bed for different bikeway designs, and Forester doesn't like bikeways.

In 1972, six years after the installation of the first set of curb-protected lanes in Davis, academics from the University of California, Los Angeles, were sent to the city to work out which, if any, of the different bikeway designs that the Davis engineers had installed actually worked. Members of the university's bicycle advocacy group—the Bicycle Safety Committee—worked with the academics, and they also trialed out new ideas, all of which went into *Bikeway Planning Criteria and Guidelines* of 1972, a document later reissued by the Federal Highway Administration. There was much theorizing over what bikeways were for. In an earlier report, faculty members Dale Lott and Robert Sommer had pointed out

Cartoon poking fun at vehicular cyclists in *Regional Workshops on Bicycle Safety*, Department of Transportation, 1978. The cyclist with the helmet is almost certainly meant to be John Forester.

the ambiguity inherent in the idea of a painted bikeway "which many automobile drivers interpret to mean 'Bikes Stay Inside' rather than 'Car Stay Out.'"

The separated bikeways in Davis required slow and complex turning maneuvers for cyclists wishing to make left turns against traffic. Everyday cyclists in Davis wanted to take the shortest and most direct routes, even when turning. They disliked being forced to make two-stage turns. *Bikeway Planning Criteria and Guidelines* stressed the need for physical separation between motor vehicles and bicycles, and admitted that "more often than not, [Davis] cyclists make left turns on the basis of convenience rather than following the right-angle method." The UCLA report added that "it should be emphasized that the efficacy of the various at-grade intersection designs presented [here] depends to a large extent on cyclists staying in their defined rights-of-way." But cyclists were not railway engines—they did not stay on their tracks, they wandered, a fact that frustrated the separated-infrastructure designers of Davis. Lott and Sommer were quoted in the *Congressional Record* saying "just as one cannot have a railroad without tracks . . . one needs special facilities and regulations for bicycle traffic." (They also wrote, "No bike paths, no bicycles.")

Forester has long been a fierce critic of the "Davis system." When Forester complained that using bikeways was slow and inefficient (and dangerous, because of side roads that had to be crossed), Sommer retorted: "It is true that a bikeway system intended to provide safe riding for children will crimp the style of more experienced riders . . . [but] the old solutions based on a small number of experienced and competent individuals no longer are effective."

The 1972 *Bikeway Planning* document was informed by Dutch bikeway designs, and it favored separation of modes. "A physical barrier between the road and the track seems more desirable than a painted line separating the road from an extra lane designated for cyclists," said Gary Fisher, lead author of the report (but not connected with the mountain-bike pioneer of the same name). Independent of Fisher's report, the City of Davis released a bikeways study later in the same year. Importantly, this recommended that cyclists should be protected with curbing on any and all streets where motor vehicles traveled at 35 miles per hour or above.

At the height of the Great American Bike Boom in 1974, the Department of Transportation released *Bikeways: State of the Art*, which was much less effusive about separation of modes than the earlier documents. A follow-up report issued in 1976 was even more dismissive of protection for cyclists. *Safety and Location Criteria for Bike Facilities* made a "general recommendation against employment of physical barriers to separate and delineate on-street bike lanes." Instead, it found that "separation of bicycles and motor vehicles by striping is assessed to be feasible and effective."

What had happened in those two years? Why did the reports vary so widely on the desirability of physical separation? The main reason was cost. In 1976, few if any localities planned to invest in amenities for cycling. The heady atmosphere of the boom years, when such spending seemed to be on the cards but never arrived, was now but a memory. And when faced with bikeway complaints from a small but vocal crowd of vehicular cyclists, including Forester, most traffic engineers and planners were only too happy to agree.

THOSE AMERICAN high-speed proficient cyclists who feared that the provision of bikeways—even shoddy ones—would mean compulsion to use such lanes, slowing them down, were perhaps statistically correct to be worried. "The laws of 36 States . . . and the ordinances of 23 municipalities provide that, where a usable bicycle path has been provided . . . bicyclists must use that path," stated a 1975 study by the US Department of Transportation, but it added that motorists were not so restricted in their habit of parking in the way of cyclists because there were only "three State laws and three municipal ordinances [that] restrict the use of bicycle lanes or paths by vehicles."

The DOT's 1974 *Bikeways: State of the Art* study had said that most cyclists at the time were "so grateful for any kind of bikeway that they were reluctant to be critical of it," adding that this was "mostly a function of cyclists' past experiences in being excluded from many roads and in having to ride in such residual road space as gutters or narrow shoulders."

However, *Bikeways* also said: ". . . experienced touring or commuting cyclists . . . were much more critical of both the concept and the form of bikeways they were on . . . and were more often resentful at what they considered the cyclist's inferior status on the roadway. One frequent comment was that 'cyclists have rights too.'" *Bikeways* focused on Palo Alto, which

> . . . provided an ideal site for evaluating cyclists' perceptions of sidewalk bikeways. . . . Although cyclists there gave sidewalk bike-ways a good safety rating, they generally felt on-street lanes were safer. . . . Nearly 75 percent of the respondents felt sidewalk bikeways were more dangerous than the lane they were on. . . . Cyclists whose use of the bicycle was for transportation . . . always complained that a satisfactory travel speed could not be maintained on the sidewalks or that traveling on them was a "pain in the neck." They said their progress was slowed by overhanging tree branches, untrimmed bushes and vines on front lawns, pedestrians, and badly tilted and cracking sidewalks.

Clearly, *Bikeways* had been much influenced by Forester and his pals.

PATRIOT SUPER-SOLDIER Captain America first appeared in 1941. With pen and ink, he fought Adolf Hitler and other World War II villains but was demobbed thanks to the postwar fug of optimism. Following the escalation of

America's involvement in the Vietnam war, he was defrosted from an ice block by Marvel Comics in 1964. Dressed in a red-and-blue costume fashioned from an American flag, and armed with an indestructible shield that he throws at foes, Captain America was—and remains—an instantly recognizable character.

Eleven years later, a look-alike superhero riding a ten-speed bike arrived on the scene. Sprocket Man—suggested by Elton John's 1972 hit song "Rocket Man"—wore a red-and-blue costume emblazoned with a five-cog, rear-wheel sprocket cluster on his head-mask. Instead of a shield, he sported an oversize sprocket cluster on his right wrist, which he could detach and throw at bike thieves. "Big man, your bike-stealing days are over," Sprocket Man predicted as he knocked bolt-cutters from the hands of "Ace," a muscular ne'er-do-well.

Sprocket Man was the defender of the good cyclists of Stanford University (the bad ones were scofflaws), and was the joint creation of Stanford's Department of Public Safety and the Urban Bikeway Design Collaborative.

Drawn by Louis Saekow, who later dropped out of Stanford's medical school to become a full-time graphic artist, Sprocket Man appeared in his own 28-page comic book in 1975. "The ANARCHY which rules the cyclist can be afforded NO LONGER" announced Sprocket Man, who, if truth be told, was more of a safety nerd than a superhero. "Don't waste your time fiddling a horn or bell," admonished Saekow's creation. "Go for your brakes and . . . SCREAM!!! Move left BUT . . . Don't swing into traffic!!"

Sprocket Man also advised Palo Alto's cyclists not to ride on the sidewalk because doing so could be dangerous for cyclists (they could be wiped out— "BLONK!"—by drivers exiting side roads) and discourteous to pedestrians— "YEOWPS!" Saekow included himself, flat on his back after being upended by a sidewalk rider. The artist also drew a hapless rider spilling a handful of carried items, including a *Playboy* magazine, and there was also a median populated not with real grass but with marijuana.

Saekow based the nannying side of Sprocket Man on Vincent Darago, a Stanford University economics teacher who taught bicycling skills to students. While studying aerospace engineering at the Massachusetts Institute of Technology in 1970, Darago had been the institution's Earth Day coordinator, and he also chronicled MIT's 1972 electric car competition. The Urban Vehicle Design Competition was the template for Darago's later Urban Bikeway Design Competition, organized in 1973 and 1974 by the federally sponsored Urban Bikeway Design Collaborative, or UBDC.

A map of Palo Alto in the *Sprocket Man* comic book focused on the town's campus-centered bikeway network, but Sprocket Man—the character and the real man—also gave tips on assertive riding. Sprocket Man was a bikeways-promoting "vehicular cyclist." The 1975 comic admonished: "When bicycles are ridden as vehicles, they are subject to the state vehicle codes . . .

> Under those laws, your status as a bicyclist is: "EVERY PERSON
> RIDING A BICYCLE UPON A ROADWAY HAS ALL THE RIGHTS
> AND DUTIES APPLICABLE TO THE DRIVER OF A VEHICLE."

The *Sprocket Man* comic book also recommended vehicular-cycling guides including Forester's *Effective Cycling* and Fred de Long's *Guide to Bicycles and Bicycling*.

Palo Alto's vehicular cyclists would have likely welcomed Darago's attempts to educate the town's university students on how to mix safely with cars on the streets, but the next incarnation of Sprocket Man was not so welcome. In 1978, the Consumer Product Safety Commission acquired the rights to the character and republished the comic. On the cover, UBDC was changed to CPSC, and a jersey-wearing cyclist inside the comic suffered the same acronym switch, but otherwise the publications were almost identical. While the Stanford original had a small print run, the CPSC distributed 250,000 copies of this new version.

Vehicular cyclists were opposed to the CPSC's interests in cycling because they feared that the relatively new consumer-safety body wanted to regulate their bicycles out of existence. The CPSC's first regulation on bicycles had become effective in May 1976 and ruled that bicycles had to sport reflectors, including large ones fitted to the front and rear. Bizarrely, the CPSC's version of *Sprocket Man* did not retrofit all of the illustrated bicycles with reflectors (although a 1990s facsimile placed a helmet on the superhero, and on all of the publication's cyclists, even those shown doing pratfalls). "This booklet had been published prior to [1976] and, therefore, the bicycles depicted do not in all circumstances conform in detail to the specifications in the regulation," said a CPSC cop-out in the new version's introduction. The CPSC alienated proficient cyclists by stating that its regulatory reach "applies to nearly all bicycles that are toys or other articles for use by children (but may also be used by adults)."

Forester, who first mimeographed and sold his vehicular-cycling teaching course in 1974 (the first edition of *Effective Cycling* included a pattern for cycling shorts), was one of the fiercest critics of the CPSC's bicycle regulations, dismissing them as created by people who had little understanding of bicycles, or cycling. He promoted his paid-for course, and the cause of vehicular cycling, by deftly aligning the CPSC's supposed attack on adult cycling with a growing bicyclist backlash against subpar bikeways. "The sheer marketing genius of marrying the still-somnolent anti-bikeways movement to the raging supernova of the CPSC controversy cannot be denied," admitted the Forester-baiting Bruce Epperson in his book *Bicycles in American Highway Planning* (2010).

The CPSC's *Sprocket Man* comic book had minor differences from the original, but to cyclists fearing for their activity these differences were magnified and pulled to pieces. Where the original said "The ANARCHY which rules the cyclist can be afforded NO LONGER" the CPSC version was a fraction more personalized, "The ANARCHY of the cyclist can be afforded NO LONGER!" (The CPSC spoilsports also airbrushed out the *Playboy* magazine, and removed the marijuana joke, too.)

Darago's Urban Bikeway Design Collaborative later evolved into a for-profit consultancy, the Urban Scientific and Educational Corporation, and produced federally sponsored cycling reports that downplayed the usefulness of bikeways, but libertarian-leaning vehicular cyclists remained suspicious of any governmental involvement in "their" activity. They were especially suspicious of losing the "right" to ride their cycles on the public highway. In 1978, John Williams of Urban Scientific and Educational Research Corporation—an offshoot from the Urban Bikeway Design Collaborative—voiced this fear:

> State legislatures occasionally write into state laws concerning the duties of bicyclists the phrase "A bicyclist *shall* use a bike path when one is available parallel to his route of travel." This means the bicyclist is not legally entitled to ride on the road if separated paths are available, even if the path is undesirable or unsafe. This leads . . . proficient cyclists to take positions against the construction of bicycle paths. This creates an unfortunate and unnecessary division from novice cyclists, anxious parents, and motorists, who often favor path construction.

A provision to force cyclists to use bike paths had been in the uniform vehicle code since 1944, declaring that "wherever a usable path for bicycles has been provided adjacent to a roadway, bicycle riders shall use such a path and shall not use the roadway." Those states that adopted this statement into their codes rarely enforced it, because cycling since World War II had been largely the preserve of sidewalk-riding children. The 1970s bike boom changed that, and a clamor grew to amend the code in those states that had adopted it.

In 1973, the Department of Transportation published a report stating that the "legal status of the bicycle and the bicyclist in relation to motor vehicles and pedestrians needs to be defined more precisely in order to avoid confusion over rights-of-way and legal liabilities associated with traffic laws." The bike boom had encouraged many more adults to start cycling—and they rode on roads, not sidewalks—but there was no legal clarity regarding where bicycles should travel, or even whether they should be on the road at all.

"The whole impetus behind the existing bicycle regulations in the code is to avoid applying harsh criminal laws to children," argued the DOT. Prior to the 1970s, the vehicle code had excluded children's bicycles from the laws governing automobiles. But "substantial use of bicycles by adults, both as a transportation and recreation device, may have rendered [the vehicle code] inadequate."

A 1975 government statement seemed to confirm that cycling on the same roads as motorists was not "normal": "Persons riding two abreast shall not impede the normal and reasonable movement of traffic and, on a laned roadway, shall ride within a single lane." And even when cyclists were allowed to ride on "motorists' roads" they had to ride as far to the right as possible, a red flag to vehicular cyclists and known to some as the "far to the right" law, or FTR for short. Under a 1944 revision to the vehicle code, the majority of US states required people on bikes to "ride as near to the right side of the roadway as practicable, exercising due care when passing."

Vehicular cyclist Bob Shanteau claims this revision was the "biggest legal challenge to bicycles using roads that has ever happened in the US." In 1976, the Stanford Environmental Law Society came to a slightly less effusive but broadly similar conclusion: "This is the worst provision in the vehicle codes. It is confusing, subject to varying interpretations, and would appear to restrict cyclists to the right curb even in situations where it is both safer and more convenient to move left."

Law enforcement officers in different states, and even in different cities, interpreted this poorly worded law in differing ways, as did courts. In 1970, an appeal was heard in a case involving fourteen-year-old paperboy Joseph

Albrecht, who had been knocked from his bike by a motorist and "permanently and totally disabled by injuries he suffered in the collision." The trial jury decided that the paperboy should not have been riding anywhere but the far right of the road, implying some negligence on his part, and the appeal court agreed. To counter such miscarriages of justice, the state of Maryland later added the words "[as far to the right of the road] as practicable and safe," but most other states did not. An Ohio court decided in 1975 that bicycles "no longer have a right-of-way to the entire right lane of a highway as do other vehicles." For many jurisdictions, getting hit by a car was proof positive that a cyclist was not sufficiently "out of the way."

Such admonitions were evident in the safety literature and films of the 1970s. The National Child Safety Council issued a 1975 pamphlet that assumed all cyclists were children. *Good Cyclist Today . . . Good Motorist Tomorrow* also assumed that all child cyclists would soon grow up and graduate to driving motorcars. A 1978 film financed by General Motors promoted the same message. *I Like Bikes* featured a young female cyclist in Kansas who preferred driving. The film's animated self-hating Ike the Bike declared that "safety-wise, please realize, you never should trust me." Ike added, "I like bikes, but THEY'RE SO HARD TO SEE! . . . LITTLE THINGS UPSET 'EM! . . . WHY CAN'T THEY PAY ATTENTION?"

A very different approach was taken by *Only One Road*, a half-hour safety film released by the American Automobile Association in 1975. Admitting "there are a lot more bikes on the road today," the film imagined that "someday there may be separate facilities provided, but for now we're confronted with the reality about mixed traffic systems." It took a robustly vehicular-cycling approach to road safety, pointing out that the lighter ten-speed bicycle of the day was now "a realistic choice for serious transportation" and that cyclists, like motorists, "have a legitimate use for the road."

Historian and academic James Longhurst has claimed that *Only One Road* was a "remarkable record of changing attitudes [that] reflected signs of change across the country," recognizing that cyclists piloted vehicles, and belonged on the road.

To many advocates at the time (and some vehicular-cycling holdouts today), people on bikes were no longer "cyclists"—they were "bicycle drivers." The Pennsylvania Department of Education issued a safety guide in 1975 entitled *The Bicycle Driver's Guide*, and the Safety Council of Maryland issued a 1978 press release with the headline "Bike Drivers! Will New Law Be Hazardous to Your Health?"

Harold Munn, the CalTrans traffic engineer mentioned in the previous chapter, was the first to talk about "vehicular cycling" and he argued that those people attracted to cycling thanks to the boom should become more skilled, and they should ride assertively in the street rather than in the gutter. Vehicular cyclists—or, as they are sometimes known, usually disparagingly, "VCers"—believe in "claiming the lane." That is, the best way to be noticed by a motorist is to ride in the center of a lane, blocking it like a motor vehicle.

Forester believed motorists thought they had a divine right to the whole road, which he called the Motorists' Superiority Phobia. Those infused with this disorder didn't want cyclists on the road at all, but rather to be siphoned off onto sidewalks or bikeways. Said Forester: "These people wouldn't succeed if they said openly that they wanted cyclists cleared off the roads. They have got as far as they have only because they are able to use arguments that mislead the public into thinking they are pro-cyclist."

Non-proficient cyclists were afflicted with the opposite, believed Forester—the Cyclists' Inferiority Phobia. Bikeways were no solution because the majority of crashes happened at junctions, not on "straight-on" roads, he believed, arguing that he had "completely demolished the logical foundations for the bikeway propaganda. There is no argument for bikeways that has not been refuted. We have been able to do this because effective cycling is so right and cycling in the bikeway manner is so wrong."

THE EARLY-1970s optimism that the nation would soon be covered with bikeways had all but dissipated by the end of the decade, and what Forester and other VCers were now proposing was music to the ears of local governments. A Minnesota government report in 1977 claimed that "bicyclists may encounter greater danger on separate facilities than would be encountered riding on the roadways with the other traffic." Bikeways were now surplus to requirements because "the desirability of separate bicycle facilities on or alongside a roadway would clearly be questionable."

Bikeways were exclusionary, said Forester, and were "based on the idea that the best way to increase the number of cyclists is to attract the people who are too frightened to cycle on the road." Those cyclists in favor of separation from motor traffic "have emotional problems which they think bike lanes will solve." Bikeways were labeled as "ghettos" or "bicycle Bantustans," a pejorative reference to apartheid-era enclaves in South Africa. Motorists, said Forester, "look on cyclists as the niggers of the roads. You can't expect them to ask for psychological treatment for it, any more than you expected the old-time racist to do so."

Forester was a suburbanite, with no interest in getting more people on bikes. For him, cycling was a "minority activity and I didn't expect it to be any more than that because I knew the difficulty. It was real fun, but on the other hand . . . it had its costs, time and social opprobrium and such."

This elitism put Forester, and some of the other hardcore VCers, at loggerheads with those who wanted to see more "bums on saddles," such as the bicycle industry and most bicycle advocates. Former transportation planner and bicycle historian Bruce Epperson calls this parting of the ways "the Great Schism," and it's still very much alive, with bikeway proponents saying the only way to grow cycling is to provide separated cycleways, and some right-to-the-roaders being opposed to any and all supposedly sidelining cycle infrastructure. Moderates— who say that both sides have valid points—are branded as apostates.

VCers MAINTAIN that it's only by retaining the right to ride on the road that cycling will be able to survive and prosper. Being provided with separate infrastructure is a slippery slope, they say, with the actual goal of such provision being the eventual removal of cyclists from the roads they have enjoyed longer than have motorists. This fear was exemplified in the way legislators treated a bikeway act in the late 1970s. Congressman Glenn Anderson, a member of the House's Public Works and Transportation Committee (and a recreational cyclist), helped push through the Surface Transportation Assistance Act of 1978. The Bikeway Program part of this act authorized $20 million to be spent on urban bikeways (thanks to belt-tightening, only $4 million was ever paid out). When Anderson started arguing for it in Congress, he said bikeways would encourage more cycling which would lead to greater health, would save gas, and would reduce pollution. His fellow politicians remained unmoved. "When he said cyclists on the roads are in the way of motorists, he got a reaction," reported *Bicycling* magazine.

Most members of Congress were motorists, and their interest in cycling was clearly only ever going to be piqued when it was pointed out that bikeways got cyclists out of "their" way. Forester has long maintained this will always be the case. He wrote that those in favor of mandatory bikeway laws:

> . . . persuaded legislators and the public that merely cycling on the road was too dangerous to be allowed and must be restricted as much as possible. . . . They say that fast motor traffic kills cyclists by hitting them from behind, but instead of these accidents being the motorists' fault they are the cyclists' fault for merely being there. They say that riding a bicycle is dangerous . . . and therefore cyclists really shouldn't be on the roads because they can't be expected to ride safely. Therefore it is legally justifiable to prohibit cyclists from using as much of the road as possible, just to protect lives. . . . It was an argument to clear the roads for the convenience of motorists.

MANY STILL claim that Forester and the other VCers were highly influential, that they stopped the progression of the US bikeways movement, and even that they "have blood on their hands" because they gave governments the excuse they needed not to spend on cycling infrastructure. According to academic John Pucher, "the most far-reaching impact of Forester's philosophy was getting an effective ban on separated paths written into the *AASHTO Guide for the Development of Bicycling Facilities* [which] was changed to denounce . . . separated path treatments. . . ."

Forester agrees that he and other "cycling spokesmen" made "scientific challenges" to the bikeways movement that prevented the United States from adopting what he called "dangerous designs":

> When bicycle traffic increased in the 1960s, motorists worried that "their roads" would be plugged up by bicycles. The motor-minded California legislature attempted (1970–72) to bring in the Dutch-

style sidepath system to get cyclists off the roads. . . . However, at this time there were cycling spokesmen able to make scientific challenges to their designs, to demonstrate how dangerous these designs are and how much safer vehicular cycling is. . . . Cyclists managed to convince the government that it would be held liable for accidents caused by the . . . dangerous designs, which were then withdrawn.

As was shown in the previous chapter, the bikeways movement faded away not because it was crowded out by vehicular cyclists but because its leading proponents melted away with the ending of the boom. Forester—no shrinking violet—doesn't believe he had the impact others claim for him. In a Skype interview, I asked him whether he stopped the building of any bikeways. "Not really," he replied. But did he at least put a stick in their spokes? "Yes." He added:

People assert that vehicular cycling is why local government didn't install bike paths. That's not true. Every election cycle since then, there has been more money put into bikeways. They've been built, at a slow rate, but they've been built. You can't stop 'em. The public is so infused with the belief that as long as you stay out of the way of traffic from behind you're safe—they'll do anything, go to any dangers rather than having a car behind them. There's no practical way in which vehicular cyclists can overturn American policy and superstition regarding cycling. It's too powerful.

Despite the copious evidence that the separation of transport modes can and does improve safety for cyclists, and encourages more people to cycle, Forester remains adamant that providing bikeways is a retrograde step for the health of cycling. He remains dismissive of what the Dutch might be able to teach others. "I have read so much damn propaganda about bikeways of one kind or another, [but] it's no basis for knowledge," he told me. "The fact is, in America, fear obscures all real knowledge about bicycle and traffic engineering."

He has also written that "the Dutch produced a very dangerous bikeway system, compared to cycling on the road, but they . . . overcompensated for those dangers by installing protective measures that make it extremely inconvenient . . . compared to cycling on the road." As Pucher and many others have asked, "If the measures used to make Dutch bikeways safe are so inconvenient, why do so many people use them?" Forester has no answer for that, other than to assert that Dutch bikeways often take the long way around, and so they are, in fact, an inconvenience for cyclists and not, as most people see them, a boon. (In fact, convenience is now baked into Dutch cycle-infra design standards—for instance, Utrecht's transport plan sets out a *minimum* average speed target for cyclists, and also specifies that high-quality bike-parking facilities have to be "a maximum of 10 minutes from home.")

Even though he no longer cycles—"My cycling experience ended five years ago. I got too many aches and pains. But I do a lot of driving . . ."—Forester still believes bikeway provision to be an evil: "If you don't fight the government, you're going to lose your right to ride on the roads. You got to keep defending that right against the impulses of both the environmentalists—bike advocates— and, of course, motordom. . . . But it takes courage to oppose society when you know what you're doing is right."

Having to mix with motor traffic is a fact of life for those cyclists who don't live in the Netherlands, but vehicular cycling is no longer seen as a code worth fighting for—it's just something that most current cyclists have to put up with. "This is not to say the vehicular cycling concept is not without merit," suggested blogger Eben "BikeSnob" Weiss in 2012:

> If you're a cyclist in America, odds are you have already been cycling "vehicularly" your entire life, since that's what you're forced to do. . . .
> But like most cycling Americans I'm a freak . . . and would still ride a bike even if the government declared open season on cyclists and people shot at us from their windows like we were deer. . . . However, try telling a normal, sane American who's interested in using a bike for transportation that all they have to do is "take the lane" and "think like a driver." They'll just come to the conclusion that if they need to think like a driver that they might as well just be a driver. . . .
> If you want lots of people to be able to use their bikes, then you copy the places where lots of people use bikes, and if you want to see one or two neon-hued dorks lost in a sea of automobiles, then you copy most of America.

Forester—if modern cycle advocates know of him at all—is today criticized for his unyielding views, but just as a stopped clock is correct twice a day, so

Forester can be right at times. Get beyond the bombast and at least one thing that Forester has said in the past appears to hold water. "Those who oppose motoring magnify the disadvantages of motoring and minimize its utility," he wrote in 2006, adding that

> . . . they argue that production of bikeways will unleash a great unsatisfied demand to switch from private motor transportation to bicycle transportation. Nowhere in America or elsewhere in the world have bikeways produced this effect; wherever there is competition between private motor transportation and bicycle transportation, the car has been winning for many reasons.

The next chapter examines this concept, and reveals how the building of extensive cycleway systems in two non-Dutch towns did not lead to an explosion in cycle use.

7 | Where It's Easy to Bike and Drive, Brits and Americans Drive

"Explanations exist; they have existed for all time; there is always a well-known solution to every human problem—neat, plausible, and wrong."

—H. L. Mencken

THE PROVISION OF A DENSE NETWORK of car-free cycleways offers no guarantee that people will flock to them on bicycles. At least not in the United Kingdom and the United States. That is if the experience from "New Towns" can be extrapolated to other urban areas, which is not at all certain, of course. Columbia, a privately owned planned community in the state of Maryland, and the English "New Town" of Stevenage are examples of where providing for trips other than car trips might only work if people are discouraged from making those car trips by use of restrictions such as pay-per-mile usage fees or circuitous driving routes. Equality of transport-mode provision does not necessarily lead to equity in use—for instance, there are many factors that either encourage or discourage the use of bicycles, and we sometimes wrongly believe separation of modes leads to equality.

Neither Columbia in America nor Stevenage in England is perfect for those who choose to pedal. Both towns have allowed their bicycle networks to wither on the vine, and there are network truncations that now make it less pleasant to cycle there, but both were originally designed—Stevenage in the 1950s, Columbia in the 1960s—to offer journey choices. Residents in each town, given a choice of transport modes, chose motoring.

There are cultural reasons for this. Cycling as transport was becoming unfashionable at the time the towns were built. Similar cycle networks built in the Netherlands in the same period saw far greater use because cycling, for Dutch people, was a normal, everyday way of getting from A to B. It still is.

The designers of Columbia and Stevenage ignored the prevailing ideas, believing that with the proper provision use would be high, and that it was, in fact, the hostile road environment that stopped people cycling. They based their cycle networks on what they had seen in the Netherlands. Situated between Baltimore and Washington, Columbia was the early 1960s dream of James Rouse, an entrepreneurial, benevolent, and forward-thinking property developer. He wanted to create a city where communities would not be segregated by race or religion, but *would* be segregated from motor traffic. A 94-mile network of pathways was planned that would weave together ten "villages" and a town center. Those who didn't want to use cars could walk or cycle on the shared-use paths, and there would be a bus service on a dedicated roadway, too. The bus service, like some of the more extravagant municipal buildings, never made it off the drawing board, but the bike and pedestrian pathways were built. Today, they are little used—in Columbia, most people drive, even for short journeys.

Columbia provided infrastructure for motorists, but it wasn't originally in love with the car. Houses in the town were equipped with modest carports, but not the sort of huge garages that were the norm elsewhere in America. Ugly gas stations, drive-throughs, and billboards were either banned or tucked away out of sight. Unusually for the era, Rouse instructed his design team to tame the car, not pander to it.

Columbia's path network (designed for cycling as well as the then up-and-coming recreation of jogging) was diffuse and—at the time—convenient to use, with underpasses and overpasses, so there need be no contact with motorcars. In 1973, a Maryland newspaper noted that "far-sighted planners" in the "model city" of Columbia had "provided [many] miles of bike paths through and around the town."

The planning for Rouse's privately funded new town started in 1962, the year after the broadcast of a TV program titled "Merrily We Roll Along," an hour-long pæan to the motorcar. The show—fronted by Groucho Marx—introduced the now-familiar cliché of "America's love affair with the automobile."

General Motors became interested in Rouse's new town, and especially in the way it would be designed for all modes of transport, not cars alone. In 1964, General Motors' marketing manager, Rufus Choate Jr., told Rouse: "We are in the business of supplying personal transportation equipment, and we view your operations as the type of thing that may well set certain trends in human settlements. Naturally, from these new trends may come different personal transportation requirements from those which exist at the present time."

In reply, Rouse said Columbia's plans would lead to "an effective separation of people and automobiles with a careful laying out of arteries, feeder roads, and neighborhood roads in such manner that . . . people of all ages can ride bicycles . . . without traffic hazard." Rouse stressed that the separation of transport modes would be in the interests of the automobile industry: "If we can plan and produce a city in which the automobile and its consumer can live free of conflict, wouldn't this be an important step forward in promoting an environment that is constructive for the automobile manufacturer?"

Columbia was built with a baked-in cycle network—albeit one shared with pedestrians—but, from the start, the provision of such a network did not lead to high cycle usage. Today, with an ambitious bicycle blueprint, there are moves afoot to radically improve Columbia's cycle-friendliness. Howard County's Bicycle Master Plan, adopted in 2016, proposes to add bike lanes, cycleways, and road crossings. It will also use the 94-mile 1960s-era wiggly path network. Welcoming the Bronze "Bicycle Friendly Community" award it was given by the League of American Bicyclists, Howard County executive Allan H. Kittleman said in 2016 that "bicycles play an important role in our transportation vision."

As they did in the 1960s, too, of course. An uptick in cycling will likely require more than a smartphone-app listing Columbia's path network and the other measures the city proposes; it will also require biting the bullet: restricting car use.

James Rouse didn't propose that in the 1960s. Equality was key, but as George Orwell put it in *Animal Farm*, "All animals are equal but some animals are more equal than others."

On what was supposed to be a family holiday in Europe in 1963, Rouse visited a number of newly built communities including Stevenage in the UK (he also visited the bomb-damaged, clean-slate cities of Coventry and Rotterdam), and saw how the British government used "Development Corporations"—and taxpayers' cash—to create New Towns. He was impressed, and incorporated in Columbia some of the features he saw in these places.

THIRTY MILES north of London and the first of England's postwar New Towns, Stevenage was widely proclaimed in the 1960s as a shining example of how the provision of high-quality, joined-up cycle infrastructure would encourage many to cycle, not just keen cyclists.

As Rouse would have seen on his visit, Stevenage had wide, smooth cycleways adjacent to the main roads, but separated from cars and pedestrians. There were well-lit, airy underpasses beneath roundabouts. Schools, workplaces, and shops were all linked by protected cycleways. Rouse's tour would have been a well-trodden one: Stevenage attracted urban planning specialists from around the world, including high-level ones from the Netherlands.

Throughout the 1960s and into the 1970s, Stevenage was held up as proof that the UK *could* build a Dutch-style cycle network. An article in *New Scientist* magazine in 1973 claimed that "Stevenage cycleways and cycle underpasses [are] premiere exhibits . . . [in a] traffic revolution."

In the first edition of *Richard's Bicycle Book*, Richard Ballantine enthused that "Stevenage . . . is a transportation dreamworld, a kind of magical Walt Disney fantasy in which everything flows with perfect smoothness and problems evaporate." The 1992 edition of the book was still in awe: "You can cycle or walk anywhere you wish in Stevenage and never encounter a motor vehicle. . . . What is the worth of never, ever, having an obstruction or aggravation in traveling? What price a mother's peace of mind, knowing that her children can walk or cycle anywhere and never encounter a motor vehicle?"

According to Tim Jones, an academic expert on traffic-free trails, the cycle infrastructure of Stevenage was designed to "produce maximum attraction, comfort, and safety." Cyclists were

> . . . provided with their own segregated junction by elevating the road by two metres and lowering the cycleway one metre to obtain a compromise in achieving the three-metre difference in level. This design was crucial in recognising that cyclists could be deterred

Cyclists in Stevenage have
their own route network.

by difficult gradients and also allowed good forward visibility to improve perceptions of personal safety. Routes were lit with overspill light from road lighting. The ten approach possibilities into the town centre were colour-coded on a signpost system and facilities for the storage of cycles were considered at end destinations such as the town centre and railway station.

Stevenage was planned by Eric Claxton, a utility cyclist. Construction of the cycleway network was given the go-ahead in 1950, and it was built at the same time as the primary road network.

The 1958 annual municipal report said: "Segregation for those who wish to avail themselves of it begins about half a mile from the centre of the Industrial Area and at peak traffic times the separation of pedestrians and cyclists from the main stream of traffic is an advantage to all types of road users."

The cycleways were mostly flat, and there were cycle and pedestrian bridges

Cyclists in Stevenage don't have to interact with motor traffic.

and underpasses that would not have looked out of place in the Netherlands at the time, mainly because they were modeled on Dutch infrastructure. Stevenage was compact, and Claxton assumed the provision of twelve-foot-wide cycleways and seven-foot-wide footways—separated at a minimum by grass strips, and sometimes by barriers, too—would encourage residents to walk and cycle. He had witnessed high usage of cycle tracks in the Netherlands, and believed the same could be achieved in the UK.

Instead—to Claxton's puzzlement, and eventual horror—residents of Stevenage chose to drive, not cycle, even for journeys of two miles or less. Stevenage's 1949 master plan projected that 40 percent of the town's residents would cycle each day, and just 16 percent would drive. The opposite happened. By 1964, cycle use was down to 13 percent; by 1972, it had dropped to 7 percent.

Claxton was chief engineer of Stevenage for the ten years until 1972. He poured scorn on those who chose motorcars rather than bicycles, complaining that motorists "seem to have a problem with their logic" because "they use their cars as shopping baskets, or use them as overcoats." Claxton complained that he had provided "cycle tracks [modeled on the] pattern of those found [in] Holland" for the residents of Stevenage, but cycle use in Stevenage never reached Dutch levels of use.

According to a 1975 municipal leaflet on the cycleway system, the town's 69,000 residents owned 15,130 cars and 14,030 bicycles, but, clearly, the use of those cars was more usual than the use of those bicycles.

The leaflet wasn't for local consumption; it was produced for those visiting the town on study tours—Stevenage attracted a great many international study tours, which invariably took in the town's cycleway system.

The leaflet stressed that the cycleway system was well maintained with "sweeping and snow-clearing procedures" and that "surface maintenance is probably more important to the cyclist than to the motorist, and the speedy repair of any imperfection is necessary." The importance of cycle parking was also stressed: "Facilities for the storage of cycles are worthy of as much consideration as the cycleway system itself."

Demonstrating that Stevenage's fame as a bike town was known worldwide, a journalist for the *New York Times* wrote in 1972 that Stevenage's "bikeways were designed to run alongside roadways, ducking under or over intersections so there is no area of conflict whatever between bike and car." Undoubtedly so, but the journalist's conclusion was wide of the mark, for he added that the "layout of

Stevenage, proves that people will give up their cars if attractive cycling routes are established." The result, said the writer, incorrectly, is that "nearly one-half of all the traveling in Stevenage is done by bike."

MOST OF the infrastructure built by Claxton in the 1950s and 1960s—and which was a mature network by the 1970s—is still there. The town's cycle infrastructure is frozen at about the same quality as that of the Netherlands in the 1970s. Very little has been done to extend the network. New housing developments and new shopping centers have been built with easy access for cars, but only standard UK "crap" infrastructure for people on bikes, with seemingly obligatory "cyclists dismount" signs where none are needed. Some cycleways that were formerly continuous are now punctuated by crossings where cars have priority. Unlike the roads that they follow, the cycleways are not named, adding to the feeling this is a hidden network. Some signage is missing, and what's there is from the 1970s, proof that this is an ossified network. Despite lighting, underpasses are dark and, for some users, less than inviting (although similar infrastructure in the Netherlands is well used). The lack of cycle access to the pedestrianized town center is a modern aberration, not one engineered by Claxton. Stevenage's low-density living, with distances between houses and shops not always terribly convenient, is no longer what urban dwellers prefer.

Today's network may be faded and somewhat less useful than the one Claxton put in place, but there are still wide, segregated cycleways next to the primary roads; glass and debris is regularly swept up by council cleanup squads; some of the cycleways have been recently resurfaced; and in many places, cyclists and pedestrians are still separated by barriers, not just paint. Squint and—where the infrastructure is intact, under the roundabouts for instance—you could be in the Netherlands. Except there are very few people on bikes.

People on bikes in Stevenage have a hidden-in-plain-sight safe and separated cycleway system all to themselves. Pedestrians outnumber cyclists, and on the roads, solo motorists in cars far outnumber both. Stevenage's 2010 master plan complains that just 2.9 percent of the Stevenage population cycles to work, which, says the plan, is "much lower than might be expected given the level of infrastructure provision."

In Stevenage, cyclists don't have to "claim the lane"; the town is laced with cycleways.

The borough council's cycle strategy—not updated since 2002—conveys no doubt as to why cycle usage is so low:

> Stevenage has a fast, high-capacity road system, which makes it easy to make journeys by car. Residents have largely been insulated from the effects of traffic growth and congestion and generally there is little incentive for people to use modes other than the private car. . . . Stevenage, with its extensive cycleway network, has largely the same level of cycling as other Hertfordshire towns, where facilities for cyclists are less developed. This seems to suggest that the propensity to cycle depends on factors other than the existence of purpose-built facilities.

Claxton may only have been chief engineer for ten years, but Stevenage New Town was largely his creation. He had worked on the New Town plan from 1946 and, despite having superiors brought in above him, much to his chagrin, it was he who was in charge of where to place the sewers; he who decided where the new roads would go; he who decided whether or not there was to be a boating lake (there was, he built it at the insistence of his daughter, a primary-school teacher who wanted somewhere scenic to take her class); and it was he who insisted that cycleways should be a key and wholly interconnected part of the town's transport system. He had to fight for funding, but, sometimes by stealth, he managed to secure permissions for his 23 miles of cycleways and his 90 underpasses. Dr. Alex Moulton, designer of the eponymous bicycle—the 1960s ride choice of society elites—said the Stevenage cycleway system was a "wonderful creation," and its designer a "prophet."

Evelyn Denington, chair of Stevenage Development Corporation from 1965 until it was wound up in 1980, said in 1992: "One important feature of the town is its segregated cycleways which duplicate the main arteries and feed both the housing and the industrial areas. Mr. Claxton was a keen cyclist and was well aware of the need to cater for this enjoyable and excellent mode of travel."

CLAXTON WAS a practical, everyday cyclist, not a racing or touring cyclist. "I didn't do my cycleways for cyclists," Claxton told an environmental magazine in 1977. "I did them for people." He had no truck with cycling campaigners. In fact, when he was a junior engineer in the Ministry of Transport in the 1930s, he wrote to the Cyclists' Touring Club asking for feedback on the main road and bypass cycle tracks he had helped to plan. "Imagine my dismay," he recalled, "when I received a rather dusty answer from the general secretary. CTC wanted nothing to do with cycle tracks and demanded the freedom to use the carriageway—it seemed I had been added to their list of devils hell-bent on snatching away such freedom." (In the 1960s and 1970s, CTC welcomed Stevenage's cycleways, and the organization gave Claxton honorary life membership for "services to cycling.")

The cycle tracks he worked on in London were substandard, admitted Claxton. "As a cyclist they gave me no satisfaction," he said in his memoirs. The engineer was determined not to make the same mistakes when given the task of shaping Stevenage. Claxton's cycle tracks—now called cycleways to differentiate them

While the roads in Stevenage are well used,
the cycleways attract very few users.

from the failed London tracks—would be designed with scientific precision: "We were in an era about to give birth to a whole new technology," cheered Claxton.

"Organised cycling rejected the [1930s cycle tracks]," he wrote. "However, organised cycling changed its opinion when the Stevenage New Town system had reached a sufficiently advanced stage to be assessed."

He wrote this paper in 1975 for the Institution of Civil Engineers. Three years after his retirement from the Stevenage Development Corporation, he was now a roving ambassador for the town, and, most notably, the town's cycleways. His cycle-infrastructure consultancy business enabled him to tour the world extolling the virtues of Stevenage's dense cycleway grid. He gave talks in US new towns such as Reston, Virginia, and made a speaking tour of the United States and Canada at the invitation of the American Society of Civil Engineers, including a talk to planners at the US Department of Transportation in Washington, DC. Louis E. Keeper, director of the Bureau of Advanced Planning at Pennsylvania's Department of Transportation, wrote to Claxton after one of his talks praising him for "adding 'human' engineering to everything."

British local authorities asked Claxton to evaluate cycleways for their towns and cities—he helped Peterborough plan 38 miles of "cross-city cycleways," separated from motor traffic, and 34 miles of "cycle priority streets."

Ladybird's *The Story of the Bicycle* of 1975 lauded Stevenage for its "careful planning" and said that the "dangers of mixing with heavy traffic on main roads can be overcome with the use of 'cycle only' roads, called cycleways." A double-page spread in the book also mentions the plans Claxton drew up for the reallocation of roadspace in Nottingham (the Raleigh-commissioned plans were not taken forward by the City of Nottingham).

Claxton's first break in the consultancy business had come from the industry-funded PR body the British Cycling Bureau, introduced in chapter 4.

ORIGINALLY FROM the county of Surrey, Claxton made his home in Stevenage, and he was a regular user of the cycleways he had brought into being. He must have been sorely disappointed that he was one of the few residents to cycle on what was meant to be the British equivalent of a Dutch-style cycleway network. There are safe cycle routes from homes to schools, but only a tiny proportion of Stevenage's children cycle to school. Many are ferried by car, a situation that Claxton abhorred: "It is pathetic to see the way some parents bring their child to school by car and later park near to the school to give them a ride home."

Where did he go wrong? Why does Houten in the Netherlands, for instance, have such a high rate of cycle usage, and Stevenage have such low usage?

There are many differences between Houten and Stevenage, but there are also many similarities. Both expanded as satellite "overspill" towns for bigger cities nearby. Stevenage was planned as a residential relief valve for London, the first of many New Towns envisaged by the motor-centric postwar Abercrombie Plan; Houten was planned as a "Groeikern"—a center of growth—close to the city of Utrecht. Stevenage's heyday was in the mid-1970s; Houten was planned from 1966 but expanded fastest in the 1980s.

A planning document on Houten said:

> In 1968 Dutch architect Rob Derks offered [Houten] a plan heavily
> focused on filtered permeability: a dense network of direct routes

for cyclists and a course network of general roads, offering limited city center access to cars. The city council, which was then made up of civilians and farmers and no politicians, approved Derk's plan, which they believed would provide a more liveable quality to their city . . . 42 percent of trips shorter than 7.5 kilometres in Houten are made by bike.

Houten was designed in such a way that it was made more convenient to walk and cycle than to drive, and faster, too.

In Stevenage, cyclists were provided with safe, segregated cycleways alongside, and slightly below, the main roads, and also with cut-throughs unavailable to motor traffic. Cyclists, therefore, had fast, direct routes connecting every part of town, and also had shortcuts. The 1975 cycleways leaflet for visiting planners said that the "cycleway system . . . starts at the edge of the residential area, uses the primary road corridor to the town centre and the industrial area, and then extends for the full length and on both sides of the spine road serving the factories. Links are made with each estate, each school, and each factory, and in addition lateral connections are made between the main routes through parkland, woodland, and along old country lanes." The people of Stevenage had (and still have) a dense network of safe routes available to them, and people on bicycles, said the 1975 leaflet, had "an advantage in time over the motorist."

But, critically, unlike in Houten, motorists in Stevenage were not constrained in any way. In fact, the UK's first New Town was designed to be highly convenient for motorists: cyclists were removed from roads so cars didn't have to encounter slower vehicles; roundabouts kept swift, motorized traffic flowing freely, and traffic lights were kept to a minimum.

MUCH OF the superlative cycle infrastructure in the Netherlands was installed in the 1980s, by which time in England it was clear that the cycleways of Stevenage were being used less and less. The cycle-path networks in the Netherlands have been expanded and improved continuously; the cycleway network of Stevenage was left as is. It wasn't expanded or improved because residents of Stevenage didn't use the network in great enough numbers.

Stevenage's 2010 master plan says the town's "compactness . . . forms the basis for sustainable movement patterns," but even though a "large proportion of the town is within a 2-kilometre cycle ride . . . of the town centre, [the] preferred mode of transport to the town centre is the car." Stevenage's dense grid of separated cycleways is used by a surprisingly low number of residents. Brits, it seems, are in thrall to the car, even when perfectly safe and convenient alternatives to motoring are provided.

In a speech in the House of Lords in 1993, civil engineer Lord Amwell used Stevenage as an example of how it was "unrealistic" to spend money on cycling infrastructure if it wasn't going to get used. "Stevenage . . . has an internationally renowned system of cycleways which completely separate the cyclist and pedestrian from the car . . . [but the] cycleways are hardly used. . . . On the basis of cost-effectiveness, many cycle provisions will be non-starters. . . . I can never see the pedal cycle as a serious competitor for Ford or Rover."

And, apparently, many residents of Stevenage thought the same. The car culture of Stevenage is not unusual. In fact, it's mainstream. The British cultural affinity with motoring—even slow, inconvenient motoring—is all-pervasive. Perhaps Claxton was trying to force water uphill by promoting cycling to motor-mad Brits in the 1960s? Maybe a cycle-friendly New Town built in the future could achieve far more than Stevenage's current 2.9 percent cycle modal-share?

Stevenage's 1970s multimodal transport system was held up—by Claxton and many others—as an example of good practice, with walking, cycling, driving, and public transport all provided for, almost equally. Yet despite all the best efforts of a chief designer with empathy for would-be cyclists, "build it and they will come" failed for bicycles and worked for cars.

Academic and cycle campaigner Rachel Aldred blames car culture:

> Stevenage didn't generate a cycling revolution primarily for cultural and political reasons. The 1950s were a terrible time to be encouraging cycling in the UK. It simply wasn't part of mainstream transport policy and discourse. The bicycle signified poverty while the car was an object of desire, particularly in a New Town with wide, free-flowing dual carriageways. The outcome—not particularly high cycling levels—wasn't just a product of infrastructure, but of infrastructure in its cultural context. Car use being so easy in Stevenage did—and does—matter a lot.

No doubt many of the commuter journeys in Stevenage are now out-of-town ones for which people will always tend to drive, but this doesn't explain why cycle-to-school levels are so low. Some children do use the cycleways to get to school (Eric Claxton's great-grandson among them), but no more than the national average (i.e., numbingly low).

BUILT FOR Londoners evicted from slums, bombed out of their houses, and, in the case of soldiers, returning from war, Stevenage was a New Town "fit for heroes to live in." The houses for these heroes and former slum-dwellers were not provided with car garages; instead, Claxton and his colleagues provided, behind the front door of every house, bicycle storage units. These cycle-cupboards were soon converted to other uses because the compact, socially engineered town attracted aspirational residents who bought into the postwar dream of car ownership for all. As soon as these residents could, they voted with their steering wheels, showing they were happy to live in a town where driving was the norm. Stevenage's Dutch-style cycling infrastructure did not, as Claxton had assumed, entice residents to keep cycling. Walking was rejected, too. Where driving is easy, Brits drive.

Today, there's a (slight) movement away from car culture and, if Claxton's cycleways were built today, in a different place, there might be a different outcome. To get the different result in a different place there would need to be a Houten-style restraining of cars. In most localities, where unfettered car use is considered a fundamental human right—a right tampered with at a politician's peril—this will require a cultural U-turn of significant proportions. "Build it and they will come" may not always work for bicycles. This does not mean cycleways should not be built. The new protected bike paths in New York, Seville, Chicago, and Vancouver show that cycle use *can* be increased after the creation of separated infrastructure and a gridded network of other safe routes, but cycle provision works best when part of a greater whole, and that usually means restricting car use. When cycling is the fastest, easiest, and safest way to get around, cycle use can grow. (And will *have* to grow—otherwise the cities of the future will gridlock themselves to a standstill.)

It's important to note that Stevenage is not a typical British town, and what failed there might work somewhere else. Nevertheless, the failure of the cycle-ways of Stevenage (and a modal-share of 2.9 percent *is* a failure) is a warning that infrastructure might not always be enough. In 1992, Claxton warned: "What a dreadful example these drivers are setting for future generations. They become selfish and almost exclusively travel alone. They do not care about others."

But by not restraining motor vehicle use—and, instead, with concrete, encouraging it—Claxton is partly to blame for the bad behavior he describes. Claxton's colleague Roy B. Lenthall, speaking in 1986, understood the deeply held desire to drive:

> If you create a system with a high degree of safety you do generate a certain amount of usage, and [Claxton] felt that the amount of usage was dependent upon the competing attraction of the car, and the car is an extremely attractive form of transport. It's warm, it's comfortable, it's convenient, it's quick, and it's quite exciting to use.

Stevenage's worldwide fame as a town with embedded cycling infrastructure started at the end of the 1950s and went through until the late 1970s. This also happened to be a period when ownership and use of the motorcar was on the rise. In 1958, there were 4.5 million cars registered for use in Britain; by 1971, that had risen to 12.5 million.

In a few areas of the UK there are pockets of high rates of cycle use, places such as Cambridge and some London boroughs, and in these places there's a clear case for installing more and more Dutch-style infrastructure. On such roads, where bicycles already dominate, it would be perverse not to provide better, safer facilities. It's a chicken-and-egg thing, but providing cycle infrastructure in places where there's not already high cycle usage could lead to underuse of such facilities, as happened in Stevenage and Columbia.

Cities without high cycle usage, but which want to gain the benefits that such usage brings, would need to restrict usage of cars. This does not require Soviet-style *diktats*; changing travel habits can be done by stealth over a number of years. How so? By removing car-parking spaces, slowly at first; by reducing motor vehicle speeds by strict enforcement; by placing bollards on rat-runs; by charging for parking and road use, and many of the other well-known measures used in cities such as Copenhagen, Amsterdam, Singapore, and others. Sadly, such measures are known collectively, by media and politicians, as the "war on the motorist," and in our short-termist political cycles it's incredibly difficult to do anything that interferes with the sacrosanct Great Car Economy. (Car ownership in the Netherlands is actually higher than the UK, but "car restraint" is used liberally—a traffic expert from the Dutch Ministry of Infrastructure said that "shifting modes . . . towards more bicycling requires a policy that reduces the possibilities of car use. . . .)

IN DESIGNING for cycle use, Claxton and Rouse were each ahead of their time, but by also designing for unfettered car use their efforts were wasted. Few foresaw the problems that mass motorization would bring.

When, in the 1980s and 1990s, British activists again pushed for the separation of cyclists and motorists, cycleways could be dismissed by planners and politicians as failures. Stevenage wasn't the only New Town to have been provided with a cycleway system that the locals didn't use in great numbers—Thamesmead in London, built in the late 1960s, had also been given an "extensive" cycleway network, said a civic leader.

Speaking to *Design* magazine in 1974, Sir Reg Goodwin, in charge of the Greater London Council, praised Thamesmead's spanking-new cycleway network. "An extensive system has been installed there, quite separate from the highway network, and connecting housing areas with schools and shops," he crowed. "Together with my colleagues, I am currently carrying out an examination of the role that the bicycle can play in London."

Earlier, a GLC report had stated that it was only in new-build places such as Thamesmead that cycling would ever likely be accommodated:

> Cyclists in London's busy and congested traffic face great difficulty. The busiest roads are not safe for them or ever likely to be and the built-up areas do not give ready opportunities for special cycleways. . . . But only in rare circumstances, for example in comprehensively planned Thamesmead, is the provision of cycleways likely.

In the 1980s, the GLC's Cycling Design Team installed reasonable-for-the-time cycling infrastructure in the center of London, but it was recognized that cycle use had not been encouraged by cycleways in working-class slum replacements such as Thamesmead. Part of the problem was Thamesmead itself: despite the hopes of planners, the residents never really warmed to the deck-access tower blocks, the concrete pedestrian ramps, or the wide cycleways. (Cycle use is pitifully low in Thamesmead—according to the 2011 census, just 0.6 percent of residents cycle to work.)

Stevenage and Thamesmead—alien, windswept, largely unloved experiments in modernist living—might be seen as atypical for Britain, but then concrete-capped Houten isn't the prettiest of towns either, and despite having the same sort of underpasses as Stevenage, Columbia, and Thamesmead, it is often held up as a cycling paradise. (Columbia is also a new town—and it is regularly voted one of the best places to live in America.)

Cycle usage is low in cycleway-dense Stevenage, Thamesmead, and Columbia, but high in Houten. If engineering alone doesn't get people on bikes, what does? That's what I shall explore in the next and final chapter.

8 | How the Dutch Really Got Their Cycleways

> *"It must be considered that there is nothing more difficult to carry out . . . than to initiate a new order of things; for the reformer has enemies in all those who profit by the old order, and only lukewarm defenders in all those who would profit by the new order; this lukewarmness arising partly from the incredulity of mankind who does not truly believe in anything new until they actually have experience of it."*
>
> —Niccolò Machiavelli

BREXIT-BESOTTED BRITS MAY HAVE VOTED—by a wafer-thin margin—to take the United Kingdom out of the European Union, but you wouldn't know it from the bus shelters on Oxford Road in Manchester: in block orange letters, and with a windmill icon beneath, those waiting are advised to "Go Dutch!" This isn't guerilla stenciling from the city's beleaguered cycle advocates; it's an official message from Transport for Greater Manchester. A £1-billion makeover has made the road—one of the busiest bus routes in Europe—safe for cyclists. Cars are funneled onto parallel roads; cyclists have their own wide curbed lanes, and buses are now faster than ever. This is what the Dutch call "unraveling":

separating the vehicle types and protecting the squishy humans. Such makeovers are normal for the Netherlands, but very much not normal for the UK.

Bicycle advocates say that the provision of Dutch-style infrastructure will result in lots more people getting on bikes, and doing so for normal, everyday journeys in normal, everyday clothes. It's too early to tell whether this will happen on Oxford Road, but it ought to because many of Manchester's academic institutions line the road and, even before the infrastructure went in, the road teemed with students on two wheels.

The acid test will be whether the separated cycleways attract *new* people to cycling. This would be welcome—not least to Manchester's bike shops—but it's by no means certain. There are many reasons why Manchester lost the culture of everyday cycling it had in the 1920s, and many reasons why it'll be tough to recreate it. According to many of those who believe in build-and-they-will-come, the elevated level of cycling seen in the Netherlands is due to engineering alone. They point to the fact that small children cycle to school by themselves on the unraveled cycleways that vein the country. Indeed, for cycle advocates, the Netherlands is considered the pink of perfection, with Utrecht just one of the Dutch cities wheeled out as a Mecca for people on bikes.

And it's easy to see why the Netherlands is so beloved by bicycle advocates. Brides, grooms, and their guests cycle to wedding receptions; pilots and aircrews glide to Schiphol Airport on butter-smooth cycleways; patients and doctors arrive at hospitals by bike; pregnant women ride until they deliver; and you don't walk a Dutch dog—you take it for a ride with its lead tethered to your bicycle saddle. Old people ride, young people ride, everybody rides. Well, not quite everyone, but the cycling levels are high compared to almost everywhere else on the planet. According to the Dutch government, the Netherlands is the only European nation with more bicycles than people. Utrecht has a three-story cycle park that houses 12,500 bicycles. A hundred thousand people ride bikes in Utrecht, day in, day out—that's almost a third of those living there. A third.

American author Pete Jordan moved to the Netherlands to be part of a cycling culture that, because bicycling is so normal, doesn't even know that it's a cycling culture (similarly, the Netherlands doesn't have any spatula magazines or vacuum-cleaner festivals). When he's asked by Dutch people why he moved to Amsterdam, Jordan explains how he once counted "927 cyclists in just 20 minutes." This usually draws blank stares. "Is that a lot or something?" is a standard response. At a University of Amsterdam summer school for international urban-planning students—all mad-keen cyclists, myself included—Jordan cheered us with this story:

> I found myself riding behind a slow-moving pair of cyclists. Looking ahead, I saw a long line of dawdling cyclists in front of me. I was stuck. It was past midnight. What the hell were all these people doing out on their bikes? That's when it struck me: It's the middle of winter; it's past midnight—and I'm stuck in a bicycle traffic jam. From then on, whenever anyone asks why I immigrated to Holland, I reply: "So I can be stuck in a bicycle traffic jam at midnight."

Dutch schoolchildren take a cycling proficiency exam when they're ten years old, having spent a number of years learning how to cope with Dutch traffic, and this exam has been an important coming-of-age ritual for more than eighty years. Cycling infrastructure in the Netherlands isn't set in aspic, it's forever being improved. The latest innovation is the *snelfietsroute*—a freeway for cyclists. Four hundred miles of these have been built since 2015, with more in the pipeline. (Keep up to speed with their Twitter feed: @snelfietsroute.) These fast cycling routes connect cities—about ten miles apart—and grant cyclists greater priority at junctions than motorists. The level of cycling provision across the nation is nothing less than astonishing.

Little wonder, then, that study tours to the Netherlands are so popular with urban planners from around the world—they flock to see how they could make their home cities "Go Dutch."

"DUTCH CYCLING infrastructure is more than 41 years ahead of other countries," one popular Go Dutch bike blogger tells site visitors. Another writes that "the 1970s was the decade in which the Netherlands' enviable infrastructure grew from nothing. . . ."

The infrastructure is most certainly enviable, but it did not grow from nothing in about 1975 or so. The Netherlands has been expanding its cycleway network since the 1890s, and has been the world's leading bicycling nation since 1906. We're not forty or so years behind the Netherlands—we're 110 years behind.

There are compelling cultural, historical, and socioeconomic reasons why the Netherlands is a cycling nation. It is not just because the Netherlands is pancake flat (as are many places), or that parking a car is difficult (the same can be said of many cities outside of the Netherlands), or that Dutch streets are wide (many world cities also have wide streets, but no cycling). It's a mix of all these reasons and more, including, of course, the fact that the Netherlands has a wonderfully dense network of cycleways, quiet streets, and "bicycle streets" where motorists are "guests." How did that dense network grow? And can those reasons be duplicated outside of the Netherlands?

MUCH OF the Netherlands was literally constructed by hand, and the building and maintenance of infrastructure is well funded and prioritized. The Dutch equivalent of "sink-or-swim" is "pump-or-drown"—*pompen-of-verzuipen*—and inundation is a constant fear for a low-lying country, much of which was reclaimed from the North Sea. Dutch people have a saying: "God created the world, but the Dutch created the Netherlands." There's a shorter word for it: *maakbaarheid*, the need to be in control of one's surroundings. Salt water has been turned into grass-and-soil polders since at least the ninth century ("nether land" means "low land," and polders are areas of reclaimed land, protected by dykes). Such reclamation requires ingenuity, hard work, and constant vigilance. They also demand communal effort—the rich man's fields get flooded at the same time as the poor man's fields, and if they don't work together to pump the water out, they would both drown. In medieval times, even when different cities in the same area were at war, they still had to cooperate to pump away seeping water. This is believed to have taught the Dutch to set aside differences for a greater purpose. There's also a deeply held sense that infrastructure is important, that access to this infrastructure should be equitable, and that maintenance of this infrastructure is something for the whole community to sweat over. Dutch people are famously brusque—often to the point of rudeness—but this no-nonsense, straight-to-the-point attitude is thought to have been shaped by finding practical, no-fuss solutions that benefit the common good. Infrastructure is both valuable and valued. It is also constantly renewed, useful for when cycleways are needed or there's a desire to turn an ugly car-park into a beautiful plaza.

Britain's Department for Transport started life in 1919 as the Department of Ways and Communications; America's Department of Transportation was born in 1967. The Dutch equivalent is the Ministry of Infrastructure and the Environment—or Rijkswaterstaat—and it was founded in 1798. The Chinese famously take the long view of history, and Dutch nation-builders take the long view of infrastructure.

Because of the folk knowledge that constant vigilance is needed against flooding, the average Dutch person's attachment to order can reach extreme proportions. When, in the past, poor maintenance of a dyke would result in catastrophic flooding, citizens had every incentive to keep things tidy and well ordered. As an English author observed in 1851: "One of the principal characteristics of a Dutch street is its scrupulous, or it would be more correct to say, elaborate, cleanliness." This obsessive cleanliness is a cliché, perhaps, but it's a national trait to want to keep life under strict control. Planning is almost a religion, and everything has to be in the right place. Mixing fast cars and slow bicycles militates against this natural order of things. An editorial in *Kampioen* motoring and cycling magazine said in 1935, "We Hollanders . . . have the finest cycle paths in the world and consider the separation of the various road users as one of the best solutions of the general traffic problem."

ON THE night of January 31, 1953, a freak combination of high spring tides, strong winds, and a fierce storm led to flooding that killed 2,000 people and washed away much of the Dutch coastline. The national response was to start building the Delta Works. This huge and costly series of floodgates, dams, dykes, and levees has been declared one of the Seven Wonders of the Modern World by the American Society of Civil Engineers. Similar projects from earlier in the nation's history helped shape the Dutch political system, with the need to coordinate the construction and maintenance of flood defenses creating the so-called polder model of consensus-based economic and social policy making. In the Netherlands, coalition governments have long been the norm: everybody gets their say. Much power is devolved locally, and those in previous decades seeking better conditions for cyclists would lobby local council members, not the national government. "We rarely talked to the minister of transport," one 1970s

Dutch cycle campaigner told me; "we talked to the municipality."

Two-thirds of the Netherlands' 16 million people live below sea level, and they are packed in tight. In the Randstad—the joined-at-the-hip cities of Rotterdam, Amsterdam, Utrecht, and Den Haag (the Hague)—4,000 people live on every square mile. If the United States were this densely populated, it would contain four billion people.

"The short distances between housing and facilities (such as offices, shops, schools, nightlife locations, stations, sports centres, etc.) in Amsterdam add to the attraction of cycling as a form of transport," says Amsterdam's tourist board. "Cycling is a fundamental part of Dutch culture," it adds.

Part of the Dutch psyche is said, by some, to be derived from religion. Roughly speaking, the northern half of the Netherlands (where most people live) is Calvinist, a strict and famously thrifty form of 500-year-old Protestantism, and the southern half is Roman Catholic. (Belief in God is not the point here; it's the cultural baggage that counts.) Cycling, goes one theory, appeals to Calvinists because it's simple, sober, and, above all, cheap. And as Calvinists—and many Dutch people—do not like ostentation or the flaunting of wealth, cycling is the perfect fit, especially on heavy, black, and anonymous Dutch bikes. Riding such a bicycle is egalitarian, not status enhancing.

Even though plenty of Dutch people do self-identify with these supposed "national characteristics," and Calvinists really do cycle more than Catholics, such explanations have to be taken with a pinch of salt. An eminent Dutch historian believes the "prudent nation" trope to be more of a foundation myth than factual. And, according to the author of *Why the Dutch Are Different*, the Netherlands has never actually been a country "where office workers smoked weed over their desks, visited prostitutes at lunchtime, and euthanised their grandparents in the evening."

WHAT'S NOT in doubt is the fact that the Netherlands has been building separated cycleways for longer than any other nation. Even the "unraveling" of modes is not modern. As early as 1595, one-way traffic for carts had been mandated in some of Amsterdam's alleys, and in 1880 *Harper's New Monthly* described a "little town in Holland in the streets of which no horse is ever allowed to come. Its cleanliness may be imagined, and its quiet repose." The first cycleway in the Netherlands was converted from a sidewalk in 1885 on the Maliebaan, a long, straight road in Utrecht. This gravel cycle path was created for high-wheel riders by 44 members of the Algemene Nederlandse Wielrijders Bond (Royal Dutch Touring Club), ANWB for short and founded two years previously. Originally a members-only racing track, it was opened for all cyclists in 1887 and was later extended to become a regular cycle path; it's still used for this purpose today.

The separation of transport modes—alien everywhere else—quickly became standard in the Netherlands. In 1898, the *Spectator* reported: "On the route from the Hague to Scheveningen there lie parallel to each other a carriage road, a canal, a bicycle track, a light railway, side-paths regularly constructed. . . ."

In the same year, the ANWB created a *Wegencommissie*, or national Roads Commission, which pressured state authorities to build and improve roads. Later this cycling club hired its own road engineer to advise on technical and legal matters regarding the construction, design, and maintenance of bicycle paths. A. E. Redelé also supplied building materials for creating these paths.

Sociologist Peter Cox has said the cycling infrastructure provided for cyclists at this time "played an important role in overcoming the unsuitability of the existing roads because as a policy it was a part of a clear intention to use the cycle roads system to raise the status of cycle users as citizens, indeed to prioritise them." Those on bicycles at this time were the elites, including those with double names indicating Dutch nobility, and there were not all that many of them. While America and Britain were experiencing the "cycling mania" of 1896–97, sales of bicycles in the Netherlands were comparatively low—there were just 94,370 bicycles being ridden in 1899, a ratio of one bicycle per 53 inhabitants. Six years later, the bicycle total had risen to 324,000, the highest ownership in the world, and by 1911 the number of bicycles owned in the Netherlands had doubled to 600,000, an ownership ratio of one in ten.

Cycle historian Kaspar Hanenbergh has said: "ANWB used their power to lobby for separate roads. Very reluctantly, local government took up this role, but in the early years private initiative was far more effective. The ANWB supported local Rijwielpadverenigingen, or bicycle path societies."

The first was formed in March 1914 in the Gooi and Eemland region, and others followed, including Drenthe in 1916 and Eindhoven in 1917. These cycle paths were rural, recreational, and largely middle-class. Following the end of the First World War, an economic slump in defeated Germany led to a flood of cheap German-made bikes into the Netherlands, encouraging wider social use of the bicycle, which had already become a national icon. (It also helped that in the same period trolley-ride prices tripled.) The excellence of Dutch bike paths was featured in a 1920 report in the German bicycle trade magazine *Radmarkt*:

> We have to thank the efforts of the [ANWB] for the extensive network of good bicycle roads that exist along the main highways of the country. There are equally good bicycle roads leaving the highway into all remote places. . . . In each street there is at least one, but generally at each side, a specially designed "clinker" pavement. . . . [In] Holland accidents fell to a minimum through the exemplary construction of these paths.

In 1921, the *Times* of London noted "the enormous number of bicycles" in the Netherlands and how it had "ideal road conditions" and an extensive bicycle path network that "testifies to the important place which cycling occupies in the life of the people of the Netherlands."

According to a Dutch newspaper in 1922, pedestrians found intersections in Amsterdam dangerous not because of cars but because of the sheer number of people on bikes. "That endless, unbroken row of three, four cyclists riding beside each other along the whole length of Weteringschans makes crossing the street deadly!" On main roads, cyclists accounted for 74 percent of the traffic, compared to just 11 percent for automobiles.

In the summer of 1924, cyclists were slapped with a "bicycle tax." Initially it paid for flood defenses and schools, but it was soon channeled to cycle-path construction and thereafter also paid for roads for motorists. According to academic Anne-Katrin Ebert, "the bicycle tax put cyclists on the political map and helped create a tradition of traffic engineering devoted to cycling paths and regulation. This would form an important basis for the 'survival' of the Netherlands as a cycling nation."

"Everyone in Holland cycles," opined a US newspaper in 1924, "and everyone can cycle everywhere" because "there is a wonderful system of roads and pathways for the cyclist. . . ."

In 1926, cyclists were paying more into the *Wegenfonds*, or Road Fund, than motorists. The following year, the government announced the *Rijkswegenplan*, a national road-building plan mostly for motorists, but paid for mostly by cyclists, although when many of the town-to-countryside arterial roads were constructed in the 1930s they were provided with separated cycleways, too. Urban cycleways were built on a few major Amsterdam streets in the same period, although cyclists complained that they were often blocked by pushcarts.

The ANWB fought for the removal of the bicycle tax, or at least reduced rates for working-class cyclists, but it's inescapable that by paying this tax cyclists became important actors on the national scene, and this influence continued even after the tax was later abolished.

Then as now, the Amsterdam cyclist did not have a very good reputation with other road users. In 1928, an American journalist wrote "traffic in Holland . . . is as completely dominated by [the bicycle] as in America it is dominated by the automobile, [but the] Dutch cyclist is even more indifferent to the rights of others than is the American taxi driver."

Because of their sheer numbers, Dutch cyclists ruled on the roads and didn't pull to one side for motorists, as was expected to happen in Germany. A German visitor to the Netherlands was amazed how Dutch cyclists had defended "with great doggedness" their right to the roadway. "In Germany, this right has long since been lost," he noted. "In Holland, this right has remained as a consequence of a true democracy."

In 1933, Karel Čapek (the Czech writer who introduced the word *robot* to the world) was impressed not only by the numbers of Dutch cyclists but also how they moved:

> I have seen various things in my time, but never have I seen so many bicycles as, for instance, in Amsterdam; they are no mere bicycles, but a sort of collective entity; shoals, droves, colonies of bicycles, which rather suggest teeming of bacteria or the swarming of infusoria or the eddying of flies. The best part of it is when a policeman holds up the stream of bicycles to let pedestrians get across the street, and then magnanimously leaves the road open once more; a regular swarm of cyclists dashes forward, headed by a number of speed champions, and away they pedal, with the queer unanimity of dancing gnats.

An American travel journalist writing in 1934 wondered: "if there really is anything in all this talk about evolution another century will see the Dutch children coming into this world on tiny bicycles." He added that in the Netherlands the bicycle had become "almost a part of the body."

A year later a Dutch newspaper proudly described the nation's "dense network of cycle paths":

> No other country has started earlier with such an elaborate and systematic construction of special roadways for cycle traffic. What we have achieved . . . commands admiration from compatriot and foreigner alike. . . . With regard to cycling traffic, our country has taken a position like no other. The traffic counts for 1932 have shown that of all traffic on national highways fifty percent is that of cyclists. In such a situation it can be considered important, not only for cyclists, but also for other road users, that cyclists have their own roadways, the cycle paths, as much as possible.

By 1938, the Netherlands had a 1,170-mile main-road network, 866 miles of which had adjoining cycleways. (By contrast, in the same year England had 200 miles of cycle tracks.) And while Dutch cycleways were found beside 74 percent of main roads, there were also 1,500 miles of off-carriageway cycleways.

No doubt these cycleways were used—fruitlessly—by the 5,600 troops of the two cyclists' regiments of the Dutch army trying to defend the Netherlands from German tanks and infantry divisions during the invasion that started on May 10, 1940. "Cyclists have a dangerous job," wrote one of these soldiers to his wife. "They seek danger and they find it." The following day he was shot from the air and killed.

During the German occupation of the Netherlands the private use of automobiles was stamped out, and even more people than usual took to riding bicycles. "For 32 years, I had not sat on a bike," one businessman told a local newspaper. "But now, with the car in the stable, I have tried it once again. And now, every evening, I pedal home on my new little bike and then again, after dinner, for another hour or so. I had almost forgotten a bike could provide so much pleasure."

Dutch cyclists were used to ruling the roads, and they continued to ride in front of motor vehicles even though those motor vehicles now contained Nazi soldiers. This came to a head in the year after the invasion, with cyclists ordered to keep their hands on their handlebars at all times, not to ride two-abreast, and

The "Bear Pit" junction in Utrecht, the first "protected" junction
to be built in the Netherlands, 1944. (Rijkswaterstaat)

to cede priority to motorists at junctions. Cyclists also had to ride in the gutter
and "snake" around any parked cars they encountered, a concept similar to the
"far to the right" rule introduced in America a few years later. "The occasional
disorderly conduct of cyclists will be curbed with the help of the new regulations,"
opined an Amsterdam newspaper. "More discipline will be expected of them."

This rankled, but what really hurt was when Germans started commandeering
bicycles for their own use. This "struck the rawest of Dutch nerves," recounts Pete
Jordan. Hostage taking and executions were accepted, but the confiscation of
bicycles was just not on. A German report marveled that "if the bicycle seizure
gave cause within the population for lively discussions and for embittered
criticism, then the shooting of five hostages was accepted with an almost eerie
silence." The theft of Dutch bicycles by German soldiers was not forgotten: from
the 1950s onwards, a common reply to German visitors from Dutch people was
"*Eerst mijn fiets terug*"—"First, return my bike."

The war didn't prevent the building of a certain large piece of infrastructure.
A giant two-level roundabout was constructed in Utrecht from 1941 to 1944—
it kept cyclists and motorists apart. The "*Berekuil*"—or "Bear Pit"—had been

designed in 1936, and is still in use today, although it has been modified over the years. This is the sort of infrastructure that, in the same period, the British government said would be too difficult and too expensive to build for cyclists in England. (However, a grade-separated roundabout to aid motorists, and supposedly protect pedestrians, was built in 1939 on the A22 Caterham bypass— the Wapses Lodge roundabout was way ahead of its time, and quite the eyesore today, so it must have looked incredibly alien in 1939. Pedestrians rarely use the underpasses. At the beginnings of the 1960s, a number of similar grade-separated roundabouts for pedestrians and cyclists were built in Stevenage— they were modeled on the Berekuil.)

FOLLOWING THE war, America helped rebuild shattered economies with the $12-billion European Recovery Program. Best known as the Marshall Plan of 1948, this pumped what would be $120 billion at today's value into European countries. The lion's share went to West Germany, but the Netherlands also received a slice. From 1950, the Dutch economy grew by 5 percent a year; living standards shot up. In 1950, there were fourteen cars per 1,000 inhabitants in the Netherlands—by 1960, this had increased to 45 per 1,000. Between 1960 and 1970, car ownership climbed to 189 cars per 1,000, and within ten years almost doubled again to 319 per 1,000. And just as there was a postwar baby boom in the United States, there was one in the Netherlands, too. By 1970, the Dutch population had reached 13 million; it had been just under 9 million in 1940.

Just as Marshall Aid helped Dutch people buy cars, it also helped them replace the bicycles they said had been stolen by the Germans. By the mid-1950s, Amsterdam's 900,000 residents owned an estimated 600,000 bikes, double the number of bikes owned just before the war. In 1958, the rate of car ownership in the Netherlands was still far below that of other European countries. In Paris, for example, there was one car for every 7.5 people. In London, it was one for every 11.5 people. But the story was different in Amsterdam, where there was just one car for every 23 inhabitants.

However, the decade between 1960 and 1970 saw the number of automobiles in Amsterdam quadruple. The use of bicycles fell off the proverbial cliff. But the cliff was high—a 60 percent modal-share cliff—and when, thanks to policies and planning, cycling's fall was arrested it landed at half its previous level. This was a huge and shocking decline, but as can be seen from the cycling usage graph in the plates section, a modal-share of 35 percent in 1973 kept enough cyclists on the streets so that cycling didn't disappear, and from this stabilized level it could, with encouragement, slowly grow again. Cities that saw more calamitous drops would find it much harder to recover. For instance, Manchester's cycle use fell from 35 percent to a gob-smacking 1 percent between 1949 and 1973 (the drop was due, in part, to public-transit improvements, the growth of automobility, and sprawl).

Despite the often awful conditions for cyclists on Amsterdam's crowded streets, cyclists were still very much visible. "You'll think the Lord has unloosed a plague of cycles upon Holland for some national sin," cautioned an American guidebook in 1950. "The visitor must . . . be careful of the countless cyclists whose agility and speed are stupefying," warned a 1964 guidebook to Amsterdam.

Perhaps these American writers might have much preferred the Netherlands to be like their homeland: full of cars and with fewer cyclists? If so, that would have chimed with the national government. "From 1950 to 1975, the bicycle was almost entirely excluded from the government's vision," chided the government's Dutch Bicycle Master Plan of 1999.

Car use might have been on the rise in the Netherlands, and cycling neglected, but cycling was so socially accepted, so "normal," and still had so many thousands of miles of cycle paths, that it didn't suffer the same fate as cycling in most other countries. "There are more and more autos in Holland," wrote Robert Nicodemus in *Bicycling* in 1972, "but surprisingly bicycle riding is on the upswing too. . . . The unique system of roads is also a boon to cyclists. The roads . . . cover the entire country."

During this relatively short period, Dutch politicians and planners were infected with motor mania, but because mass motoring arrived in the Netherlands some years later than in other countries—and because the Netherlands didn't possess a domestic car industry that the government would feel duty-bound to feather-bed—the damage was not as bad as many of the plans of this period proposed. Nevertheless, Dutch cities steadily filled with cars, and there were plans to rip out city centers to cosset them even more. The Safer Traffic Party—a one-trick pony—fielded pro-motoring candidates in the 1962 municipal elections in Amsterdam, calling for more on-street parking, the replacement of electric trolleys with diesel buses, and the filling in of the city's canals to make more space for cars. When party boss Ton Hamers was asked what he'd do about Bloemgracht, a picturesque canal, he replied, "It should be filled in." When asked about Lauriergracht, the picture-postcard canal where his business stood, Hamers gave the same answer. "Then, at least, I'll have a place to park my car." His party won a seat on the city council.

AND THEN began the fight-back against the car. In Utrecht this started in 1965, when cars were banished from a number of major shopping streets in the city center. "Traffic cannot be constrained by half measures," stated a newspaper, arguing that it would be a "hard task to get the public to change [the] habit of shopping by car" and that the full cold-turkey would be necessary. What had started out as a six-month trial was extended to a year, and then the municipality announced the ban on cars would be permanent. "The general public particularly appreciates that there is now at least one area where it can shop quietly and undisturbed by motor traffic," reported a newspaper in 1966.

In the same year and the same city, a new cycle advocacy organization was founded to campaign for facilities for cyclists. Today this is known as the Fietsersbond, the Dutch Cyclists' Union. It was launched as ENWB, "the First Only and Real Cyclists Union," a dig at the ANWB which, although it had been founded as a cycling club in 1883, had opened to motorists in 1900 and had all but been taken over by motoring interests within ten years. ENWB was run by baby boomers and was explicitly pro-environment and anti-automobile. The organization's slogan—"The ENWB demands priority for modes of transportation which are safe, use limited amounts of energy, and are environmentally friendly; more possibilities for cyclists (as well as pedestrians and public transport)"—no doubt sounds pithier in Dutch.

"Our aim is to stimulate people to take back possession of their streets," said the ENWB's young chairman, Jan Wittenberg, in 1975. "The cycling tradition is still alive here," said William Drees, a former Dutch transport minister in the same year. "If we had strong political leadership, the bicycle could return as the main means of urban transport in six to eight years."

"Everyone thinks the Netherlands is a cycling paradise, but if we didn't put bikes on the agenda they'd be forgotten," said a Fietsersbond official in 2005.

"Taking the lane," Amsterdam-style.

"It's natural to cycle, but it's not natural to make policy." And to stimulate the provision of that policy required agitation, believed the founders of the ENWB. The organization's magazine was named *Vogelvrije*—"Free as a Bird"—but, more colorfully, it also meant "outlaws."

Many from this new breed of campaigners were agitating for the same sort of social and environmental issues that were exercising the eco-aware baby boomers in America and Britain. In the first half of the twentieth century, the Netherlands had been held in place by a system of *zuilen*, or "pillars"—distinct but opposing cultural groups that, by the equal exertion of pressure, kept each other in check. Although restrictive in some ways, this multifaceted approach ensured that respect for other peoples' opinions—from minorities, too—was baked into the system. Equality reigned; tolerance was sacrosanct. When these social pillars began to tumble in the 1960s and 1970s, the baby boomer generation saw an opportunity to ridicule and reject the conservatism of their car-owning parents.

Han van Spanje, a Fietsersbond official and a former chair of the 1970s Stop de Kindermoord campaign (which I'll explain below), told me:

> There was a shift in society [in the 1960s], something in the air. People wanted to do what they wanted. Women wanted the right to abortions, and they wanted the [contraceptive] pill. Young people wanted to change the world. We quarreled with our parents, arguing with fathers especially. There were "happenings"—where you made noise in the evenings and people grouped together shouting "away with the cars!" We wanted to control our own lives; we wanted to smoke our own products.

Amsterdam became the *magisch centrum*—or magical center—of Europe's countercultural movement, with drugs, free love, environmentalism, homosexuality, and a few more drugs all on the menu.

The year 1965 saw the birth of the "Provos," a lighthearted, arty, anarchist-leaning group that took its name from the Dutch word *provoceren*, meaning "to provoke." The short-lived group—consisting of perhaps eighty members, of whom twenty were hard-core—printed a magazine that sold up to 20,000 issues per monthly edition. According to this magazine, the Provos were:

> . . . beatniks, pleiners, scissors-grinders, jailbirds, simple simon stylites, magicians, pacifists, potato-chip chaps, charlatans, philosophers, germ-carriers, grand masters of the queen's horse, happeners, vegetarians, syndicalists, santy clauses, kindergarten teachers, agitators, pyromaniacs, assistant assistants, scratchers and syphilitics, secret police, and other riff-raff.

The group said it was against "capitalism, communism, fascism, bureaucracy, militarism, professionalism, dogmatism, and authoritarianism" and "realises that it will lose in the end, but it cannot pass up the chance to make at least one more heartfelt attempt to provoke society."

Provo became most famous for their "White Bicycle Plan," a proposal to close central Amsterdam to motorized traffic and create a free bicycle-sharing scheme, using bicycles that had been (poorly) painted white. "The asphalt terror of the motorized bourgeoisie has lasted long enough," mused a Provo poster promoting the coming of the White Bicycles (the idea of which would later go on to inspire city bike-share schemes around the world).

> Every day, human sacrifice is made to the newest authority that the bourgeoisie are at the mercy of: the Auto-Authority. The smothering carbon monoxide is their incense. . . . Provo's Bicycles Plan presents liberation from the car-monster. . . . The White Bicycle can be used by whomever needs it. More White Bicycles will follow until . . . the automobile danger is eliminated.

There were only ever a handful of these free bicycles in circulation—the Provos were stumped by a Dutch law that said all bicycles had to be locked when not moving—although a legend claims thousands were on the streets. What the Provos did manage to do was get international press coverage for their ideas.

A four-page piece on the Provos in the *New York Times* in 1966 said the group appealed to "beatniks, students, rockers, misfits . . . and those who feel like cyclists on a motorway." The White Bicycle plan "sounds zany, especially if you are not aware of what the bicycle means to the Dutch: the 870,000 inhabitants of Amsterdam are said to own 600,000 bicycles." The Provos, said the piece, were protesting to show that "streets are for people . . . not traffic."

Some of the group's ire was aimed at American traffic engineer David Jokinen, a Robert Moses acolyte hired in

"Fight against jackbooted authority." Provo campaign poster, 1965.

by the auto lobby to produce a plan that was to transform Amsterdam into a car city. (In fact, the plan was a feint, produced to tip the city over the edge and commission a subway that the auto lobby believed would free up the streets for automobiles.) The protests worked, although not immediately.

In 1967, the political wing of the Provos—that would be Luud Schimmelpennink, an industrial designer—won a seat on the city council of Amsterdam. The election result didn't provoke any change at that time, except that the group realized that with an office, phone number, post office box, monthly magazine, and a seat on the council—it had gone mainstream. For anarchists this was anathema; they agreed to disband.

Inspired by the spirit of protest, other groups sprang up including De Lastige Amsterdammer—"The Troublesome Amsterdammer"—which, in 1970, campaigned for cyclists' rights. Made up mainly of students from the University of Amsterdam, the group rented 25 bakfietsen (trikes with large cargo boxes on the front) and pedaled them through the city, holding up motor traffic around Dam Square, the historical center of Amsterdam (which was then choked with traffic but is now car-free, partly because of protests such as those from The Troublesome Amsterdammer). The students handed out flyers that read:

> On a bakfiets, we're taking up as much room as a small car, but we aren't spewing exhaust; we aren't honking; we aren't mowing down children . . . So now who's the crazy one?

Later events would attract even more cyclists, and more bakfietsen, this time emblazoned with "RATHER LIVE THAN DRIVE" and "CARS HAVE BEEN A NUISANCE TO US FOR YEARS."

In a newspaper interview, one of the event's leaders said:

> There's but one solution for the parking problem: shove those cars out of the city. An end must be put to the terror of the so-called experts who believe the city can't be closed off [to cars]. Nonsense. It's not me but they who are radical. What's more radical than continually tearing down chunks of the city to appease the traffic?

Another group active in the city, founded by a former Provo, was De Kabouters—"The Gnomes"—who rode bikes and established a "Car-Elimination

Service" as part of its self-styled Ministry of Environment and Hygiene. The Kabouters, too, rode in packs through the traffic, a form of bicycle protest that would later inspire the Critical Mass events started in San Francisco in 1992. The Kabouters blockaded a major shopping street on four different days in April 1970, and were taken aback when the city agreed that, as an experiment, cars would be banned from driving on the street. Two months later, in a municipal election, the Kabouters won five places on the city council. Political success took the wind out of their sails, but other protest groups took their place, and all with the aim of massively reducing the automobile's impact on the city.

In a follow-up piece on the Provos in the *New York Times*—headlined "Avant-Garde Right at Home in Amsterdam, City of Canals and Bicycles Is Also a Hippie Haven"—the "original hippie, anarchist flower people" were said to have left to "marry, have babies, and go mainstream."

Many of the former radicals did, indeed, settle down and become parents, but that didn't stop them agitating. Where the Provos left off, Stop de Kindermoord took over.

IN 1971, Dutch motorists killed 3,000 people, 450 of whom were children. One of these was the child of Eindhoven-based journalist Vic Langenhoff, a senior writer on the national newspaper *De Tijd*. In anguish, he wrote an article headlined "*Stop de Kindermoord*"—"Stop the Murder of Children." He urged that children be taken to school by bus rather than walk or cycle. His article hit a nerve, and urban activists were inspired to create the Stop de Kindermoord campaign organization. Led by Maartje van Putten, a 23-year-old new mother, the new body advocated not for school buses but protection from motorists. This poignant campaign—along with the others that had preceded it—persuaded the authorities, drip by drip, to extend and improve the already extensive cycling infrastructure in some parts of the Netherlands.

This persuasion was done at a face-to-face local level, Stop de Kindermoord's Han van Spanje told me:

> We always started locally, not nationally. We were a campaign group, but also an information source. School governors would contact us

and ask what to do to improve the safety outside their schools. We told them: "Contact the press. Talk to the traffic engineers." Most of us were cyclists, but it wasn't a cycling campaign. When you say you want to save kids, who can oppose that?

Stop de Kindermoord organized demonstrations across the nation, usually with many children in tow. Crucially, it didn't just shout and moan—it also offered practical solutions. The protest group recruited traffic engineer Steven Schepel as technical advisor. He drew up child-friendly street designs specific to whichever local authority or municipality asked for them. Stop de Kindermoord did a pillar-style deal with the national government: it paid Schepel's salary. (In 1989, Stop de Kindermoord changed its provocative name to Kinderen Voorrang— "Priority for Children"; in 2001, it was subsumed by the road safety campaign, Veilig Verkeer Nederland—"Safe Traffic Netherlands"—which continues to campaign for road safety. The Dutch Institute for Road Safety Research reports there were 621 road deaths in 2015, a third of whom were cyclists, but "relatively few children are killed in traffic.")

One of the other protest groups of the time benefitted from national television exposure. The Wijkgroep de Pijp—"the Neighborhood Group of De Pijp"—was filmed for a 1972 documentary on the proposed redevelopment of the De Pijp area of Amsterdam. The area's working-class children were filmed asking for safer roads. When parents took the law into their own hands by closing off streets, enraged motorists were shown getting out of their cars, removing the barricades, and fighting with parents. Because of newspaper articles inspired by the documentary, the area's children were provided with "play streets" where motor traffic was much reduced. The run-down De Pijp area was later gentrified and is now an exclusive neighborhood.

Stop de Kindermoord! ("Stop the Murder of Children!") logo.

TWO LONG-RUNNING grassroots road-safety campaigns in Britain had many of the same features as Stop de Kindermoord, yet they did not result in nationally safer roads for pedestrians and cyclists. The first was a two-year campaign staged by worried Londoners who lived beside Western Avenue, the busy 1920s arterial that was—and remains—a motorway in all but name.

The road, introduced in chapter 1, was the first in Britain to be retrofitted with cycle tracks, and was designed to be a swift motor road from the center of London to "the west." Western Avenue—the Westway—had a starring role in *Crash*, J. G. Ballard's disturbing 1973 novel about a group of people who share an erotic obsession with car crashes. (A pre-publication report on the manuscript advised the editor that the author was "beyond psychiatric help," a description Ballard cherished.) It's no wonder the road has inspired such strong feelings, because almost from the outset it was a dystopian road. Though it was originally meant to be an expressway, developers had other ideas, and the houses and factories erected beside the road quickly made it a frustrating stop-start journey for motorists (and cyclists on the cycleway) who chafed at having to slow down. Seeking to alleviate these delays, the Ministry of Transport erected barriers to stop pedestrians crossing the road. Residents bristled at such restrictions and demanded, instead, slower speeds from the passing motor cars, which, reported a newsreel, were "killing kiddies."

"Parents are organising demonstrations to protest against the 'slaughter' of school children by speeding motor cars," reported a newspaper in July 1937: "A procession of 250 strong crossed and re-crossed the [Western Avenue] in pouring rain, holding up the traffic on a busy Saturday afternoon. Motorists were confronted with banners bearing slogans 'Make Westway Safe' and 'It May Be Your Child Next Time.'" The plummy voiceover for news footage shot by British Pathé said that the "West Way has a bad record for accidents so the local mothers and fathers are at war with the authorities." The newsreel showed parents carrying placards with illustrations of a dead child carried by a policeman, printed with "Driver—don't take a chance." The newsreel added: "Who says that as a nation we are not demonstrative?"

Residents wanted the Ministry to reduce the speeds on Western Avenue, and they suggested a variety of methods of doing so, most of them involving the speeding traffic coming to a complete halt. They most certainly did not want a bridge, as shown by posters carried by protestors in 1938. A photo published in the *Daily Herald* showed a wheelchair-bound woman carrying placards reading "A victim of Western Avenue" and "My friends was killed; I was seriously injured." A poster carried by a pram-pushing woman stated "Road bridge won't help us."

The local authority was also aghast at the injuries and deaths caused by motorists on the road. "The time for talking is over," called the Acton mayor at a protest meeting, urging locals to gather and "do their duty in no half-hearted way." T. H. Foley of the Pedestrians' Association was more forceful: "We have had months of terror, death and injury. . . . We must stir the dictators to a recognition of our rights!"

At 5:45 p.m. on July 21, 1938, locals gathered at The Approach, the most dangerous section of the road. A procession led by Reverend Race Godfrey filed across the road, blocking cars. Within minutes there was a long queue of motor vehicles.

The next day the minister of transport ordered two footbridges to be erected, but this failed to satisfy the demonstrators: they believed elevating pedestrians out of the way would merely encourage motorists to go even faster. Instead, they wanted to be able to carry on crossing the road without using the hastily erected bridges. Women with prams demonstrated how they struggled to climb the stairs. A week later, a thousand people assembled at The Approach and once again blocked the road. Foley said the demonstration was of "national importance" for, if the people of Acton allowed pedestrian bridges to remain, then Western Avenue would forever remain a "speed track," and bridges would be introduced elsewhere—pedestrians and cyclists would become interlopers on roads. The bridge at The Approach was nicknamed *Pons Asinorum*, Latin for "Asses' Bridge." Protests went on for months—in October 1938, torchlit processions held up the traffic night after night. Pallbearers carried a mock coffin—placards read "We want crossings, not coffins." The Ministry of Transport remained unmoved: the hated bridges stayed put. The demonstrations became weaker and weaker, until they finally petered out. Two years of Stop de Kindermoord–style protests in motor-centric Britain had come to nothing.

Stop de Kindermoord had other equivalents in the UK, including ones happening at the same time as the Dutch one. "Local people should insist that children should not unnecessarily be exposed to risk to cut a few minutes off commuters' journeys," thundered a 1971 editorial in *De Beaver*, the newsletter for residents of the De Beauvoir Estate and town in Hackney, London. The secretary of the De Beauvoir Association was Doris Kibblewhite, known locally as "the lady on the bicycle" (she delivered copies of the newsletter from the wicker basket of her bike). Residents "argued strongly" that De Beauvoir Road and others should be closed to through-traffic: "Mrs. Rose said the road was uncrossable at peak hours and was too narrow for parking and the weight of traffic."

A plan for road closures drawn up by residents and the Greater London Council would "improve the neighbourhood by creating traffic-free streets. . . ." Residents voted in favor of a number of road closures and restrictions on car parking, but in 1972 the GLC decided not to go ahead with the road closures. "If you, your children, or your old folk [have to cross roads in the area] then the council's decision should be of real concern to you," suggested *De Beaver.* "Let's get ready to protest about it." The protests were tame: nothing much more than letters to the local press. But, with the GLC dragging its heels, residents became increasingly confrontational. In April 1974, residents—organized by the De Beauvoir Association—blocked a road with homemade banners to protest at traffic. The banner slogans included "This road is unfit for children" and "Homes before roads." By June, the residents started taking direct action more frequently. Beneath the De Beaver headline "Militant mums demand action now," Mrs. Hubbard wrote that "the first demonstration . . . was a great success. The drivers did not know what had happened and this came as a surprise to them." She also offered some advice to future protesters: "Make sure it is the busiest time of day, and do it unexpected as the police . . . will divert the traffic. Never let them know too soon or else you are left with no traffic. . . . Make sure you have plenty of banners and make sure you have all the parents behind you."

Terry Hemmstead, the Association's leader, was equally unbending: "We all want action and nothing else." Roads should be closed "before a child dies."

De Beaver reported that a "mums' chorus" went up at one meeting against the council: "All these committees are no good. We'll close roads ourselves." A councilor mocked the anarchy: "You need someone to show you how to make Molotov cocktails." One mum replied: "We know how to do that already!"

Some of the roads that the campaigners wished to see closed *did* get stopped up, but one of the main ones took until 2016. A pedestrian crossing—one of the other demands—was later installed, but the 1970s protests in London did not have the same national effect as the similar Stop de Kindermoord campaign in the Netherlands. Why did the Dutch campaign work while the British ones didn't—at least, not to the same degree? Partly it's to do with Britain's motor-centrism, but it's also because the Dutch system of government is more amenable to face-to-face campaigning, with local politicians having meaningful power.

THE POTENTIAL fragility of mass motorization was brought vividly to life for Dutch people during the OPEC oil crisis of 1973. The Arab oil embargo affected the Netherlands far more than any other European country, because the Netherlands was targeted thanks to its being home to the oil company Royal Dutch Shell. Faced with dwindling oil supplies, the Dutch national government decided that the best way for the nation to conserve fuel would be to limit Sunday driving. All of the country's 3 million motorists were instructed to stay at home on Sundays, with the only exceptions being diplomats and 16,000 motorists belonging to "essential professions," such as doctors.

To promote a travel mode that didn't require oil, Prime Minister den Uyl rode his bicycle through the grounds of his official residence in front of news cameras. The first no-drive Sunday was held on November 4, 1973. Cities went quiet; people held picnics on motorways. The no-drive days were later halted, but people had magically done without their cars for whole days without ill effects, and they had enjoyed riding their bicycles, too. During the oil crisis, sales of bicycles doubled.

The following year a new lobby group was formed to rid Amsterdam of cars, and it was organized by some of the leaders from earlier protests, including Schimmelpennink. "Amsterdam Autovrij"—Car-Free Amsterdam—staged a mass bike ride in May 1974, and 1,000 riders turned up. The following month 2,000 turned up. In October 1974, a "die-in" was held, with a minute of silence to honor killed cyclists and pedestrians. Three thousand riders turned up at the event in 1975; it attracted 4,000 in 1976. On June 5, 1977, 9,000 Amsterdammers staged a die-in in front of the Rijksmuseum.

Schimmelpennink said the 1978 event would be the last: "We now want something to show for the time, money, and energy we've expended," he said. Fifteen thousand riders took part. Four days later, members of the newly elected city council said they believed the city's Traffic Circulation Plan centered too much on private motoring, and in November 1978 a new plan was adopted—this called for the reduction of motor traffic, and car-parking spaces in the city center,

Amsterdam's cyclists aren't protected with curbs everywhere in the city, yet people still cycle. The words on the truck door warn cyclists to "Beware of blind spot."

with more space given over to cyclists. "In the coming years," the revised plan stated, "the policy must strongly focus on improving conditions for cyclists."

THE PROTEST groups—the Fietsersbond, the Provos, Stop de Kindermoord, and the rest—had all played a part in creating a culture of street-level awareness for everyday cycling. This—slowly—changed minds and influenced policies. From the mid-1970s, more investment was made in cycling infrastructure across much of the Netherlands, with federal policies put in place that entitled municipalities to receive payment for 80 percent of the costs of new cycling infrastructure. But where did the Dutch get the cash to expand the nation's cycleway network? From Groningen, that's where. Or more specifically, from underneath the region surrounding the city of Groningen. A mammoth reserve of inland natural gas was discovered close to the city in 1959. The Groningen gas field turned out to be the largest natural gas field in Europe. Its discovery was a boon for both the Dutch government and Dutch citizens. After it came on stream in 1963, Groningen's gas paid for a great deal, including the famous social welfare policies of the Netherlands. The national *potverteren*—or treat-like "spending pot"—also helped pay for much of the other immense infrastructure projects of the period, such as the Delta Plan's flood defenses, and the expansion of the country's motorway and cycleway networks. With gas revenues—and the influx of overseas investment cash—Dutch people became richer, and bought more cars, but they also bought more bicycles. In 1960, 527,000 bicycles were bought in the Netherlands; by 1972, that had doubled to 1,086,000.

The city of Groningen has one of the highest cycling modal-shares in the country: up to 60 percent of journeys are done by cycle. The city has had a long tradition of cycling, and this was enhanced in 1977 by the implementation of Groningen's Traffic Circulation Plan, which divided the city center in four quadrants. Private motor traffic could only go from one quadrant to the other via a ring road. A system of one-way streets was installed literally overnight, much to the annoyance of the city's motorists. The plan was forced through by the 24-year-old left-wing politician Max van den Berg. In effect, motorists were banned from the center of Groningen.

US bicycle advocate and filmmaker Clarence Eckerson Jr. describes today's Groningen as a "bicycle nirvana" where he "couldn't stop smiling at what I saw around me." Fellow advocate Jonathan Maus from the *Bike Portland* blog was equally effusive, describing cycling around town as like being in "a fairy tale."

However, Dutch bicycle advocate Mark Wagenbuur points out that a great deal of cycling in Groningen is "all too often shared with motor traffic," and that the city has "almost no protected intersections." Furthermore, says Wagenbuur "even articulated buses, go right through the narrow streets of the old city centre."

Despite the sometimes less-than-optimal infrastructure, cycle use in Groningen remains at levels that British and American cycle advocates can only dream about. And, for the Netherlands as a whole, this elevated modal-share for cycling is the result not just of hard infrastructure but also a 110-year tradition of cycling.

Even in 1972, when many of today's British and American cycle advocates say cycling was supposed to be in the doldrums, an American engineer explained how the Netherlands was still very much a cycling nation:

> In 1972, there [are] 3.5 million cars, 1.85 million mopeds, 7.3 million bicycles of which 5 million are regularly in use, and 13.5 million residents in The Netherlands. . . . Everyone rides a bicycle: young, old, rich, poor, in all manner of dress, and carrying additional passengers. . . . The Dutch even "walk their dog" on a bicycle.

BRITON DAVID HEMBROW moved to Assen with his family in 2007 and now leads a popular ten-year-old study tour. He schools cycle advocates from around the world on his adopted hometown's cycle-friendliness. But he's not the first to offer such study tours to Assen.

In the 1970s, the Netherlands National Tourist Office in New York encouraged Americans to visit the country on bikes. The organization produced "Holland-Cycle Land" and other pamphlets extolling the virtues of cycling in the Netherlands. Cycling author Rob Van Der Plas—a naturalized American born and raised in the Netherlands—visited in 1974, and particularly liked the cycling infrastructure centered on Assen which had "bikeway systems [that] are really bicycle freeways: They have well-designed crossings with other roads, often form the most direct link between towns and villages, are well surfaced. They are used [for] transportation . . . because they do not delay the cyclist. . . ."

New Yorker writer H. P. Koenig went on a cycle holiday two years later and came back with glowing reports of a country where "bicycling is still a way of life. . . ." and where "paved bicycle lanes run alongside main roads." Many of these paths, said Koenig, had been "built 60 years ago . . . ," including a "surge of building" in the 1930s. "A master plan for 250 miles of paved paths [near Assen] was devised in the mid-'50s, most of which has been completed."

Koenig wrote that, in Assen, he "enjoyed the kind of bicycle riding that doesn't exist anywhere else in the same satisfactory way." He added that the cycleway network of Assen was a "model being studied by engineers from Japan, the United States, France, and West Germany." Cycling study tours of Assen have a history that is longer than is usually appreciated.

Before and after photographs of Mient & Appelstraat, The Hague, 1975.

WHILE THE cycleways of Assen were good in the 1970s, an evolving series of amendments since then has improved them nearly beyond all recognition. The 1950–75 period saw few upgrades to the cycleway networks of the Netherlands. In fact, many cycleways were ripped out during these years.

Among the most important network upgrades in the mid-1970s was the "pilot project" for The Hague. "The Hague announced in future the interests of road traffic would be subordinate to the maintenance of the quality of urban life: in accordance with this aim, the growth in private-car use would have to be restricted in favour of public transport [and] bicycles," said the mid-1970s cycleway plan for the pilot. "The planning of the cycleway goes back to 1973, when a residents' organisation in the Zeeheldenkwartier district put forward plans for the provision of cycle tracks in three shopping streets," said the report.

However, progress was slow. "The first public meeting . . . took place in an emotional atmosphere: the shopkeepers . . . with the support of the Chamber of Commerce . . . called the whole route into question. Frequently heard statements were that shopping streets were not suitable for the construction of cycleways and that restraints in motor traffic meant lower turnovers." (This is a complaint many of today's cycle advocates in Britain and America are painfully familiar with.) "On 11 October 1975 . . . angry shopkeepers protested by blocking . . . the intersection with their cars."

The retailers backed down only when they were offered compensation should the cycleways lead to a loss of takings: "After consultations . . . retailers were prepared to cooperate if certain conditions could be met [including] that shopkeepers' incomes should be guaranteed in the event of the experiment's failure. . . ."

The cycleways were opened in 1978. None of the retailers ever had any cause to apply for compensation—in fact, the construction of the cycleways, and the journeys they encouraged, increased their takings.

TO KEEP their souls topped up with bicycling goodness, many cycle advocates make pilgrimages to the Netherlands. It's the bike version of the *hajj*. They—and that includes me—gawp, applaud, and take endless photographs in places such as Utrecht, Assen, Groningen, and, for a bit more of a manic time, Amsterdam. Such "study tours" to the Netherlands have been taking place for a long time, yet we non-Dutch often still don't seem to "get it." Even when we *think* we're going Dutch we usually don't go the whole hog. Dutch planners and engineers think diffuse networks, while too often we fixate on curb-protected cycleways, believing that's the Dutch way. There's even an epithet for this: *curb-nerdery*, the belief that all cycleways must be lined with curbs because that's how they do it in the Netherlands. But that's not how they do it in the Netherlands.

Here's the tick-box that Dutch road engineers use:

> **Coherence:** cycling infrastructure should provide good connectivity between all origins and destinations in the area.

> **Directness:** road authorities should minimize detours and delays for cyclists.

> **Safety:** road authorities should minimize the number of conflicts between motor traffic and cycle traffic and minimize the outcome of remaining conflicts.

> **Comfort:** cycling infrastructure should allow for comfortable maneuvering and minimize the use of (precious) human energy.

> **Attractiveness:** as slower modes of movement are more sensitive for the quality of urban space, cycle routes should preferably use varied small-scale environments.

It's not a pick'n'mix—all five policies are required. Too often we think that a flagship route, costing millions but beautifully curb-protected, will encourage eight- to eighty-year-olds to start cycling. We are then perplexed when this does not happen. The real secret to the success of the Dutch cycle networks is not that they are all *protected* but that they are *connected*. Flagship routes can become white elephants if they don't link in with a wider network. We wouldn't expect a freeway to be used if no roads joined up with it.

But even providing a perfect network still isn't enough to encourage people to start cycling. In their wonderfully titled report *Making Cycling Irresistible*, the American academics John Pucher and Ralph Buehler wrote that "The most important approach to making cycling safe and convenient . . . is the provision of separate cycling facilities along heavily traveled roads and at intersections. . . ." However, they add:

> . . . separate facilities are only part of the solution. Dutch . . . cities reinforce the safety, convenience, and attractiveness of excellent cycling rights-of-way with extensive bike parking, integration with public transport, comprehensive traffic education, and training of both cyclists and motorists, and a wide range of promotional events intended to generate enthusiasm and wide public support for cycling. . . . The key to the success of cycling policies . . . [is] the coordinated implementation of [a] multi-faceted, mutually reinforcing set of policies. Not only [does the Netherlands] implement far more of the pro-bike measures, but [it] greatly reinforces their overall impact with highly restrictive policies that make car use less convenient as well as more expensive.

The Netherlands has had a long time to work on all of this. They made many mistakes along the way. We have the benefit of being able to learn from their experience, and then shape it to fit our localities. For the many cultural, historical, financial, social, and perhaps even religious reasons I discuss in this chapter, it will be tough to replicate what the Netherlands took more than a hundred years to perfect. This does not mean we should not try.

Many Dutch people think of their bicycles as simple tools, not something to get excited about ("You're writing a book about the historical use of toothbrushes? Weirdo!"), but the Dutch method of providing for cyclists is an export industry. The Dutch Cycling Embassy is a public–private network for "sustainable bicycle inclusive mobility" and is said to represent the "best of Dutch Cycling: knowledge, experience, and experts offered by private companies, NGOs, research institutions, national and local governments." (It also states that it has "over 40 years of experience in bicycle policy and practical bicycle solution." Yes, a lot "over"—it should calculate from 1906, not 1976.)

Members of the Dutch Cycling Embassy travel the globe sharing "best practices." Sometimes even they are surprised at some of the exemplary cycling infrastructure that is being installed around the world. Take, for example, the Te Ara I Whiti cycleway in Auckland, New Zealand. This replaced a freeway on-ramp, is startlingly wide and, just like some of Britain's 1930s cycle tracks, it's shockingly pink. About riding upon the cycleway—which is embedded with Maori symbols—Mirjam Borsboom, director of the Embassy, told a local magazine: "It's very impressive infrastructure; I think every city needs an iconic cycling path . . . but this is really exceeding expectations."

Meredith Glaser, a cycle-infrastructure consultant and one of the lecturers on the summer school mentioned at the beginning of the chapter, told me that cities need to show their appreciation of cyclists. "Many cities have built 'wow' infrastructure, such as the Cykelslangen ["Cycle-Snake"] bridge in Copenhagen, or the Hovenring in Eindhoven. These iconic pieces of cycle infrastructure make people go on detours to get to them, and make them feel loved and cared for."

The Te Ara I Whiti cycleway—Maori for "Light Path"—isn't just a pretty face, it's strategically intelligent. It joins up with three existing cycleways, and there are plans for another cycleway to link in soon. It's this sort of network thinking that is the most effective way to "go Dutch."

Epilogue

New York City's Protected Bikeways: Then and Now

THE PROVISION OF BIKEWAYS IN NEW YORK CITY has had a checkered history. Congressman Ed Koch was all for bikeways in the early 1970s, and he rode on demonstrations calling for their creation—demonstrations such as those organized by activists like the *Village Voice* columnist David Gurin, friend of urbanist Jane Jacobs, and cofounder of the confrontationally named Action Against Automobiles. Koch became mayor and Gurin became assistant transport commissioner, but in 1980s-America *keeping* the protected bikeways they had both long called for didn't pan out.

"Special four-foot-wide lanes for bicycles will open . . . along Broadway and the Avenues of the Americas in midtown Manhattan," reported the *New York Times* in July 1978. The painted lanes—three miles in length, and the result of an eighteen-month federally financed study—were announced by Mayor Koch, and "could pave the way for some 500 miles of such lanes in [New York City]," predicted the paper.

"We want to make people realize that bicycle riding is a serious business, a valid way of getting around the city," Gurin told the *Times*.

However, within days of the lane-striping, the newspaper expressed its displeasure, saying the "bikeways were created by stealing space from [a] parking lane. . . ." Not that the newspaper need have worried—the painted lanes soon filled with trash, hot-dog stalls and, of course, parked cars and trucks. Bicycle messengers avoided the lanes, as did most of the people who got on their bikes during an eleven-day transit strike in April 1980, when bike commuting tripled.

"One of the things we did every morning during the strike was to have our volunteers put up cones that created bike lanes on Fifth and Sixth Avenues," said "Gridlock Sam" Schwartz.

In mid-April, Mayor Koch's executive administrator Ronay Menschel told the *New York Times*: "We want to take full advantage of the momentum for bicycle travel that built up during the transit strike." The newspaper said the city was "studying ways of segregating bicycle lanes on a permanent basis without using traffic cones, which were frequently knocked aside during the transit strike."

In August, raised islands started to be installed on Manhattan's Fifth, Sixth, and Seventh Avenues and on Broadway, creating six- and eight-foot-wide protected bikeways. The two-foot-wide islands—described as "permanent" by the *New York Times*—were made from concrete curbs filled with asphalt.

Archival photos show that the one-way lanes offered ample protection, but they were often blocked by cars at intersections and were used too by street vendors, who also valued the protection they offered. Many cyclists stuck to the streets, upsetting motorists who believed they should now stay in the bikeways. Nevertheless, according to the New York City transportation department, 3,000 cyclists a day used the bikeway on Sixth Avenue (the Avenue of the Americas). But Koch warned that if an unspecified "larger" number of cyclists did not start using the bikeways, "we're going to pull these lanes up again and give them back to the cars." Koch said he was "getting a lot of flak" for the installation of the protective curbing, "yet cyclists do not appear to be taking advantage of it in significant numbers."

Cyclists said the lanes were infrequently used "because pushcarts lumber along them, because pedestrians block the paths as they step off curbs to wait for traffic lights to change, and because garbage accumulates near the curbs."

Motorists, meanwhile, were "convinced that traffic has slowed on avenues with the bicycle lanes, and figures from the City Transportation Department confirmed their suspicions," reported the *New York Times*. "According to tests on the Avenue of the Americas . . . it takes cars from five to ten minutes longer than it did a few months ago to travel from 30th Street to Central Park South."

Gurin responded: "There always are problems in the beginning." With an ironic smile, he added: "Traffic always returns to its normal great speed of five miles an hour."

Dressed in a suit and wearing a reflective vest and a helmet, Mayor Koch straddled his roadster bicycle on October 15 to formally inaugurate the protected bikeway on the Avenue of the Americas.

New York Governor Hugh Carey accused Koch of having a bike "fetish." In a traffic-snarled limousine ride up Sixth Avenue with President Jimmy Carter, Carey pointed to a bike lane empty of cyclists and snarked, "See how Ed's pissing away your money?"

By November 12, Koch had decided to demolish the bikeways. He told the *New York Times*: "My own gut tells me they're not working. And if they're not working, rip them up." The previous weekend he had seen "a total of two bikes in the lanes each day—one of them going the wrong way."

After hearing from Transportation Commissioner Anthony R. Ameruso that daily use of the lanes had declined from 3,000 cyclists in mid-September to 1,700 in November, Koch ordered the lanes to be destroyed. "I was called into Koch's office and told to remove the paths," recalled Schwartz.

Work crews appeared on November 14. "The bicycle-lane barriers installed over the summer on avenues between Washington Square and Central Park began to disappear yesterday," reported the *New York Times*. "Wearing armbands smeared with ketchup to simulate blood, some . . . protestors lay down in front of bulldozers."

By nightfall the concrete-and-asphalt islands were gone, with the curbing carted away to be used elsewhere and the asphalt sent for recycling.

THE REMOVAL of the bikeways was bad, but there was worse to come: in his third term, Mayor Koch planned to prohibit cycling on some streets altogether.

Flanked by his police and transportation commissioners, the New York City mayor stood on the steps of City Hall on July 22, 1987, to unveil the ban, which he said would take effect six weeks later. The ban was described as an "experiment," and was designed to "reduce accidents caused by speeding bicycle messengers," reported the *New York Times*. The ban would prevent the riding of any bicycles on Park, Madison, and Fifth Avenues in midtown Manhattan between 10:00 a.m. and 4:00 p.m. on weekdays. Ross Sandler, the city's transportation commissioner, said the hours of the ban were selected so as not to interfere with commuter cyclists—as if they didn't move around during the day.

Messenger cyclists, meanwhile, "imperil the lives of New Yorkers every single day," said the bicycle-riding mayor.

"What they're doing is scaring the public to death," said Police Commissioner Benjamin Ward, "and we've got to do something about it."

Charles Komanoff of Transportation Alternatives saw it differently: "Singling out cyclists, a small part of the traffic stream, was ludicrous from a pragmatic standpoint and indefensible from a moral one. Moreover, targeting vulnerable, working-class bike messengers qualified as scapegoating and class warfare."

"Hundreds of thousands of safe bicycle riders would be inconvenienced by a few daredevil riders," cycling organizations told the *New York Times*.

Cyclists protested the ban, and not just "scofflaw bicycle messengers." Rolling demos started to take place at the end of the messengers' workday, with hundreds of cyclists riding slowly along city streets, remembers Komanoff:

> As we streamed up Sixth Avenue, cries of "What do we want? Our streets back!" reverberated through the glass canyons, alternating with "Join us! Join us!" Before long, riders were holding signs and banners lampooning the mayor—"Koch Can't Ride"—and calling on New Yorkers to "Clear the Air: Cyclists and Pedestrians Unite!"

The Association of Messenger Services sued the city, and in September, a New York State Supreme Court judge invalidated the ban because it had been issued without sufficient public notice.

Koch said the victory was "short-lived and foolish." He promised that the city would appeal. In the end, City Hall threw in the towel.

Stuart Gruskin, the messengers' lawyer, said: "You don't solve a problem of overcrowding by putting the same number of people in less space. Banning bicycles will not cause them to vanish."

THE DESTRUCTION of New York's protected bikeways and the attempt to ban cycling in Manhattan can be regarded as battles. The war is not over. In truth, the war will never be over. Streets do not stay the same; cities are constantly reinventing themselves (for instance, the run-down, crime-scarred New York of the 1980s is a world away from the New York of today). Cars may seem dominant in many towns and cities right now, but that's because choices were made to allow such dominance. Choices can be remade; minds can be changed.

Janette Sadik-Khan became New York City's transport commissioner in 2007, and in her six years in charge she was able to reduce at least some of the motorcar's dominance. She tamed Times Square and she (re)installed protected bikeways in Manhattan and installed others elsewhere in New York. Her task was not an easy one, which is why her 2016 book about her time in charge is called *Street Fight*.

Hers was a fight against vested interests, a fight against inertia, a fight against "that's just the way it is." But streets *can* be changed, and they can be changed radically and for the better. Dutch retailers once fought against the installation of cycleways; they now fight to extend them. An eye-opening and inspiring exercise is to look at "then" and "now" photographs of Dutch streets. Many were clogged with cars in the 1970s, but then decisions were made to remodel the streets, blocking access for cars. Today these streets are designed for people, not engines, leaving many people to assume they were always this civilized. They were not—they were changed. And it's not just a Dutch thing—streets around the world are being transformed, with cars removed entirely or their dominance reduced. (Where are the cycleways going to go if streets are full of parked cars?)

There's a wonderful online resource that shows street transformations in action. It's a collation of Google Street View images collected by Brazilian urban design collective Urb-i. More than a thousand street makeovers are listed on urb-i.com, and the archive grows daily. New York City's Times Square is on there, of course. The Street View image from 2009 shows a car-dominated scene; the 2014 image doesn't. The 2011 image shows "tactical urbanism" in progress, with planters temporarily—and cheaply—blocking the way, and people starting to dominate.

Google Street View is ten years old this year. Take heart that, during those ten years, many towns and cities have taken the plunge to transform themselves. Much of this book has been about the fading away of bicycling cultures. It does not have to be like this. History is a lesson, it is not a template. Fight.

Acknowledgments

THANKS TO ALL at Island Press, including but not only Heather Boyer and Mike Fleming.

For their patience, thanks are due to the loves of my life—my wife, Jude, and my children, Josh, Hanna, and Ellie Reid.

Thanks also to my Kickstarter backers, listed overleaf.

As much of this book is based on original research, it has involved wading through personal papers and dusty archives. Librarians in America and the UK proved to be exceptionally helpful. It was wonderful—albeit distracting—to work in such gob-stoppingly beautiful libraries such as the Library of Congress in Washington, DC, and the library at the Royal Automobile Club in London. I paid numerous (fruitful) visits to the National Cycling Archive at the Modern Records Centre at Warwick University, and while this doesn't have the architectural splendor of the former libraries, it more than made up for it in the wonderful array of records deposited by the Cyclists' Touring Club and other bodies. I also looked at Ministry of Transport papers held in The National Archives in Kew, London (which is the most technologically advanced archive I have ever visited, but the concrete building leaves a lot to be desired).

Portions of chapters 1 and 6 were previously published in *Roads Were Not Built for Cars* (Carlton Reid, Island Press, 2015). However, I have expanded the content, including adding more period sources.

Kickstarter Backers

Philip Bowman
Trickhand
Chris Niewiarowski
Stewart Duncan
Chelle Destefano
David Goodstein
Graham George
Irene McAleese
Simon Woodward
Chris Murphy
Allen Dickie
James Grant
Jnik
Ken Callan
Edouard Guidon
Mike Skiffins
Mark Philpotts
Andy Fox
Edgar Fernandez
Jaime Lee Pabiloña
Jon H Ballentine
Jonathan Winston
Maree Carroll
Michael Charland
Tim Doole
Ray
Lea Tui
The Warmans
Richard Evans
Steffen Lohrey
John Cooper
Alan Couchman
Richard Ashurst
Bristolpedalrevolution
Shaun Connor
Dr John Darling
Michael Josephy
Kevin Hasley
Adam Bower
Thomas NIcol
Paul Tildesley
Sara Rich Dorman
Frankie Roberto
John Boyd
William Chong
Donald Pillsbury
Kyle Griggs
Jim Baltaxe
Bruce Lewandowski
Ian Clark
Martin Packer
Melvin Bailey
Tedder

Robin Holloway
James Johnston
Chris Dorling
Charles Frazer Harvey
Chris Whiley
John Donnelly
Andrew Lamberton
Anthony McDougle
Nigel Oulton
Fredrik Jönsson
Alan Cragg
Richard Worth
Ken Neal
Paul Shortland
John Grocock
Peter Hawkins
Don Springhetti
Christopher Fox
Rick Rubio
Darren Steele
Catherine Bedford
Graham Parker
Jacqueline Campbell
Dave Robinson
Jonathan Streete
Hans Dorsch
Terry Coaker
David Houghton
Seamus Kelly
Ben Wooliscroft
Tina Bach
Michael Beverland
Graham Connor
Mark Carlson
Miles Rickelton
Pj roon
Barista
Graham Robinson
James Evans
Frode P. Bergsager
Mark Chopping
Kerry Chin
FlyKly
D Wiegand
Darran Shepherd
Mark Silcox
Jim Stahl
Daniel
Gabor
Patrick Finley
Fiona Campbell
Ed Wojtowicz
Alasdair Sinclair

Sumei Toh
Christian Amoser
Heikki Rautanen
Sylvia Aitken
Paola Vedana
Sam Joslin
Richard Guy Briggs
Jacob Curtis
Nick Orloff
Graham Powell
Davide Zulli
John Pitts
Martin J.
Ed Ames
Joe Wiederhold
Tam
Mark Dwight
Thomas Hoffmann
Tore Simonsen
Torben Finn Laursen
Tino
Kerry Palmer
Fabien Fivaz
Alec McCalden
Ron Grosinger
Bernardo Pereira
Ferran
Pål Steinar Berg
Douglas Carnall
Suso del Rio
Ben Martin
Hugh Wilson
Curtis Corlew
Erin McWalter
Greg Hostetler
Kelvin Kwan
Paul Deaton
Hans-Erhard Lessing
Ulf Göransson
Robert Seidler
John Junta
Kris Wills
Richard Masoner
Kirsten Shouler
Josh Miner
Belen Vivanco M.
Giulia Cortesi
Thomas Jenkinson
Jeffrey Dallas Moore
James Eldridge
SW
Ed Loach
Robert Weeks

Sam Jordison
Rosie Bell
Robert Dingwall
Mary Manning
Nunuboogie
Brian Brunswick
Mark Dempsey
Matthew Hardy
Nick Lewis
George Coulouris
Terry Duckmanton
Richard Warren
Adam Bowie
Ian Hollidge
Peter Clinch
Steve Fagg
Paul Dyett
John Blackie
Patrick Wadsworth
Mark Harrison
Calum
Philip Henderson
G Swanson
Lesley G. Craddock
Toby Adam
Darryl Rayner
Graham Clark
Brenda Broughton
Grant Mason
Keith Stephen
Roy Cuckow
Graeme Wilson
Icicle19
Gemma Rathbone
Andrew Harker
Paul Kohn
Andrew Knights
Toby Churchill
Jonathan Sanderson
Patrick Mcloughlin
David Davies
Giles Cudmore
Yoav Tzabar
Jan Foniok
Will Crocombe
Peter Veasey
Jamie Scahill
Peter Silburn
Peter Whitelegg
Vivienne Gray
Philip Ashbourn
David Priestley
Matt Bridgestock

Jonathan Simpson
Peter Blakeman
Mark Heal
Brian Carlin
Rob James
Ian Hull
Pete Abel
Paul Fulbrook
Matthew Little
Neil Barron
Michael Pospieszalski
Brian Mackenzie
Don Muir
Jonathan McGarry
Phyll Hardie
Andrew Russell
Richard Pelling
GODtower
Graham Jones
Edward Fitzgerald-Clark
Rms cycling services
Andy Walker
Roger Suddaby
Andrew Grimbly
les crook
Stephen Carleysmith
Tim Mullett
Jamie Radford
Jeremy Strutt
Vicki Berry
Jenni Gwiazdowski
John Krug
Juliet Blackburn
Mark Sanders
Chris Emerson
Iain Peacock
James Shepherd
Andrew Martin
Pierre Riteau
Oly Shipp
Gaz
Marc Eberhard
Thomas Heller
Graham Smith
peter kershaw
Piers Hawksley
Philip Johnston
Kevin M Ablitt
Tim Blackwell
Graham Fereday
Jim Stuart
Tim Warin
Eric Schneider
David Ryan
Anthony Morley
Daniel Glassey
Richard Dean
Robert Feakes
Keith Richmond
Joe Clarbour

Stephanie Creasey
eric ludlow
Robert Harber
Alexander Allan
Jonathan Rowland
Wil Symons
Ivor Hewitt
John Olson
Eifion Francis
Paul Wilkinson
Sigurd Gudd
Gary Dawes
Chris Hinchliffe
David Ramkalawon
Philip Passmore
Peter Lyons-Lewis
Martin Hart
Lukas Georgiou
Peter Dixon
Tom Ryan
Alister Barclay
Christopher Peck
Dave Minter
Peter G. Taylor-Anderson
Daniel Wrightson
Grant Sandilands
Ben Cooper
Johnathan Calvert
Lazerblade
Rob Wachowski
Chris Smith
Derek Vickers
Amaryllis Courtney
Jez Higgins
Mark Strong
Jakob Whitfield
Anthony Cartmell
Nigel Shoosmith
Lin Tuff
Keith Day
Dave Warnock
Alex Ingram
Wiethege
James Spinks
Neil Webster
Eviltoystealer
Hugh Willliams
Jonathan Bennett
Ian Denton
Warren Isaacs
Gwenda Owen
David Hartley
Clement T. Cole
Leslie Reissner
Tom Sulston
Kasey van Puijenbroek
Karey Harrison
Lisa Adolphe
John Peterson
Trainmanusa

Christof Damian
Aaron Spencer
Ashley Burrows
Norman Oxtoby
David Gibbon
Mark james
John Waterworth
Mathieu Davy
Jerry Ash
David Wellbeloved
James Holloway
Graeme Howell
Paige Mitchell
John Wills Lloyd
Michael Oxer
K.A. Moylan
Gregor Buchanan
PurpleCyclist
Santiago Gorostiza
Langa
Kim Schönfeld
Jason
Keith Byrne
Peter Owen
JCorvesor
Philip Howard
Neil Richardson
Richard Palmer
Peter Rohde
Michael Gaze
Neville Jones
Mark Appleton
Cheryl Churm
Ian E Hall
Craig
Samuel Quemby
Andrew Wood
Kevin Green
Jerry Lawson
Chris Hill
Christopher Allan
zanf
Nigel Land
Philip Benstead
e_bruton
David Squires
Derek Noble
John Saunders
Francis King
Jason Wood
Alasdair Alexander
Amos Field Reid
Ollie Dwnwrd
James Clarke
Jonathan Dow
Mark Martin
Guy Joel Ripley
Joe
Chris Clayton
Erik Daems

Brian C
Sean Carter
David Bernstein
David Tuttle
Ralph Metcalf
Jim Vincent Jr.
Adam Lennie
Karl
Pedro Fradique
Michael Richters
Simon Schupp
Jonathan Gradin
Jerry McKinley
Spotwood Vance
duncan r jamieson
Patrik Lundquist
Tom Lindsay
Paul Jorgensen
John Galbraith
Bruce Devlin
Andrew Reeves-Hall
Charles Halliday
Susan E Spinks
Tibs
Shaun McDonald
John Richards
Michael Schooling
Anthony Lister
John Conway
Gregg Hillmar
Edward T. Burke
Ben Fields
Martin Donkin
Keith Robertson
Steve Knattress
Richard Wilson
Vivek Krishnan
Lorenz Zahn
Bryan Lorber
Fred_dot_u
Roland Backhouse
Paulo A.Franke
Phillip Darnton
Nigel Clark
Michael Barnstijn
Mike Dunn
Mark Redmond
Dave Walker
Phil Clarke
Brent Johnson
Robert Prior
Greyson
Zvi Leve
Albert Reid
Jim Denham
Jon Cotton
Sean O'Sullivan
Gary Fisher

Appendix A:
"Bike Boom" Mentions,
1896–2016

BELOW I LIST A SELECTION OF THE various "bike boom" media mentions down the years. But first, let's zoom out to look at the bigger picture with Google's Ngram Viewer. This is an online book-scraping tool developed by Google in 2010 with the help of scientists at Harvard University. The massive searchable database comprises more than 5 million books—both fiction and non-fiction—published between 1800 and 2000. Plotting the search terms "cycling boom," "bike boom," and "bicycle boom" throws up three mountain ranges, peaking at 1940, 1980, and 2000. (Quite why the 1895–97 boom doesn't spike in Ngram is anybody's guess.) The 1940 mountain, peaking after the stellar sales of the mid-1930s, is K2, with Everest being the 1980 mountain. Mount 1980's climb started at the end of the 1960s, and climbed steeply through the 1970s. This tallies reasonably well with bicycle sales, as well as bicycling's popularity.

The Ngram results are English-language only; a Dutch-language Ngram would result in different peaks and troughs. Clearly, the Dutch bike booms are of a different order of magnitude to the booms elsewhere in the world. The US and UK bike booms are also different although it may be a surprise to many to discover that there were any pre-1970s bike booms in either country.

1890s
The phrase "bike boom" was first used in the 1890s, when the word *bike*—once frowned upon as a slang word—started to become more generally used, even in

We are overdoing the Bicycle Boom.

Bicycle boom, 1896. Cartoon from
Puck magazine, January 1896.

polite society. "Cyclomania" was greatest in America and Britain, but the "cycling craze" also spread to France, the Netherlands, and Germany, as can be witnessed by the phrases "la mode de la bicyclette," "de wielermanie," and "den Siegeslauf des Fahrrads." In this era, cycling was for the elites, from the middle classes to royalty, not yet the workers. The boom started in 1896 and was over by 1897.

1925

By the end of the 1920s, cycling was a popular form of transport for working people all over Europe, most especially in the Netherlands and the "cycling city" of Copenhagen. This boom—an actual and steady boom—was woefully underreported in the media.

There had been a "Boom in Bicycle Sales" reported the *New York Times*, quoting DeWitt Page, vice president of General Motors. Sales had increased by 25 percent, Page told dealers at the 21st annual convention of the Cycle Trades of America, being held in New York. Page said that "friends of mine who find it difficult to locate parking space for automobiles near their offices ride bicycles from the parking place to the offices. It saves time and provides good exercise." (DeWitt Page may have been a motor-man but—via his leadership of the New

Departure bicycle bell company, absorbed by General Motors after part of it had become a motorcar maker—he was president of the Cycle Trades of America.)

1932

Reporting from the Lightweight Cycling, Hiking, and Camping Exhibition being staged in the Royal Horticultural Hall, Westminster, the *Guardian* glowed: "The surprising bicycle 'boom' of the last 18 months is shown here in all its glory. . . ." The newspaper added that the exhibition had been opened by Labour party leader George Lansbury, who declared that it "was a good thing that some machinery should be so adapted that men and women could use their own limbs," and that he was glad to "see this rebirth of interest in cycling."

1934

When, for recreation, horses were replaced by bicycles at the Desert Inn in Palm Springs, California, the resident Hollywood film stars "began to wheel madly around." This led to cycling becoming a "raging West Coast fad," which "spread rapidly to the East," claimed *Time*. "Thus was born last year's bicycle boom which dropped unsought into the laps of U.S. bicycle makers."

1935

The "Boom in Bikes" had succeeded in "bringing back to popularity the rubber-tired bronco of the late Victorian days," wrote cowboy-chronicler Wayne Gard in *Real America*. "From Hollywood to Park Avenue, ladies in shorts have taken up that favorite pastime of the 'nineties."

1936

"The Bicycle Comes Back," headlined a double-page spread in *Popular Science* in July 1936. "News items from all parts of the country tell the story of this dramatic boom in popularity. . . . Instead of subsiding, the tide of cycling popularity continues to rise." The bicycle, said the magazine, had been a "forgotten vehicle" but, since 1932, had made an "amazing comeback"—thanks, in part, to Hollywood film stars flocking to two wheels. "What started as a mere publicity stunt, turned into an authentic cycling craze," wrote the magazine's John E. Lodge. "The bicycle craze spread up the California coast to San Francisco. Society leaders took up cycling as a novelty, and ended by adopting it as a regular activity. The popularity of cycling spread inland. Before it could reach the Atlantic coast, Boston, New

York, and Washington had already been bitten by the bicycle bug from another direction. . . . Today, hardly a city or state is untouched by the bicycling wave which has swept the country." Lodge continued: "Another outstanding development of the bicycle boom is the establishment of cycle paths in city parks." He concluded: "The bicycle, economical and dependable, has got its second wind."

1939

"The bicycle is back," reported *Collier's Weekly* in 1939. "The current bicycle bug bit hard out in Hollywood in 1934 when the movie stars took to wheels for the sake of fun and their figures." The American news magazine continued: "The present bicycle boom has put on the road in the past three years over three million bicycles . . . ." The Second World War saw cycle usage grow massively in both the United Kingdom and the United States, but the media no longer talked about "bike booms," cycling merely became the normal thing to do for countries where fuel was rationed. It would take another 25 years before cycling became boomy again—from the media perspective, at least.

1956

Hollywood "movie folks" were making bicycles popular once again, reported a US newspaper. In a news story headlined "Big Boom in Cycling," the paper reported that a bicycle shop in Beverly Hills did a "thriving business" selling bikes to Marilyn Monroe and Tyrone Power. "Clark Gable has long been a good cyclist," stated owner Hans Ohrt. "He pedals around Encino, where he lives." While many stars cycled for transportation, others—such as Bob Hope and Bing Crosby—"pedal around the [studio] lots," said Ohrt.

1971

"Bicycle Business Is Booming," headlined the *New York Times* in August 1971. "Big Adult Market Is Bringing Euphoria to Industry." A marketing executive with Schwinn told the *Times* reporter: "There is a recession going on but I forget it. Until I talk to someone out of our industry." Schwinn had sold out of its 1.225 million production for 1971 by May. "If we could have increased our production by 50 percent or even 100 percent, we [still] couldn't have met the demand," said Peter Kaszonyi. And it wasn't just Schwinn doing well—the *Times* said the whole industry had found itself in a "Jack-and-the-beanstalk state of growth," selling 8.5 million bicycles before the year was out, compared with 3.7 million in 1960 and 5.6 million in 1965. And the industry was "dreaming impossible dreams" because a third of the new sales were to adults. "The demand for adult bicycles is accelerating its growth rate so fast even the acceleration is an acceleration," said Gene Bierhorst, who had opened three discount bike stores in Manhattan.

1972

"The continuing bicycle boom [is] beginning to be heard by city, state, and federal bureaucrats," said a nationally syndicated article in an American newspaper in 1972. "In Oregon, the 'bicycle bill' passed last year by the state legislature directed the state to spend one cent per dollar of its highway money to build bicycle trails. . . . Chicago has just added 50 more miles to its network of bike ways. . . . The list goes on . . . a new bikeway in Ft. Wayne, Ind. . . . 27 more miles of paths in Tampa, Fla. . . . a Maryland bill that would incorporate bike lanes into all new road and highway construction."

1973

In a letter to the nationally syndicated "Dr. Bicycle," W. T. of Ottawa wrote: "Bicycle writers keep talking about the U.S. bike boom as if no one else had ever heard of two-wheels. Well, there's a bicycle explosion going on up here, too. . . . Bikeways are being built." A line drawing of Dr. Bicycle had him saying, "I'm geared for the bike boom."

1974

"Today, bicycles are booming," said TV presenter Michele Brown in a British government PR film, released in 1974. The boom had come for the bicycle "after years of being scorned as the motorcar's poor relation." An Associated Press film of 1974 also talked about a "bike boom." It predicted that "in Britain alone one million people will switch from four-wheels to two." This was because the "cost of motoring has given a fresh boost to cycling." The film added that "finding a route to ride in safety is one of the biggest obstacles to pedal power, but the new English town of Stevenage incorporates twenty-five miles of tracks . . . without crossing the tracks of motorists." *CycleTouring*, the magazine from the Cyclists' Touring Club, warned: "Get Ready for the Bike Boom."

1975

"There is a bicycle boom throughout the world," wrote Richard Ballantine in the third edition of his best-selling *Richard's Bicycle Book*. "In America it is like the 1849 California Gold Rush . . . and now there is a boom in Great Britain." Ballantine wrote that line in 1973 when there most definitely was a boom; by the following year the boom was over.

1976

ITV broadcast a program to cash in on the 1970s bicycle boom. *The Big Booming Bicycle Show* was produced by Tyne-Tees Television, and aired a number of times on Saturday mornings in 1976. It was fronted by Sally James who, the following year, became the presenter of the Phantom-Flan-Flinging *Tiswas*. One episode of the show focused on the separated cycleway network of Stevenage.

1979

Newsweek reported that injuries sustained by people on bikes were on the rise, and would increase still further "if the cycling boom continues."

1981

The "bicycle boom is bringing in benefits to enterprising local businesses," stated SPOKES, the newsletter of the Edinburgh cycling campaign group, reporting that the number of bike shops in Edinburgh had doubled in 1981. "We are in the middle of a cycling boom, the like of which has not been seen for a hundred years," claimed the *Municipal Journal*, published by Britain's Ministry of Housing, and anticipating one of the subjects in *Roads Were Not Built for Cars* when it added that the previous boom had been "when the dust problem caused by cyclists using unmetalled roads first led to pressure for road surfacing." A Department of Transport consultation paper puffed that the UK was experiencing a "boom in cycling."

2004

"Cycling is booming in London with an increase of 23 per cent in the past year alone," claimed Peter Hendy, Transport for London's managing director of surface transport, in a press release. "It's National Bike Week and cycling is booming," stated a 2004 headline in the *Independent*.

2006

The "cycling boom" was a "Revolution!" blurted the front cover of the *Independent* in June 2006. "Britain embraces the bicycle," continued the newspaper's reporter Cahal Milmo, who stated that "clogged roads, concern at global warming caused by air pollution, and the quest for improved fitness" was persuading "millions to opt for pedal power" in an "explosion in bike use." The lofty rhetoric notwithstanding, Milmo admitted that "despite the phenomenal growth, Britain remains near the bottom of the European league of cycle use with just 2 per cent of all journeys made by bike."

2009

"Cycling is booming," said the UK government's culture secretary—and member of the All-Party Parliamentary Cycling Group—Ben Bradshaw in 2009.

2014

"Cycling has boomed," wrote the BBC's Ben Dirs in 2014, stating what he called the "anecdotal truism" that "cycling is the new golf."

2016

"People are aware at the moment that there is a boom in cycling," Olympian Sir Bradley Wiggins told Peter Walker of the *Guardian*. "But as that boom becomes the norm and 20 years pass we may get to a stage where we're like an Amsterdam." The gold medalist added: "Cyclists aren't going to go away. As the issues grow with cars, and emissions, and all these things, and roads getting busier, cycling is only going to get more popular, become more of a means of transport." Reporting on London's bike boom for *BikeBiz* trade magazine in 2016, I described the "utterly amazing growth of cycling." A document from the mayor of London's office and the Greater London Authority said: "It is sometimes suggested that cycling is a marginal or fringe activity. In London, this is no longer true. In zone 1, during the morning rush hour, 32 per cent of all vehicles on the roads are now bicycles. On some main roads, up to 70 per cent of vehicles are bicycles." According to Transport for London, motorists entering central London during the morning peak in 2000 outnumbered cyclists by more than eleven to one. By 2014, the ratio was 1.7 to 1. "If these trends continue, the number of people commuting to central London by bike will overtake the number commuting by car in three years," said a statement from TfL.

Appendix B:
How the Bicycle Safety Institute Was Formed from a 1970s-era Cycle Advocacy Organization

IT IS OFTEN ASSUMED that the main cycle-helmet information source must have been started by a cabal of money-grubbing helmet manufacturers in cahoots with automobile interests aiming to make cycling look dangerous. In fact, the Bicycle Helmet Safety Institute of America was born from a cycle-advocacy organization that, from its foundation in 1972, lobbied for separated cycleways. Today, those in favor of cycleways are often opposed to cycle helmets, citing that in countries where cycling is common helmets are not.

The BHSI was founded in December 1988, but its roots go back to 1974 when the then two-year old Washington Area Bicyclist Association (WABA) collected bicycle helmets from nine brands, and set out to test them. Randy Swart, a former State Department economist, approached the Snell Memorial Foundation to arrange a comparative test, but the helmet-testing organization declined (at the time it tested only motorsports helmets). WABA's helmet committee approached Snell again in 1979, and the outcome was WABA's Bicycle Helmet Wearability Study which tested and rated eleven helmets. "Without one, you are always in danger," wrote Swart in the helmet committee's first communication; "with one, you stand a good chance of surviving even a bad crash."

In June 1980, 22-year-old Washington bicycle messenger Mary Gaffney was killed by a truck. While the BHSI website acknowledges that cycle helmets offer little protection in a crash with a truck, Swart echoed the DC Coroner's belief that Gaffney's death "might have been prevented by a safe helmet." The WABA's board created the Mary Gaffney Memorial Fund "which would solicit donations to be used to promote helmet use." The Fund paid for the helmets used in a 1981 helmet comparison carried out by Swart and WABA's Tom Balderston, a cyclist and motorcyclist. Balderston convinced Snell that the quality of cycle helmets had advanced enough for them to warrant cycle-helmet-specific tests.

Helmet manufacturers were not keen on WABA's helmet committee efforts. "Some of the manufacturers got worried when they heard what Swart and Balderston were doing, and tried to scare them off," claims a WABA history. Swart recalls: "Skid Lid sent us a page and a half of obscure references thinking they could bury us. But Tom went to the Library of Congress and looked up everything, while I called a professor in Sweden, and we found out they were just blowing smoke."

Balderston wrote up the results of the study for *Bicycling* magazine but, according to the WABA history, the "publication date for the article kept slipping, possibly because some of the manufacturers threatened to sue." Swart informed *Bicycling* that WABA's lawyers wanted to see the communications from the manufacturers. The study was eventually published in 1983, and, thanks to a PR push by WABA, the *Bicycling* article "generated a great deal of interest in the media," said Swart. "It was reviewed in *USA Today* . . . and on several television and radio programs."

Snell urged WABA to join the helmets committee of the American National Standards Institute. According to Swart, this had "already drafted a bicycle helmet standard, but it was bottled up by members who were manufacturers of helmets that did not meet the standard." A bicycle helmet standard was adopted in 1984, and Swart started to travel the country addressing "bicycle rallies about the importance of bicycle helmets. . . ." He figured that if he "could convince the serious bicyclists who attended these rallies, others would follow their lead." WABA also paid for the production and dissemination of brochures promoting helmet use.

In 1987, WABA president Bill Silverman embarked on a campaign to compel advertisers who used bicycling themes to show riders wearing helmets. He wrote to advertising associations, syndicated newspaper columnists, national magazines, and Fortune 500 firms such as Chrysler, Stanley Tools, Sears, and MCI.

WABA's helmet committee became the Bicycle Helmet Safety Institute in 1988. Swart is still the BHSI's lead volunteer. The BHSI's much-visited website—

helmets.org—went online in 1995, and despite its antediluvian design is still the main go-to source for cycle-helmet information or, as some opposing advocates would have it, cycle-helmet propaganda. The helmet issue is one that can divide cyclists almost like no other. Pro-helmet campaigners say the wearing of cycle helmets saves lives. Opponents say the promotion of helmets makes cycling— which is statistically safe—look dangerous, and therefore less appealing, especially to would-be cyclists.

The BHSI is still part of the cycleways-lobbying Washington Area Bicyclist Association, although it is not supported by members' subscriptions (BHSI is run on a shoestring budget funded by consumer donations). In a 2013 blog posting, WABA president Jim Titus appeared to diverge from some of BHSI's positions. In particular, Titus wanted the federal government to withdraw its long-standing claim that bicycle helmets prevent 85 percent of head injuries. This statistic— pointedly called "bad information" by Titus—is from a 1989 Seattle study, and is frequently wheeled out by pro-helmet campaigners. Titus said:

> Efforts to replicate . . . results during the 1990s confirmed that helmets reduce injuries, but not nearly as much as the Seattle study suggested. Yet public health advocates, government web sites, and the news media have continued to repeat the 85 percent factoid to the point that it has become a mantra. Bad information can cause problems. . . . If people think that helmets stop almost all head injuries, consumers will not demand better helmets, and legislators may think it makes sense to require everyone to wear one.

In response to WABA's petition, the National Highway Traffic Safety Administration and the Centers for Disease Control dropped the 85 percent claim. Swart continues to claim that the 1989 study was a "landmark" one, and despite its many critics, he believes it and another from the same researchers with a lower estimate to be "still valid" and "based on field experience."

(Disclosure: *Bike Boom* publisher Island Press is a corporate member of WABA.)

Appendix C:
Vive la Vélorution!

Cars, cars everywhere
What a stink!
Packed together
Street by street
Usurping our space
Eliminating our feet
We had nothing to like
Then we rediscovered the bike
—Bicycle Bob

WITH ALMOST 400 MILES OF CYCLEWAYS—including a two-mile curb-protected cycleway smack-bang in the Central Business District—Montreal is considered to be the best cycling city in North America. The city was twentieth out of twenty in the Copenhagenize Report's index of best cycling cities in 2015 but, significantly, it was one of only three non-European cities included on the list.

Montreal became bicycle-friendly because of people power. Le Monde à Bicyclette was founded in April 1975, and many of the campaign tactics employed by this bicycle-advocacy group are still used by advocacy groups around the world. Montreal's first "stop killing cyclists" demonstration—modeled after play-dead protests in the Netherlands from earlier in the 1970s—used black humor, urging protestors to "Come die-in with me." A placard at one of these die-ins demanded *"vélo pour la vie"*—"bicycle for life."

Le Monde à Bicyclette—literally, "The World of the Bicycle," or Citizens for Cycling, or just MAB—was a motley collection of francophone nationalists and anglophone anarchists who, after a number of years of campaigning, successfully

Robert "Bicycle Bob" Silverman, cofounder of Montreal's
cycle advocacy group Le Monde à Bicyclette, on the Claire
Morissette cycleway in the center of the city.

persuaded the left-leaning politicians of Montreal to provide for people on bikes.
The anti-automobile activism group was cofounded by Claire Morissette and
Robert "Bicycle Bob" Silverman. The curb-protected cycleway in the Central
Business District was built in 2007, replaced a car lane, and was named for
Morissette, who had died from cancer earlier in the same year. Signs on the Piste
Claire-Morissette state proudly that she was a "militante écologiste."

Morissette was the creative brains of the organization while Silverman was
the lead actor, he told me when I visited him in Montreal. To protest at the lack
of a safe bridge crossing for cyclists over the St. Lawrence River, he dressed up
as Moses and, clasping the Ten Bicycle Commandments ("Thou shalt not Kill,
Thou shalt not Pollute . . ."), he attempted in vain to part the "Red Sea" for a
gaggle of waiting cyclists. Of course, the local media loved that, as well as other
stunts the group pulled, such as attaching wings to bicycles and attempting to

fly over the river, and towing bicycles on rafts behind canoes. In 1990, Montreal built a pedestrian and cyclist bridge, and added bike lanes to other bridges.

Perhaps because many members were comfortably bilingual, and because Silverman was at heart a poet, MAB used words as weapons, although always humorously. MAB's guerrilla protesters were "*vélo*-Quixotes," "*vélo*-holy rollers," and "*vélo*rutionaries"; they fought against "*auto*cracy" using "*cyclo*dramas."

Silverman wrote poems and songs for the group's newsletter, *Le Monde à Bicyclette*, such as this one from 1976:

The World of the Bicycle

Forward bicycles
Listen to the echoes
The future of bicycles
It's the end of cars

Le Monde à Bicyclette
Wants to change the planet
Le Monde à Bicyclette
Will save the planet

It's the end of the scourge
No more plots
No more pollution
For it is the revolution.

The group's longest-running cyclodrama was when activists carried bulky items onto Montreal's metro—a ladder, skis, a papier-mâché hippopotamus—while those with less bulky bicycles were refused access. After three years of these "cyclo-provocations," MAB won the subway access for cyclists it had sought.

MAB also constructed car-sized wooden frames for placing over moving bicycles to demonstrate how much space Montreal would save if it catered to cyclists, and not just to automobiles. "Motorists got really mad at that," remembered Silverman, with a twinkle in his eye.

Always willing to suffer for the cause, Silverman was sentenced to eight days in the clink for refusing to pay a small fine levied after he was caught illegally painting a cycle lane on a residential street. (He was released after two days.)

"Bicycle Bob" is now 83, partially blind, and no longer able to cycle—I pedaled him around his old haunts with the help of a cargo bike—but he remains passionate about what he and Morissette were able to achieve as the leaders of Le Monde à Bicyclette.

In 1998, despite being salaried, they wound up the group. "We'd achieved all our aims," Silverman told me. "There was nothing else to campaign for."

MAB was later revived, and the group's mission is continued by a new generation of *vélorutionaries*. Among other things, they campaign to open a long-closed gate on one of the hard-fought-for bridge bike paths.

Select Bibliography

Ballantine, Richard. *Richard's Bicycle Book*. Ballantine Books, 1972.

Barker, Theo, and Dorian Gerhold. *The Rise and Rise of Road Transport, 1700–1990*. Cambridge University Press, 1995.

Berto, Frank. *The Dancing Chain: History and Development of the Derailleur Bicycle*. Cycle Publishing/Van Der Plas Publications, 2013.

Bijker, Wiebe. *Of Bicycles, Bakelites, and Bulbs: Toward a Theory of Sociotechnical Change*. MIT Press, 1995.

Blue, Elly. *Bikenomics: How Bicycling Can Save the Economy*. Microcosm, 2013.

Brendon, Piers. *Motoring Century: The Story of the Royal Automobile Club*. Bloomsbury, 1997.

Coates, Ben. *Why the Dutch Are Different: A Journey into the Hidden Heart of the Netherlands*. Nicholas Brealey Publishing, 2015.

Dodge, Pryor. *The Bicycle*. Flammarion, 1996.

Epperson, Bruce D. *Bicycles in American Highway Planning: The Critical Years of Decision-Making, 1969–1991*. McFarland, 2014.

Forester, John. *Bicycle Transportation: A Handbook for Cycling Transportation Engineers*. MIT Press, 1994.

Furness, Zack. *One Less Car: Bicycling and the Politics of Automobility*. Temple University Press, 2010.

238 | BIKE BOOM

Hadland, Tony, and Hans-Erhard Lessing. *Bicycle Design: An Illustrated History*. MIT Press, 2014.

Heitmann, John. *The Automobile and American Life*. McFarland, 2009.

Herlihy, David. *Bicycle: The History*. Yale University Press, 2004.

Horton, Dave, Paul Rosen, and Peter Cox. *Cycling and Society*. Ashgate, 2007.

Hudson, Mike. *Bicycle Planning*. Architectural Press, 1982.

Hurst, Robert. *The Cyclist's Manifesto: The Case for Riding on Two Wheels Instead of Four*. Falcon, 2009.

Jordan, Peter. *In the City of Bikes*. HarperCollins, 2013.

Kirk, Andrew G. *Counterculture Green: The Whole Earth Catalog and American Environmentalism*. University Press of Kansas, 2007.

Lightwood, James T. *The Cyclists' Touring Club: Being the Romance of Fifty Years' Cycling*. Cyclists' Touring Club, 1928.

Longhurst, James. *Bike Battles: A History of Sharing the American Road*. University of Washington Press, 2015.

Mapes, Jeff. *Pedaling Revolution: How Cyclists Are Changing American Cities*. Oregon State University Press, 2007.

McCann, Barbara. *Completing Our Streets: The Transition to Safe and Inclusive Transportation Networks*. Island Press, 2013.

McGurn, Jim. *On Your Bicycle*. John Murray, 1987.

McShane, Clay. *Down the Asphalt Path: The Automobile and the American City*. Columbia University Press, 1994.

Mionske, Bob. *Bicycling and the Law: Your Rights as a Cyclist*. Velo Press, 2007.

Norton, Peter. *Fighting Traffic: The Dawn of the Motor Age in the American City*. MIT Press, 2008.

Oakley, William. *Winged Wheel: The History of the First Hundred Years of the Cyclists' Touring Club*. Cyclists' Touring Club, 1977.

O'Connell, Sean. *The Car and British Society: Class, Gender, and Motoring, 1896–1939*. Manchester University Press, 1998.

Oldenziel, Ruth, Martin Emanuel, Adri Albert de la Bruhèze, and Frank Veraart, eds. *Cycling Cities: The European Experience: One Hundred Years of Policy and Practice*. Published by Foundation for the History of Technology and LMU Rachel Carson Center for Environment and Society, 2016.

Penn, Robert. *It's All about the Bike: The Pursuit of Happiness on Two Wheels*. Bloomsbury, 2010.

Perry, David B. *Bike Cult*. Four Walls Eight Windows, 1995.

Plowden, William. *The Motor Car and Politics in Britain*. Bodley Head, 1971.

Pucher, John, and Ralph Buehler, eds. *City Cycling*. MIT Press, 2012.

Reid, Carlton. *Roads Were Not Built for Cars*. Island Press, 2015.

Rosen, Paul. *Framing Production*. MIT Press, 2002.

Sadik-Khan, Janette, and Seth Solomonow. *Street Fight: Handbook for an Urban Revolution*. Viking, 2016.

Wray, J. Harry. *Pedal Power: The Quiet Rise of the Bicycle in American Public Life*. Paradigm, 2008.

Index